Images of Dictatorship

Images of Dictatorship
Portraits of Stalin in literature

809.93351
M354i

Rosalind Marsh

Routledge
London and New York

First published 1989
by Routledge
11 New Fetter Lane, London EC4P 4EE
29 West 35th Street, New York, NY 10001

© 1989 Rosalind Marsh

Printed in Great Britain by
TJ Press (Padstow) Ltd, Padstow, Cornwall

British Library Cataloguing in Publication Data

Marsh, Rosalind J.
  Images of dictatorship: Stalin in literature.
  1. Soviet Union. Stalin, I. (Iosif), 1879–1953.
  Portrayal in literature. Portrayal of
  Stalin, I. (Iosif), 1879–1953
  I. Title
  947.084′2′0924
  ISBN 0-415-03796-4

Library of Congress Cataloging in Publication Data

Marsh, Rosalind J.
  Images of dictatorship: Stalin in literature/Rosalind Marsh.
  Bibliography
  Includes index.
  ISBN 0-415-03796-4
  1. Stalin, Joseph, 1879–1953, in fiction, drama, poetry, etc.
  2. Dictators in literature.   3. Literature, Modern—
  20th century—History and criticism.   4. Soviet literature—
  History and criticism.   5. Solzhenitsyn, Aleksandr Isaevich. 1918–
  —Criticism and interpretation.   1. Title.
  PN57.S82M37   1989
  809′.93351—dc19   88-26815
                                                                          CIP

For my parents

Contents

Preface

Little research has hitherto been done on the literary presentation of historical character; indeed, the historical novel itself is a relatively neglected genre. The aim of this study is, firstly, to develop a historical and theoretical framework within which literary portraits of major twentieth-century European historical figures can fruitfully be analysed; and secondly, to discuss the depiction of Stalin in literature, particularly in the works of Russian writers living both within and outside the USSR. Stalin has been selected as an exemplary figure because of the immense influence which he exerted on the history of the USSR and of Europe as a whole, and hence on the consciousness of Soviet and western writers.

Although thirty-five years have now passed since Stalin's death, his name still possesses an enormous emotional impact: he is either the object of the fiercest loathing or the deepest veneration. Portraits of Stalin are still commonly to be seen in the shops and houses of his native Georgia and gifts are sent in homage to the Stalin Museum at Gori, while elsewhere his name is synonymous with oppression and genocide. For more than two decades Stalin arbitrarily controlled the life of his nation and people with an authoritarian cruelty that has few equals in history, but at the same time he presided over the transformation of the USSR into a powerful state capable of defeating Nazi Germany and ultimately of rivalling the USA in industrial and military might.

This book will analyse the many different ways in which Russian and European writers have sought to come to terms with Stalin, both in his lifetime and after his death. The main focus of the book will be prose fiction, although particularly important poems and plays will also be discussed. Recent events in the USSR have made it more difficult than before to classify literary works in definite categories. Since Gorbachev's accession some works previously only published in the west have now appeared in the USSR, and the boundary between permitted and 'dissident' literature has begun to break down. For the purposes of this book, however, a distinction has been drawn between works first published in the USSR and those which originally appeared only in the west. The chapters on fiction first published in the USSR will be concerned not only with the figure of Stalin himself, but also with the way in which different aspects of Stalinism could be treated in Soviet literature at different times. Soviet fiction containing references to Stalin and Stalinism provides valuable insights into the reappraisal of the Stalinist past and the discussions about the future development of Soviet society which have formed the major subject of political and cultural debate in the post-Stalin period, generating a prolonged and enduring conflict between 'anti-Stalinists' and 'pro-Stalinists' in the USSR.

Particular attention will be devoted to two novels which contain the most interesting and detailed portraits of Stalin in modern fiction: Anatoly Rybakov's controversial *Children of the Arbat*, published in the USSR in 1987, and the revised, 96-chapter edition of Alexander Solzhenitsyn's *The First Circle* (1978), which has as yet been published only in the west and has received only limited critical attention. An attempt will be made to analyse the historical, philosophical and literary treatment of the figure of Stalin in the new version of Solzhenitsyn's novel and to consider what light a comparison between this portrait and that in the earlier 87-chapter version of the novel published in 1968 sheds on Solzhenitsyn's literary and political evolution.[1]

A consideration of the treatment of Stalin and Stalinism in literature affords valuable insights into the development of Soviet fiction, changing official attitudes to history in the USSR and the different perceptions held by Soviet. Russian *émigré* and European writers about the past and future development of the USSR.

Acknowledgements

I should like to acknowledge my debt to the Russian and East European Center of the University of Illinois at Urbana-Champaign for granting me a fellowship at the Summer Research Laboratory. My thanks are also due to Daniel Rancour-Laferrière, Neil Cornwell, Peter Henry, Lesley Milne, Robert Lewis, Michael Pursglove, Julian Graffy, and my colleagues in the Irish Slavists' Association and the Scottish Slavonic Seminar.

For permission to quote poems, as specified in the text, acknowledgement is made as follows: B Okudzhava (from *65 pesen: 65 Songs*) to Ardis publishers; Y. Aleshkovsky, V. Vysotsky, A. Galich (from G.S. Smith, *Songs to Seven Strings*) to the author and Indiana University Press; A. Tvardovsky (from *For the Right of Memory*) to *Novy Mir*.

Note

Translations are my own, unless otherwise stated. The transliteration system is a modified version of that used in the *Cambridge Companion to Russian Literature*. Proper names have been rendered in simplified fashion, and the surnames of well-known figures such as Khrushchev, Beria, Ehrenburg, Mandelstam and Gorbachev are given in their more familiar, rather than their more strictly transliterated forms. The titles of literary works will be given in English translation, and accompanied, wherever possible, by the original date of publication in Russian, although reference in the notes may be to subsequent, more accessible editions.

List of abbreviations

AATSEEL Journal	*Journal of American Association of Teachers of Slavic and East European Languages*
GPU	Designation for Soviet secret police in 1922; acronym for Russian words meaning State Political Administration; continued to be used popularly after 1922.
KGB	Acronym for Soviet secret police after 1953; stands for State Security Committee
LG	*Literaturnaya gazeta*
MGB	Initials for Soviet secret police, 1946–53; acronym for Ministry of State Security; succeeded by KGB
MVD	Russian acronym for Ministry of Interior; performed secret police function briefly in 1953
NEP	Acronym for New Economic Policy, a period of limited private enterprise, 1921–8
NKVD	Designation of Soviet secret police, 1934–43; acronym for People's Commissariat of Internal Affairs
SEEJ	*Slavic and East European Journal*
Sob. soch.	*Sobranie sochinenii*
Vestnik RKhD	*Vestnik Russkogo Khristianskogo Dvizheniya*

An approach to the presentation of historical character in European prose fiction

Georg Lukács admitted in his pioneering work *The Historical Novel*, first published in Russian in 1937 and reissued in English in 1960, that a study of the historical novel was 'almost virgin territory'.[1] The majority of critics concerned with historical themes have chosen to discuss individual writers of historical fiction, such as Shakespeare, Scott, Schiller, Goethe and Tolstoy. There are still relatively few general studies of the European historical novel, and in these works the portrayal of historical characters is only mentioned in passing.[2] Even fewer studies have been devoted to the general development and separate periods of the historical novel in Russia.[3] Moreover, of those studies of the historical novel which have appeared, the majority have concentrated on works of the eighteenth and nineteenth centuries. The importance of history for the twentieth-century European novel is, however, demonstrated by the fact that many modern writers – Thomas Mann, Arthur Koestler, Paul Scott, Graham Greene, André Malraux, Olivia Manning, Victor Serge and Solzhenitsyn, to name but a few – have chosen to deal in works of fiction with historical events in the present or the recent past because they themselves have experienced historical cataclysms in their own lives.

Literary scholars have been divided in their approach to such works, expressing uncertainty as to whether they can be defined as 'historical novels'. Harry E. Shaw, in a book on historical fiction which is mainly concerned with Walter Scott, deliberately avoids discussing the representation of history in novels set in the recent past or the present. Gilles Nélod goes even further, dismissing works on contemporary historical periods which the author lived through as 'memoirs', 'eye-witness accounts', 'documentary reports' or 'polemical works aimed at their contemporaries'.[4] Lukács, however, convincingly argues that the fictional treatment of contemporary lived history has, since the time of Balzac's *Comédie Humaine* and Tolstoy's *War and Peace*, been a legitimate literary genre, an extension of the social novel. Xenia Gasiorowska, in her study of portraits of Peter the Great in Russian literature, considers a novel to belong to the historical genre 'if it is set in a time recent to the author but historically completed and closed so that a perspective of events can be achieved and so that research becomes necessary'.[5] This definition can usefully be applied both to Tolstoy's *War and Peace* and *Hadji Murat* and to Solzhenitsyn's *The First Circle*. The works of Solzhenitsyn and other writers who treat the theme of Stalinism can be regarded both as 'novels of the recent past',[6] a subclass of the wider genre of the historical novel, and, in Irving Howe's wide definition, as 'political novels . . . a novel in which we take to be dominant political ideas or the political milieu'.[7]

Avrom Fleishman regards the inclusion of at least one 'real' historical personage as an essential element if a novel is to qualify as historical: 'The historical novel is distinguished among novels by the presence of a specific link to history: not merely a real building or a real event but a real person among the fictitious ones'.[8] However, this is an arbitrary requirement which excludes from the genre many important novels with a historical setting such as *Middlemarch* and *Nostromo*. Fleishman's definition leads to confusion, because he fails to distinguish between different kinds of historical novels. The useful term 'documented historical novels' has been coined by Joseph W. Turner in order to describe novels in which actual people from the past occur, emphasising their direct links with recorded history.[9] The novels and stories containing portraits of Stalin which will be considered in this study all fit into the category of 'documented historical fiction'.

There has been little theoretical writing on the fictional presentation of historical characters. Lukács established that the 'world-historical personage' in the classical historical novel appears as only a minor character compositionally, a figure described from the outside, in action, whose character is not developed throughout the novel, but whose presence, words and

actions have a significant effect on the other fictional charac-
ters.[10] Lukács's analysis can usefully be applied to the depiction
of such episodic characters as Richard Coeur de Lion, Louis XI,
Elizabeth I, Mary Stuart and Cromwell in the novels of Walter
Scott, and to the portrayal of Pugachev and Catherine the Great
in Pushkin's *The Captain's Daughter*, which was influenced by
Scott. This technique of 'external characterisation', to use Harry
Shaw's term,[11] was also used to portray such historical tyrants as
Marat, Danton and Robespierre in Victor Hugo's *Quatre-Vingt
Treize*, Robespierre in Anatole France's *Les Dieux ont Soif* and
Tolstoy's caricatures of Napoleon in *War and Peace* and
Nicholas I in *Hadji Murat*.

To some extent Lukács's analysis held true for the presentation
of Stalin in the first (1968) version of Solzhenitsyn's *The First
Circle* : he was a minor character whose entrance was, nevertheless, carefully prepared, and whose influence was felt throughout
the novel. However, Lukács's interpretation breaks down, even
for the first version of *The First Circle*, because of Solzhenitsyn's
great interest in the psychology of his 'world-historical personage', which is more typical of the twentieth-century historical
novel than of earlier historical fiction. A useful distinction has
been drawn by Gasiorowska between conventional historical
novels, in which historical characters remain outsiders whose
role is limited to ensuring in the reader's imagination the
authenticity of the period, and 'biographical novels' where they
are protagonists and personalities whose image is of paramount
importance to the plot, and in which milieu becomes secondary.
In this sense *The First Circle* could be considered a 'biographical
novel': the image of Stalin dominates the novel, although he
himself only appears in a few chapters.

When referring to both genres, Gasiorowska makes a totally
unjustified generalisation: 'A historical novelist should not
become involved in an in-depth psychological study of the
inhabitants of his fictional world', justifying her view by the
argument that historical characters 'are too remote for complete
empathy'.[12] Such prescriptive comments by critics on what a
novelist should or should not do are not particularly useful.
Harry Shaw is on less controversial ground when he points to the
difficulty involved in depicting historical characters in fiction:
'We are likely to resent the intrusion into the minds of actual

3

historical figures of thoughts we suspect are placed there because they serve the ideological or moralistic needs of the author. We want, in other words, no more information than can be inferred from the historical record'. Shaw also argues that whereas with many fictional characters the depiction of the inner life is the most important evidence about a character, and in many novels the character's consciousness *is* the character, 'With actual historical figures in historical novels, by contrast, the direct portrayal of consciousness can *never* have such a significance. It most properly serves as a summation of what we learn about the character by other means'.[13] It is certainly true that in the majority of historical novels writers are less concerned with the character's inner consciousness than with the social and historical significance of the character, and that for this purpose Scott's 'external characterisation' is still a useful device. However, Taine's criticism of Scott also possesses some validity: 'Walter Scott pauses on the threshold of the soul and in the vestibule of history'.[14] It is this lack of psychological and historical depth which some twentieth-century writers have attempted to remedy.

The evolution of the documented historical novel is related both to the development of the novel form and to changing attitudes towards historical scholarship. Although in practice such twentieth-century novelists as Anthony Powell, with his vignette of Field-Marshal Montgomery in his series *A Dance to the Music of Time*, and Philip Roth, with his depiction of Nixon in *Our Gang*, have conformed to Lukács's classical model, the twentieth century has also seen an increase in fictional representations of historical characters based on a close reading of historical sources, testifying to a much greater concern for historical authenticity on the part of modern writers and to their aim of recreating a whole socio-political and moral world. Some twentieth-century novels probe deeply into the inner consciousness of historical personages, tracing their psychological development. This is true, for example, of Robert Graves's *I, Claudius* and Marguerite Yourcenar's meticulous *Les Mémoires d'Hadrien*, and also of some works closer in time and conception to Solzhenitsyn's *The First Circle*, for example Richard Hughes's novels *The Fox in the Attic* and *The Wooden Shepherdess*, which contain a fascinating psychological portrait of Hitler.

Perhaps the main reason for the lack of a separate theory of historical characterisation is that all characters in a novel are fictional; since there is no difference between 'real' historical personages and any other characters in 'invented' fictions, there can be no general theory. All novels are forms of literary discourse; the very presentational form chosen ensures that it can contain only different degrees of unreality. As Käte Hamburger says, 'The form of fiction in and of itself posits a demarcation from reality of any kind'. Hamburger also makes a general point about historical character when she refers to the difference between an invented content and a fictive one. Historical characters in a novel, such as Napoleon in *War and Peace*, are not 'invented', but nevertheless in their capacity as figures in a novel they are fictive. Just like purely invented characters, they 'are' only by virtue of their being narrated. What does vary is the degree of 'feint', to use Hamburger's term, which authors use in their presentation of historical characters. Certain writers take pains to invest their works with a high degree of historical authenticity, and use literary techniques such as first-person narration which diminish the amount of 'feint' involved in characterisation. As Hamburger states: 'If historical figures become first person narrators, then it depends on the nature of the narrative to what degree the author renders them feigned'.[15] In *Les Mémoires d'Hadrien*, for example, which is formally presented as a genuine autobiography of the Emperor Hadrian and backed up by extensive documentation, Yourcenar takes care to ensure that the degree of feint is very slight by avoiding all fictionalising techniques such as dialogue.[16] As we will see, authors who paint portraits of Stalin also vary considerably in the degree of 'feint' which they employ.

Solzhenitsyn's portrait of Stalin, particularly the new portrait which presents an imaginative reconstruction of Stalin's entire biography up to 1949, is deeply influenced by classical models, especially by the caricatured portraits of historical characters in the works of Pushkin and Tolstoy. It also bears the imprint of the twentieth-century interest in psychology which has affected not only writers of fiction, but also historians: Joachim Fest's biography of Hitler, Max Gallo's study of Robespierre and Robert Tucker's biography of Stalin are prominent examples of the genre of 'psycho-history'.[17]

Chapter two

Tyrants in twentieth-century literature

Before discussing the literary portrayal of twentieth-century tyrants, it may be useful to consider the more general question of the strategies employed by writers in presenting the terrible events of recent or contemporary history. Many authors who attempt to treat such subjects as the Nazi holocaust or Stalin's terror are fully conscious of the magnitude of the task they have undertaken, since there are certain enormities which it is impossible to depict adequately in fiction. In the words of Lionel Trilling, 'The great psychological fact of our time which we all observe with baffled wonder and shame is that there is no possible way of responding to Belsen and Buchenwald'.[1]

Some writers, aware that certain things are literally unspeakable, make a conscious decision to avoid the subject completely. Boris Pasternak, for example, breaks off his *Essay in Autobiography* (1956) before the dreadful years of the Great Purge with the words: 'to continue it would be immeasurably difficult ... one would have to talk in a manner which would grip the heart and make the hair stand on end'.[2] One method of presenting evil in fiction which avoids the melodramatic piling of horror on horror is extreme factuality. A simple documentary approach is used by Anatoly Kuznetsov in his novel *Bab'ii Yar* (1966), which is based on contemporary documents, newspaper cuttings and the testimony of eye-witnesses, including the remarkable account of Dina Pronicheva, a Jewish woman who survived one of the mass executions at the ravine of Babi Yar near Kiev in 1941.[3] Kuznetsov reports her account verbatim, without adding anything of his own; and the same memoir was subsequently used, with very few changes, by D. M. Thomas in

The White Hotel. Similarly, Primo Levi's eye-witness account of Auschwitz, *If This is a Man* (1947), is couched in a quiet, calm, almost gentle tone. Such restraint and understatement give a good idea of what Hannah Arendt has termed 'the banality of evil'. However, many writers feel that mere realism is not a sufficiently powerful medium to provide an adequate evocation of evil. A more common approach is the use of satire, the grotesque, hyperbole and humour, as, for example, in the works of Mikhail Bulgakov. Satire is able to convey evil by pointing to the distinction between the ideal and the real, while at the same time diminishing the weight of negative phenomena by teaching the reader to laugh at them. A third strategy is the use of allegory and fantasy, as in George Orwell's *Animal Farm* and *1984* and Georgy Vladimov's *Faithful Ruslan*. As we will see, writers who attempt to depict either Hitler or Stalin have adopted one, or a combination of these literary techniques.

An examination of portraits of Hitler in fiction suggests some interesting parallels with literary portraits of Stalin. In the first place, during the period of Hitler's ascendancy German writers exalted their Führer in similar eulogistic tones to those of Soviet writers glorifying Stalin: a prominent example is Will Vesper's poem of 1943, *Dem Führer*.[4] It is, however, significant that since Hitler's death there have been very few portraits of Hitler in German literature in comparison with the number of portraits of Stalin in Soviet literature since 1953. A major reason for this is the fact that German historians were free to investigate the truth about Hitler after the war, so there was no need for writers to play the role of historian, as there was in the Soviet Union, where even at the height of de-Stalinisation under Khrushchev only half-truths about the Stalin era were cautiously disclosed. Moreover, Hitler's life was generally much more public and better documented than Stalin's; he was in power for a much shorter time; and after his death documents were made available to historians. In contrast with Stalin, whose early life remained mysterious and who stayed aloof from the public for many years, Hitler's life contained fewer secrets to attract the novelist. The Nuremberg Trials were a cathartic experience for the German people and brought many facts into the open, in contrast with the secrecy surrounding Stalin's purges.

There are several other possible literary or psychological

explanations for the dearth of literary portraits of Hitler. Western Europe possesses a less developed tradition of historical and political novels containing real historical characters than Russia, although, in compensation, it has a strong tradition of historical biography. Since the Second World War the political novel has not been particularly popular in western Europe; most writers have concentrated on private themes: individual human beings and their personal relationships. Perhaps German writers, in particular, find the subject of Hitler too horrific and too daunting for fictional treatment, or feel that the depiction of Hitler in a work of fiction would humanise him – something they may not wish to do. The majority of literary works on the subject of the Holocaust have dealt with the victims rather than the perpetrators of the tragedy.

Most German writers who have depicted Hitler did so in his lifetime, as a warning to their contemporaries; and the majority have been less concerned with the character and impact of Hitler as an individual than with the general effect of the Nazi regime on the lives of ordinary German people. Lion Feuchtwanger, for example, said that his *Wartesaal* (*Waiting Room*) trilogy, of which the first part, *Erfolg* (*Success*) (1930), was the first novel to attack Hitler openly, had as its purpose to 'bring to life for future generations that bad time of waiting and transition, the darkest age Germany has experienced since the Thirty Years' War'.[5] Of those artists who do depict Hitler, some choose to approach their subject obliquely, through allegory or caricature. Bertolt Brecht, writing in exile during the era of the Third Reich, felt that Hitler and his associates needed a crude, unobjective literary treatment. In *The Resistible Rise of Arturo Ui* (1941) he draws a satirical analogy between Hitler and a Chicago gangster chief. Brecht's *Schweyk in the Second World War* (1943) contains a caricatured giant-sized figure of Hitler who appears fleetingly at the beginning of the play determining the fate of the 'little man', but whose absurd pretensions are finally exposed when he is swallowed up by the Russian steppe. A similar approach was adopted by some foreign artists: Charlie Chaplin, for example, felt that 'Hitler must be laughed at', and in his film *The Great Dictator* (1940) portrayed Hitler as a ludicrous cartoon character, ridiculing the Nazis' 'mystic bilge about a pure-blooded race'.[6]

Perhaps it is easier for foreigners to attempt an objective psychological portrait of Hitler than Germans, since they are not as emotionally involved with their subject. David Puttnam's film *Swastika*, for example, includes clips from Eva Braun's home movies in a deliberate attempt to depict Hitler as a human being, not merely as a monster. Interestingly enough, the most extensive fictional treatment of Hitler is contained in the unfinished novel sequence *The Human Predicament* by the English writer Richard Hughes. The first novel of the series, *The Fox in the Attic*, published in 1961, portrays Hitler at an early stage in the Nazi movement: before, during and after the unsuccessful Munich putsch of 1923. In contrast with Solzhenitsyn and other Soviet writers, Hughes demonstrates his concern for historical accuracy by citing his sources, which include both secondary published material and private papers. He has evidently done extensive research, because he thanks the only living person (unnamed) who was in a position to describe to him at first hand the whole 48-hour period when Hitler was in hiding in Uffing. Hughes, like Solzhenitsyn, claims to be doing something different from other writers and historians: 'At certain points my narrative of the "putsch" differs materially from others compiled'. This is, however, because of his deep concern for historical authenticity: he says he 'has imported almost nothing fictitious except the little dog in the plaid waistcoat'. Much of the narrative of the Munich putsch itself is based on a vivid contemporary account by an actual Nazi participant, Major Goetz.[7] The literary presentation of Hitler is well prepared and more subtle than most portraits of Stalin by Russian writers. Hitler is first seen from the outside, by other people: initially as an insignificant figure who poses no threat, and later as a stirring, though somewhat grotesque, speaker on the eve of the putsch: 'Wagner staged by Hieronymus Bosch'.[8] It is not until Chapters 9 and 10 of the second part of the novel that Hughes attempts to reconstruct Hitler's psychological state – and this is during his two days' hiding in Uffing when the author has a personal memoir of the father of Baroness Pia von Aretin on which to base his portrait. Hughes uses a mixture of authorial narration, narrated monologue in the third person and occasional direct discourse. We witness Hitler's interior monologue, but the author's guiding voice is always heard, ironising and interpreting Hitler's character for us, and in particular, showing how Hitler's adult 'I' has developed directly from the child's supreme ego.

The second novel of the series, *The Wooden Shepherdess*, first published in 1973, describes Hitler's rise to power, culminating in his disposal of his rivals in the 'Night of the Long Knives' of 1934. Once again Hughes claims to have presented historical facts as accurately as possible, but honestly admits that the Nazis destroyed all official records bearing on the Blood Purge of 1934: 'thus surviving contemporary sources tend to be the work of known liars on both sides, so that disproof of one version cannot be taken as establishing any other. This reduces "belief" at certain points in the narrative of the Night of the Long Knives to a matter of choice'. He frankly confesses that he has used certain stories which he considers psychologically plausible, but not necessarily historically verifiable, such as the strange story that Otto Strasser saw Banquo's Ghost on the stairs before he was killed.[9] Once again, Hitler appears as an episodic character in the novel, often seen through the eyes of others, such as his four-year-old nephew, his supporters and opponents. Hughes builds up a picture of Hitler's personal life, evoking his kindness to children and his erotic relationship with his niece Geli, who eventually committed suicide. For the most part, Hitler is presented from the outside, in action, or through the author's third-person narration; his thoughts are only rarely conveyed through indirect interior monologue. Towards the end of the novel, when the pace of events quickens, Hitler is almost entirely depicted through external characterisation, as in Lukács's classical model.

Hughes's portrait of Hitler provides a useful measure by which to judge portraits of Stalin, since it is a very successful example of the depiction of a twentieth-century tyrant. Hughes's Hitler is a less caricatured, more multi-faceted character than Solzhenitsyn's Stalin. Such a comparison is, however, only of partial value, since, although Hughes is deeply concerned about historical authenticity, his portrayal is less ambitious in scope than Solzhenitsyn's. He selects certain historical incidents for detailed consideration and makes no attempt to cover Hitler's entire career.

Chapter three

Historical treatments of Stalin and Stalinism

An investigation of historical biographies of Stalin will help to highlight the problems facing all authors who treat the subject of Stalin. In the USSR the real facts of Stalin's life have, until recently, been too sensitive for unbiased enquiry, and an elaborate tissue of myth and counter-myth has grown up around the dead dictator. Any discussion of Stalin and Stalinism, whether in the USSR or in the west, is likely to raise highly controversial issues and evoke contradictory historical opinions and judgements. Analysts of Stalin and Stalinism are concerned with one of the most important phenomena of modern times, and their subject rouses powerful feelings. Biographers of Stalin are, almost inevitably, trying to prove a point rather than merely to establish a dispassionate historical analysis. Since they have either to accept or reject the versions of Stalin's biography propagated by the dictator himself, their aim is either to create a legend or to debunk a myth. A brief examination of the different types of biography of Stalin which have hitherto appeared will give some idea of the problems of interpretation, bias and conflict which this subject has aroused.[1]

There have been more biographies of Stalin than of any other man in history, but most of these have been propaganda pieces published in the USSR in more than 300 languages; serious historians have been frustrated by the secrecy, distortion and terror surrounding the figure of Stalin. In the period 1929–53 – particularly from 1934 onwards, the period later condemned by Khrushchev as the 'period of the personality cult' – many laudatory biographies of Stalin were published, each more extravagant than the last. Stalin's secret police chief Lavrenty

Beria, for example, called Stalin 'the closest colleague of our great Lenin'; for the French Communist Henri Barbusse he was 'the most important of our contemporaries' and for E. Yaroslavsky 'the friend, the teacher, the leader of nations'.[2] History was rewritten to create a legend about Stalin's early life, especially with regard to the period 1899–1917. According to this legend, Comrade Stalin had, from his schooldays, been a heroic underground revolutionary who soon became the most prominent Bolshevik in the Caucasus, a major leader of the all-Russian Bolshevik movement, a close collaborator and disciple of Lenin. It was alleged that before 1917 Stalin had been not only a leading ideologist, but also a man of action involved in all the main revolutionary initiatives, and that, with Lenin, he was the chief architect of the Bolshevik revolution of October 1917. Subsequently he did more than anyone else to win the Civil War of 1918–21; and he was Lenin's most faithful ally and comrade-in-arms during Lenin's last years. All these claims are false or grossly exaggerated, while many details used to back them up are totally bogus.[3]

Other biographies fall into two main categories: the popular and the Marxist. In the 1920s Stalin rose to power so unobtrusively that very little was known about him, especially about his early life; indeed, Trotsky said that Stalin made as much impression as a 'grey blur'. By 1929, when Stalin had risen to the position of uncontested leader of the Communist Party of the Soviet Union, there was a demand for more information about him – a need recognised by *Pravda*, which in 1929 published an article entitled 'Stalin the Enigma'.[4] The first western biographies, such as those by Stephen Graham and Isaac Don Levine, were written to provide more information about Stalin.[5] Subsequent western biographies published during the 1930s, the period of the 'popular front', for example that by the French Communist Henri Barbusse, were also mostly favourable. During the Second World War, when Stalin was the major ally of the western powers, some official Soviet biographies, such as Yaroslavsky's *Landmarks in the Life of Stalin*, were translated into English 'in response to the wide demand for more detailed information about Joseph Stalin's noble and courageous life'.[6] Some interesting personal memoirs were written in Stalin's lifetime, such as that by his boyhood companion, the Georgian

Menshevik Josef Iremaschwili.[7] However, some of these popular memoirs, such as Budu Svanidze's *My Uncle Joe* and Ahmed Amba's *I Was Stalin's Bodyguard*, were largely spurious, containing conversations which were alleged to have occurred some thirty to fifty years previously.[8]

Another important strand of biographies published in the West was by Marxists hostile to Stalin. One of the best is by Boris Souvarine, a French Communist who was sympathetic to Trotsky and inspired by hatred of his subject.[9] The most famous is the unfinished work which Trotsky was writing at the time of his murder in 1940. Trotsky saw Stalin as 'an Asiatic despot, a tyrant', but also advanced an impersonal, class-based explanation of Stalin's advancement: 'Stalin took possession of power, not with the aid of personal qualities, but with the aid of an impersonal machine. And it was not he who created the machine, but the machine that created him'.[10] Isaac Deutscher's interesting and scholarly biography also closely follows Trotsky's interpretation.[11]

Stalin was such a controversial figure that since his death in 1953 no full-length biography of him has been published in the USSR; his achievements have, however, been subject to drastic revaluations. In the 1950s a gradual de-Stalinisation took place, culminating in Khrushchev's 'Secret Speech' to the Twentieth Party Congress of 1956, which told some of the truth about Stalin's crimes, and was followed by Khrushchev's further, public revelations about Stalin's purges at the Twenty-Second Party Congress in 1961.[12] After Khrushchev's fall the Brezhnev-Kosygin regime, composed of party and state bureaucrats, was unprepared to make any more revelations about Stalin and the 'Anti-Party Group', but was also unwilling to permit the total rehabilitation of Stalin at the Twenty-Third Congress of 1966 and on the centenary of Stalin's birth in December 1969. The issue of Stalin and his rehabilitation was gradually shelved by the party leaders; it was not mentioned at either the Twenty-Fourth or Twenty-Fifth Congresses (1971 and 1976). Under Brezhnev, Andropov and Chernenko the official Soviet line was to minimise Stalin's personal role in Soviet history and to play up the role of the Communist Party, but at the same time to describe many of his policies as the necessary and proper development of Marxism-Leninism and the dictatorship of the proletariat.[13] It is only since Gorbachev's accession in 1985 that Stalin's abuses of power have once again been officially condemned.[14]

In recent years many interesting memoirs of Stalin have been published, notably by the Yugoslav leader, then dissident Milovan Djilas, and by Stalin's daughter Svetlana Allilueva.[15] Roy Medvedev, a historian and former dissident who still lives in the USSR, produced the first scholarly analysis of Stalinism inside the USSR using previously unknown archival material and the testimony of eye-witnesses. As the book could not be published in the USSR, Medvedev authorised its publication in the West.[16] His view is that Stalin was totally responsible for the aberrations of Soviet rule; Stalin distorted Leninism. In the West, a steady stream of sensational popular biographies has continued to appear, such as those of Levine and Alexander Orlov, as well as the more scholarly work by Edward Ellis Smith, all of which contend that Stalin was a Tsarist police agent.[17] There have also been some interesting biographies by western scholars, notably Bertram D. Wolfe, Ronald Hingley, Robert C. Tucker and Adam B. Ulam, which are based on an extensive use of primary sources. These works express individual viewpoints, although they all aim at historical accuracy and do not disguise Stalin's ruthlessness and criminality.[18] Tucker's work, the first volume of a longer study, is a biographical and psychological survey of Stalin's early life up to 1929; Ulam analyses the Stalin era, as well as the dictator himself; and Hingley concentrates on Stalin the man, emphasising his intelligence and political acumen.

One interesting development in recent years, not only in the USSR, has been the renewed attempts to emphasise the positive side of Stalin's achievement. The 'Cold War revisionists', one group of western historians, have been inclined to a more sympathetic view of Stalin;[19] and the biography by Ian Grey has an epigraph from Shakespeare's *Julius Caesar*:

Why, man, he doth bestride the narrow world like a
  Colossus . . .
The evil that men do lives after them;
The good is oft enterr'd with their bones.

Grey's aim is to provide a more balanced assessment of Stalin distinct from the extravagant eulogies of the 'cult' period and the moral indignation of western biographers.[20] Another approach to

Stalinism has been adopted by some scholars who argue that, at least in the 1930s, Stalin's system was not completely totalitarian; Stalin himself could not control everything, and his regime displayed the inefficiency typical of any bureaucratic organisation.[21] The only whole-heartedly 'Stalinist' biography of Stalin to appear in recent years has been the memoir of the Albanian dictator, the late Enver Hoxha, which commemorated the 'centenary of the birth of the great Marxist-Leninist Joseph Stalin', the 'much-beloved and outstanding leader of the proletariat and the world, the loyal friend of the Albanian people, and the dear friend of the oppressed peoples of the whole world fighting for freedom, independence, democracy and socialism'.[22]

During the 1970s and 1980s Stalinist sentiment grew gradually more fulsome among Soviet officials. It became easier to publish works containing qualified praise of Stalin than criticism of him; the use of Khrushchev's phrase 'the period of the personality cult' was forbidden, and censure of Stalinism was largely banished from the official press. Under Brezhnev, Andropov and Chernenko Stalin was no longer regarded as a demi-god, but a revaluation of his historical role took place, especially in relation to the war. Stalin was seen as a great national leader who manifested 'devotion to the working class and the selfless struggle for socialism', and the whole Stalin era was regarded as a necessary, heroic period of Soviet development.[23] Stalinist sentiment, which was prevalent not only among military and political officials, but also among broader sectors of the population, was partly related to the resurgence of Russian nationalism, and partly generated by a nostalgic desire to return to an age of law and order, stability and efficiency, to counteract what some perceived as the moral decay of contemporary Soviet society.

Because of the partial rehabilitation of Stalin within the USSR after 1964 and the ban imposed on any discussion of questions of guilt and responsibility for past crimes, some dissident and *émigré* Russian writers felt it their duty to return to the issue of Stalin and Stalinism in the name of historical justice. Many of the most important *samizdat* chroniclers of Stalinism – Solzhenitsyn, Roy and Zhores Medvedev, Evgenia Ginzburg, Nadezhda Mandelstam, Lydia Chukovskaya, Varlam Shalamov, Lev Kopelev, Evgeny Gnedin, Alexander Nekrich, Mikhail Baitalsky, Suren Gazaryan and Anton Antonov-Ovseenko – had

15

themselves suffered in Stalin's terror or were relatives of victims.[24] Like survivors of the Jewish holocaust, they wanted to tell the truth about the Stalin era, so that the past should never be forgotten. The lasting importance of bearing witness to Stalin's crimes before present and future generations has been eloquently expressed by Antonov-Ovseenko: 'It is the duty of every honest person to write the truth about Stalin. A duty to those who died at his hands, to those who survived that dark night, to those who will come after us'.[25] Since the accession of Gorbachev, a similar view has been taken by writers who still live in the USSR, notably Anatoly Rybakov. In the contemporary USSR the issue of Stalin and Stalinism has again become highly topical both in fiction and in debates in the official press about how best to overcome the legacy of the past and promote Gorbachev's new policies of *glasnost'* (openness) and *perestroika* (reconstruction).

In view of the controversy surrounding the figure of Stalin and the system he created, fictional portraits of Stalin by Russian writers possess a significance transcending the world of literature; they also represent a contribution to a historical debate which is still continuing both in the USSR and the west.

Chapter four

The image of Stalin in Soviet literature during Stalin's lifetime

With the exception of Lenin,[1] no historical figure in modern times has been the subject of as many literary and dramatic portrayals as Joseph Stalin. Many writers in the USSR, including both hack writers and the best writers in the country, have chosen – or been forced – to treat this subject. In Stalin's time Soviet writers were obliged to contribute to the ever-growing cult of Stalin's personality; and after his death Stalin became a subject of intense speculation by Soviet writers, as a result of the party's reassessment of Stalin's achievements and the need of individual writers to come to terms with their own and their country's past. Hence a sharp dichotomy exists between literary portraits composed in Stalin's lifetime and after his death. Another useful distinction can be drawn between works published in the USSR, where portrayals of Stalin are subject to a rigorous scrutiny for ideological purity, and works published elsewhere, where there are no such restrictions. The latter group includes a wide spectrum of western writers and dissident and *émigré* Russian authors with different approaches to Stalin, but they are all united by their freedom to depict Stalin in any way they wish.

Solzhenitsyn's portrait of Stalin in the new version of *The First Circle* manifests some similarities to, but also considerable differences from, other fictional depictions of Stalin both in the USSR and in the west. An examination of other literary portraits of Stalin will help to highlight the originality of Solzhenitsyn's conception, as well as to provide a measure by which the literary qualities and historical accuracy of his portrait can be judged.

Early hostile portraits

Not surprisingly, few Soviet writers are known to have expressed opposition to Stalin during his lifetime, since derogatory references to Stalin could mean persecution, imprisonment, or even death. Paradoxically, this reflects the high regard in which literature has been held in the USSR: as Osip Mandelstam said in the 1930s, 'Poetry is respected only in this country – people are killed for it. There's no place where more people are killed for it'.[2] Nevertheless, in the 1920s, before Stalin's rise to uncontested leadership of the party, three prominent Soviet authors, Kornei Chukovsky, Evgeny Zamyatin and Boris Pilnyak, inspired by the long-standing Russian tradition of using literature for the scrutiny of socio-political issues, were drawn to treat the subject of Stalin.

One of the first Soviet writers to make an oblique allusion to Stalin was Chukovsky, in his narrative poem for children, *The Big Bad Cockroach* (1923).[3] Chukovsky paints an allegorical picture of an idyllic animal kingdom terrorised by 'a dreadful giant ... A big bad cockroach' which rages and twitches its moustache, snarling 'I'll devour you, I'll devour you, I won't show any mercy'. As Lev Loseff has shown, the tyrant-cockroach is an image common in Russian folklore: the etymology of the Russian word 'cockroach' (*tarakan*) is linked with the Turkic word 'dignitary' (*tarkan*); and the figure of Torokanchik, the representative of an alien and hostile power, appears in a number of folk epics.[4] The Russian cockroach has whiskers, so 'Tarakan' is often used as a nickname for any man possessing a thick, bristly moustache. Moreover, the word 'moustache' (*usy*) was in use up to the nineteenth century as a slang term for 'thieves' in a cycle of folk ballads depicting thieves who pillage and torment the simple people, the *muzhiki*. Thus the images of 'moustache' and 'cockroach' combine to form a single, powerful image evoking coercion and unlawfully acquired power. Chukovsky composed his poem before Stalin became dominant, at a time when several of the contenders for power in the party had moustaches (Zinoviev and Trotsky, for example, as well as Stalin), so his satire was aimed not at any specific ruler, but at any dictatorship imposed by a small political faction against the will of the majority of the population. It was only with hindsight that Chukovsky's vision could be seen as prophetic, and was clearly regarded as such in the USSR. Stalin's nickname 'The Cockroach', which was in use from the beginning of the 1930s, was taken from Chukovsky's poem; and in the 1950s, in a performance based on *The Big Bad Cockroach* at the Leningrad Young People's Theatre, the title character was played as an undisguised caricature of Stalin. Chukovsky's work, moreover, established a whole genre of successful anti-Stalinist Aesopian satire in the guise of children's literature.

One of the first Soviet prose writers to portray a character bearing some resemblance to Stalin was Zamyatin, in his comic story *X* (1926), a satire on the superficial adaptation of some people to the new Soviet environment.[5] Zamyatin depicts Comrade Papalagi, a terrifying member of the Cheka (secret police), whose foreign-sounding name and huge, black, pointed moustache are reminiscent of Stalin (whose real name was Djugashvili). Zamyatin emphasises Comrade Papalagi's ruthlessness: his moustache is like 'a pair of horns ready to gore' his hapless victims, and he shouts 'Confess!' to Deacon Indikoplev, who admits to making the sign of the cross in public.[6] Stalin was not formally connected with the Cheka in the 1920s, but since 1919 he had been Commissar of the Workers' and Peasants' Inspectorate which supervised the machinery of government, and, as General Secretary of the Central Committee from 1922, he had co-ordinated the work of the Central Control Commission, the body responsible for purges in the party. Although there is no definite proof that Zamyatin had Stalin in mind, by 1926 he would have had some reason to express hostility to Stalin, because his anti-utopian novel *We* (written in 1920–1), with its idea of 'infinite revolutions' (an echo of the concept of 'permanent revolution' advocated by Stalin's rival Trotsky), had been banned in the USSR in 1924.[7] Moreover, the prophetic talent displayed by Zamyatin in *We*, which proved to be a fairly accurate prediction of some aspects of Stalinist Russia, renders it legitimate to interpret the character of Papalagi, who shines a light into his victims' eyes and forces them to confess to absurd crimes, as a precursor of Stalin and his NKVD interrogators during the purges of the 1930s.

Zamyatin's *We*, which has often been interpreted as a powerful satire on Stalin's Russia, cannot be cited as the first Soviet novel to contain a portrait of Stalin, since it was written too early for the figure of the all-powerful Benefactor to bear any direct relation to Stalin. Zamyatin's Benefactor can rather be seen as a generalised picture of a dictator of the future, and his 'Socratically bald' head gives him, if anything, a greater resemblance to Lenin. However, Zamyatin's frequent use of metallic imagery in his portrait of the dictator, and, particularly, the repeated image of 'steel' to describe the Benefactor's supporters and the One State that he rules: 'Everything was new, of steel: a steel sun, steel trees, steel people', make it not entirely fanciful to suspect a veiled reference to Stalin, who chose the revolutionary name 'Man of Steel'. More significantly, Zamyatin's portrait of the Benefactor demonstrates that already, in the early 1920s, he was keenly aware of the dangers of a 'cult of personality'. By 1926, when *X* was written, the cult of Lenin was growing, and excessive reverence for the party leaders was becoming a more serious problem in the USSR. Zamyatin's contempt for the burgeoning 'cult of personality' is evident in *X*, when he comments ironically: 'Before Papalagi stood a plate with the most ordinary millet gruel, and it was a marvel to see him eating it in the most ordinary manner, like everybody else'.[8]

A character more obviously recognisable as Stalin was depicted by Boris Pilnyak, in his *Tale of the Unextinguished Moon* (1926).[9] This story was closely based on the death of M. V. Frunze, People's Commissar for Military and Naval Affairs, who died in October 1925 during an operation for a stomach ulcer undertaken at the behest of the party. It was rumoured that Stalin had ordered Frunze to be murdered because he resisted the domination of the army by the GPU, and because his power and popularity represented a threat to Stalin's ambition. Although in real life Stalin's complicity has not been proven, Pilnyak suggests in his story that Commander Gavrilov was killed on the orders of his superior, the shadowy 'Number One' (*Pervyi*).[10] Pilnyak uses the epithets 'Number One' and 'the Unbending Man' (*negorbyashchiisya chelovek*) interchangeably to evoke the powerful bureaucrat in whom many Soviet readers recognised a resemblance to Stalin. Vera Reck contends that Pilnyak depicted this Stalin-like character because of 'his artist's instinct rather than any deliberate attempt at portraiture'[11]; he did, however, take pains to inform himself about the details of Stalin's life and conduct during Frunze's illness, acquiring information both from the newspapers and from two friends, the critic A. K. Voronsky and the Communist leader Karl Radek. Pilnyak's Unbending Man shares several characteristics with the real Stalin: his posture is stiff, his movements quick and angular; he lives like a recluse in Moscow in a silent, curtained room whose only luxuries are a carpet and a fireplace;[12] and he justifies the liquidation of people in the name of the Revolution: 'It is not for us to talk about the grindstone of the Revolution, Gavrilov. The wheel of history, unfortunately, I suppose, is turned mainly by blood and death – particularly the wheel of revolution'.[13] The epithet 'Unbending Man' is reminiscent of the Soviet phrase 'inflexible Bolshevik' (*nesgibaemyi bolshevik*); and Number One is the senior figure in the ruling *troika* at a time when Stalin too was a member of a *troika*, but rapidly gaining ascendancy over his colleagues Zinoviev and Kamenev. Although Pilnyak 'covers' himself by crediting Number One with several traits which differentiate him from Stalin – he does not smoke, and is an educated man with a knowledge of foreign languages – these differences only serve to accentuate the parallel. In particular, Pilnyak's evocation of the dictator's ruthless lust for power, indifference to human life and willingness to annihilate his rivals, who were old revolutionaries, former comrades in the 'glorious band of 1918',[14] testifies to the author's prophetic talent.

Vera Reck considers that Pilnyak was only able to write such a work as a result of 'political naïveté';[15] and indeed, Pilnyak's preface, which warns the reader: 'It is not at all the point of my story to report on the death of a Commissar of Military Affairs. I feel I must inform the reader of all this, lest he seek real persons or events in my story',[16] seems to be an example of extreme naïveté, since it had just the opposite effect from that explicitly intended: many readers associated Gavrilov with Frunze and his murderer with Stalin. Pilnyak's camouflage is so thin that it is legitimate to speculate that the preface may have been an attempt to alert readers to the reasons for Frunze's death, or to point to other, wider philosophical ideas in the text. As Elena Semeka has demonstrated, it is an oversimplification to view the Unbending Man as merely a portrait of Stalin; with his angular movements, his monotonous speech in which 'every phrase was a formula',[17] his absence of emotions, immobility, loneliness and silence, he is associated both with machinery and with death. The Unbending Man is more than Stalin: 'a generalised portrait of the dictator of the future who has ceased being human and has become a machine'.[18] Everything in his study is red, the colour of blood and violence; and when he travels in his car, the embodiment of soulless mechanisation, which is like a spaceship or a 'whip', he gazes with 'a cold glance' on the city which suffers under his scourge.[19] The moon in Pilnyak's story is an ambiguous symbol with multiple possible meanings, which has variously been interpreted as signifying death, or the unfathomable spirit of nature and eternity which cannot be extinguished.[20] When Number One rushes out of the city in his car, he is able to change the direction of the moon, which, like him, remains solitary and immobile until it is eventually chased beyond the clouds. The Unbending Man can be seen as the master of the universe who glimpses higher eternal values, but is unable to sustain the vision; he is able to stop life and set death in motion, although he is ultimately powerless to exert full dominion over nature and death.

The wider philosophical significance of Pilnyak's story was ignored when the author's personal fate was being decided. Although many details of Pilnyak's case remain obscure, it would seem that Stalin recognised himself in the story; Pilnyak's tale was not republished in the USSR for over half a century; and Pilnyak himself, despite his contacts with senior party and secret police officials, including Ezhov, disappeared in mysterious circumstances in the purges (he was probably shot in 1937). It has been assumed that Pilnyak's fate was sealed because Stalin never forgave him for the unflattering portrait; but since he was arrested on other charges, and so many other literary figures were purged at the same time, the precise contribution made by *The Tale of the Unextinguished Moon* towards Pilnyak's ultimate fate still remains unclear.

Another writer who dared to express a hostile attitude to Stalin was Osip Mandelstam. According to Nadezhda Mandelstam, her husband composed his famous epigram on Stalin in November 1933,[21] at a time when the cult of Stalin was beginning to blossom, because he had been deeply affected by collectivisation and 'the terrible sight of the hungry, wraith-like peasants he had recently seen on the way through the Ukraine and the Kuban'.

The opening lines of the poem:

We live, deaf to the land beneath us,
Ten steps away no one hears our speeches,

express Mandelstam's feeling that he could no longer remain silent about the evils of Stalinism, as exemplified by the mass deportation of the peasantry and the herding of writers into a single Union of Soviet Writers, subservient to Stalin. Mandelstam's wife relates that, although he suspected that his fate was already sealed, 'he did not want to die before stating in unambiguous terms what he thought about the things going on around us'. The poem, which was written in a comprehensible, accessible style 'with a view to a wider circle of readers than usual', was a deliberate act of suicide on Mandelstam's part; it led directly to his first arrest in 1934, although after Stalin's personal intervention he was only sentenced to exile. Mandelstam describes Stalin with imagery taken from the most primitive forms of life. His reference to Stalin's fat greasy fingers like grubs has a basis in reality: the poet Demyan Bedny fell into disgrace because he was unwise enough to note in his diary that he did not like lending books to Stalin because of the dirty marks left on the white pages by his greasy fingers.[22] Mandelstam's line 'his great cockroach moustache laughs' is a highly condensed and powerful use of the image first employed by Chukovsky; and Stalin's cronies are depicted as subhuman creatures who fawn around their master mewing and whining like animals. In the first version of the poem which came into the hands of the secret police Mandelstam had emphasised Stalin's responsibility for the tragedy of collectivisation, calling him a 'murderer and peasant-slayer'[23] (the word *muzhikoborets* again evokes the 'moustaches', or thieves in folk tales who robbed the peasantry). Stalin's unlimited power and ruthlessness are evoked by imagery of heavy metal; his words resemble 'lead weights' and, like some infernal blacksmith, he forges iron laws like horseshoes which are flung at vulnerable parts of the human body. He takes a malign pleasure in terror: 'Every killing is a treat'. The epithet 'Kremlin mountaineer' applied to Stalin has been explained by Nadezhda Mandelstam: 'In Russian there is a clear phonetic trail of association leading from "Kremlin" to "mountain" via the words *kremen'* ("flint") and *kamen'* ("stone")'.[24] In this poem, as in one of Mandelstam's later poems of 1936 describing an idol living in the middle of a mountain which tries to remember the days when it still had human shape,[25] the image of the mountain evokes Stalin's remoteness, immobility and isolation.

The personal interest which Stalin took in Mandelstam's case, as in Pilnyak's, once again demonstrates the seriousness with which Stalin regarded literary references to himself. Mandelstam recognised this when he said, 'That poem of mine really must have made an impression, if he makes such a song and dance about commuting my sentence'.[26] It has been claimed that the question Stalin asked Pasternak on the telephone after Mandelstam's arrest, 'He is a genius, he is a genius, isn't he?', and Stalin's initial decision to spare Mandelstam's life, were a result of his desire to be immortalised in verse by a real genius, rather than by innumerable hacks.[27] The epigram of 1933, however, represented Mandelstam's true feelings about Stalin; as we will see, when in 1937 he forced himself to write an ode glorifying Stalin it turned out to be an artistic failure and did not save his life.[28]

The highly personal manner in which Stalin read fiction is also demonstrated by the experience of the satirist Mikhail Zoshchenko. In the original version of his story *Lenin and the Sentry* (1940) Zoshchenko had presented Lenin as a kind, gentle, wise man; for contrast, he had described a crude party official with a moustache and beard. His editor suggested that in subsequent editions the beard should be omitted, in case people thought the crude official was based on Mikhail Kalinin, the President of the USSR. Unfortunately, however, Zoshchenko made the horrific mistake of removing the beard, but leaving the moustache. Allegedly Stalin read the work and took offence, imagining that it was about him; subsequently a series of troubles began for Zoshchenko, culminating in the famous attack on him by Andrei Zhdanov, Stalin's aide on cultural matters, in 1946.[29] Whether or not this story is true, it aptly illustrates Stalin's sensitivity to any slight, real or imagined, and the extreme caution with which all Soviet writers had to operate in Stalin's time.

The cult of personality

The cult of Stalin's personality in the 1930s grew out of and became integrated into the cult of Lenin, which Lenin himself opposed and managed to keep in check until incapacitated by a stroke in March 1923. The Lenin cult, while undoubtedly based on the Bolsheviks' genuine veneration for their leader, whose personal influence had been vital from the formation of the movement to the seizure and consolidation of power, was also a result of the party's need for a unifying symbol after Lenin's death. Moreover, as Robert Tucker and Nina Tumarkin have convincingly shown, the Lenin cult, with its religious overtones which clashed with the professed secularism of the Soviet state, also grew out of certain elements of the Russian past, notably traditional peasant respect for personal authority, and, particularly, veneration for the Tsar as a divinely appointed ruler.[30] Stalin had been fully conscious of the power of such feelings from the moment of Lenin's death, ensuring that he posed at Lenin's funeral as Lenin's faithful disciple and natural successor. Although he possessed considerable support and even popularity within party circles in the years after Lenin's death, Stalin knew that his prestige was not remotely comparable with Lenin's; hence it was in his interests to associate himself as closely as possible with Lenin. The Stalin cult was already in evidence by 21 December 1929, Stalin's fiftieth birthday, when the press was full of adulation of Stalin, the 'glorious leader' and 'staunch fighter'. During the ceremonials of 21 January 1930 to mark the anniversary of Lenin's death an idealised view of Stalin's close relationship with Lenin was frequently expressed.

Since Stalin's popularity subsided somewhat in the early 1930s as a result of forced collectivisation and the concomitant famine of 1932–3, he resolved to prevent the growth of opposition to him by making his political position more unassailable. Conscious that his elevation to a status similar to that of Lenin would be useful for this purpose, he actively assisted the creation of his own cult. Stalin's letter to the journal *Proletarian Revolution*, 'On Some Questions of the History of Bolshevism', published in October 1931, was a turning point in the building of the cult.[31] The underlying aims of this letter, which attacked an article by A. S. Slutsky suggesting that Lenin had underestimated the Centrist danger in the German Social Democratic Party before the First World War, were to solicit a Stalin cult in party history; to assert the infallibility of Lenin, and hence of Lenin's successor; and to falsify the position of other revolutionaries by proposing that they be judged by their deeds, rather than by documents discovered by 'archive rats'. The influence of this letter was so

far-reaching that idolatry of Stalin became universal in all fields
of culture in the 1930s, rising to heights of extravagance on such
occasions as the Seventeenth Congress of 1934, the promulgation
of the Stalin Constitution of 1936 and the purge trials of 1937
and 1938. Political expediency alone, however, does not explain
why Stalin found it necessary to allow the cult to grow after his
power became increasingly absolute later in the 1930s. It must be
assumed that Stalin had a psychological need for adulation; as
Tucker suggests, 'Boundlessly ambitious, yet inwardly insecure,
he had an imperative need for the hero worship that Lenin found
repugnant'.[32] The image of Stalin projected in the cult must have
borne some relation to Stalin's own self-image, since, while
outwardly assuming a demeanour of modesty, he was angry when
Louis Fischer suggested in 1930 that he should put a stop to the
personal glorification.[33] Evidently Stalin, the ordinary man,
needed the idealised picture of 'Stalin' evoked by his sycophants.
Once the cult had been established, its continuation can be
ascribed to several factors: Stalin's personal encouragement, the
servility of his followers and the psychology of mass conformism
engendered by a totalitarian state. Above all, the cult persisted
because it was highly effective; just as tyrants of the past had
solicited flattery and worship in order to retain their power, the
personality cult enabled Stalin to survive until his death in 1953.

It would be an impossible and thankless task to attempt to
encompass the ceaseless flood of hack literature eulogising Stalin
which flowed from the pens of Soviet writers from the early
1930s to the end of the dictator's life. Nevertheless, it is worth
considering certain literary genres which were specifically engendered by the cult of Stalin's personality. Alexander Tvardovsky,
the poet and editor of the journal *Novy Mir* in the post-Stalin era,
had these in mind when he said scornfully: 'By 1936 every issue
[of *Novy Mir*] opened with a portrait of Stalin, a *skaz* [folk tale]
on Stalin, "folk songs" on Stalin'.[34]

The 'poem' or 'song about Stalin', which attributed exceptional human virtues or even superhuman powers to him, was a
unique new genre which emerged in the 1930s.[35] Such tributes
were produced in great quantities in all the languages of the
USSR, particularly by poets from the east, where the tradition of
flattering rulers in verse dates back to ancient times. An early
example was *To the Leader, to Comrade Stalin*, a long poem by

A.A.Lakhuti, an Iranian who emigrated to the USSR and became a Soviet citizen, which was translated from Persian into Russian in 1932:

> Wise master, Marxist gardener!
> Thou art tending the vine of communism.
> Thou art cultivating it to perfection.
> After Lenin, leader of Leninists.[36]

Other exponents of the genre who received decorations and prizes were the Kazakh bard Dzhambul Dzhabaev, to whom were ascribed the oriental dithyrambs *My Stalin, I Sing this Song to You* and *The Immortal Name – Stalin*;[37] and Suleiman Stalsky from Dagestan, who received a special ovation when he was presented to the First Congress of Soviet Writers in 1934. Deutscher describes their conquest of Moscow: 'Both were the last of the oriental tribal bards, illiterate nonagenarians, long-bearded, picturesque composers of folk-songs, belated native Homers. From their highland and steppe they came to Moscow to sing, to the accompaniment of their harps, Stalin's praise at the Lenin Mausoleum'.[38]

The case of Dzhabaev is particularly curious and instructive. As Shostakovich relates in his memoirs, Dzhabaev was entirely a creation of the 'personality cult'; he embodied the strange phenomenon of 'a great poet, known by the entire country, who doesn't exist'. The promotion of Dzhambul began in the 1930s when a Russian poet and journalist working on a Kazakh newspaper brought to his editor a few poems which he claimed to have written down from the words of some folk singer and translated. The party leader of Kazakhstan happened to read the poems of the 'unknown poet', whereupon he ordered him to be found and immediately made to write a song in Stalin's honour. At this point the journalist admitted that he had lied and that the poems he had submitted were his own, but he managed to extricate himself from the dilemma by discovering Dzhambul, a picturesque old man who sang and played the *domba*, a Kazakh folk instrument. Shostakovich relates: 'They found Dzhambul and a hurried song in his name praising Stalin was sent to Moscow. Stalin liked the ode, that was the main thing, and so Dzhambul Dzhabaev's new and incredible life began'. Dzhambul was illiterate, but he was handsomely paid for his poems, which existed only in Russian translation, not in the Kazakh original. Shostakovich comments sarcastically, 'An entire brigade of Russian poetasters laboured for Dzhambul, including some famous names like Konstantin Simonov. And they knew the political situation well and wrote to please the leader and teacher, which meant writing mostly about Stalin himself'. After Dzhabaev's death some young Kazakh poets wanted to expose the myth, but they were ordered to keep quiet, and the non-existent poet's anniversary was celebrated with pomp.[39]

Apart from labouring for Dzhabaev, many well-known Russian poets produced in their own names popular lyrics about Stalin intended to be sung. These included Mikhail Isakovsky, Aleksei Surkov, who likened Stalin to 'the flight of our youth' (a phrase later used ironically by the dissident Alexander Zinoviev as the title of his 'literary and sociological study of Stalinism'),[40] and Vasily Lebedev-Kumach, whose famous *Song of the Motherland*, written in 1935 and published in editions of 20 million copies, quotes Stalin's 1936 Constitution:

A person always has the right
To study, rest and labour.

(this verse was omitted from the 1977 text of the song).[41] The Soviet national anthem, which was composed in 1943 by the poet Sergei Mikhalkov and the journalist Gabriel El-Registan after taking Stalin's corrections into account, and set to music by A. Aleksandrov, after a national competition, contained a third verse eulogising Stalin:

Stalin raised us – faithfulness to the people,
Work and heroic deeds he inspired in us.[42]

When the 'cult of personality' was exposed in the post-Stalin period the anthem became known as the 'song without words', until in 1977 a new text was approved in which Stalin's name was replaced by Lenin's.

Songs about Stalin are highly stylised in language and imagery, using elements divorced from popular speech. The emotional range is very restricted: no satire or humour could be included, and the poet could only express positive emotions such as joy, happiness, gratitude, veneration, pride and fidelity, or defiance towards the enemies of the USSR. Some epithets and images are those associated with God or gods in religious literature: Stalin is constantly addressed as 'father', and is seen as a 'sun', a 'star', a source of light; and the words 'immortal' and 'eternal' are sometimes used in connection with his youth or his fame.[43] Other images evoke the earthly power and majesty of the ruler and shaper of human destinies: he is an architect, a helmsman, a military leader ('our fighting glory'),[44] or an incalculable treasure:

> You are more dear than all diamonds
> You are more valuable than all pearls.[45]

Other images are more closely connected with Stalin's own life and achievements. He is frequently depicted against a specific geographical background: either the mountains, sun and snows of his native Georgia[46], or the fields and steppes of Russia.[47] Bird imagery is also commonly used to evoke Stalin's Georgian background and soaring genius. Stalin had once characterised Lenin as a mountain eagle, and in the 1930s this image was taken up by the Old Bolshevik N. Antonov-Ovseenko to eulogise Stalin.[48] Subsequently, innumerable poets employed the image of the eagle, sometimes coupled with a reference to aeroplanes, to evoke Stalin's paternal encouragement of the long-distance pilots such as the Arctic flier Valery Chkalov, popular heroes whose feats enhanced Soviet national prestige in the 1930s, and who were known as 'Stalin's falcons' or 'Stalin's fledgeling children'.[49] While most imagery is taken from archaic rural folklore rather than from modern urban life, Stalin is sometimes depicted in Moscow, where he is seen as the embodiment of Russia's capital city and of the Kremlin, the symbol of imperial Russian power;[50] the light in the Kremlin window at night symbolises his fatherly concern for his people.[51] In the 1940s, in homage to Stalin's interest in Lysenko's agricultural schemes and his sponsorship of the 'Great Stalin Plan to Transform Nature' (1948), another set of images depicted Stalin as a 'gardener' before whom the abundant kolkhoz fields extend in sunny profusion;[52] the promise of new life which he offers is conveyed by images of dawn and spring. While most poets treat Stalin with awe, some present a more approachable Stalin, describing him as a 'friend', a genial figure who blows smoke rings;[53] and his role as the mentor of youth is frequently evoked:

> He loves youth
> He himself is young.[54]

Another unique genre engendered by the cult of personality in the 1930s was the folk tale in prose or verse about Stalin and other Soviet leaders. A renewed interest in folklore was stimulated by Gorky, who in his speech to the First Writers' Congress of 1934 called on literature to model its heroes on those of 'folklore, i.e. the unwritten compositions of the toiling man'.[55] Considerable resources were invested in the collection and dissemination of oral folklore; and an attempt was made to create a genuine contemporary folk literature. The main aim of these latter-day *byliny* (traditional heroic poems) or folk tales was to extol and legitimise the Stalin leadership. In 1937 the publishing house 'Two Five Year Plans' invited some singers of *byliny* to travel from their remote villages to Moscow to create new tales in praise of the present age. Professional writers were usually assigned to the bards to help them compose their epics or tales. The best known example is *Tale of Lenin* (1937) by Marfa Kryukova, the granddaughter of the *bylina* singer used as a source by the great nineteenth-century collector of folklore, Rybnikov.[56] Kryukova's epic poem depicts three meetings between 'the red sun Vlademir' (Lenin) and 'Stalin-svet' (light), after which Lenin sends Stalin out into the world to accomplish his work. The poem, which closely follows the Stalinist version of Bolshevik history, is intended to legitimise Stalin's succession.[57]

Other folk tales are either designed to provide a general eulogy of Stalin as a wise leader, or to glorify specific aspects of his life and achievements. In *The Dearest Thing* (1937) by F. A. Konashkov, a story-teller from a Karelian kolkhoz, the three best workers from a collective farm are sent to resolve an argument about the identity of 'the dearest thing'. They follow an enchanted ball of thread until it leads to Moscow, to Stalin; and the moral of the story is: 'The best and dearest thing we have on earth is the word of Comrade Stalin'.[58] The Chuvash tale *About Happiness* (1935) is designed to praise Stalin's collectivisation policy. An old Chuvash sends his son away to find happiness; he meets an eagle (Stalin) who tells him to kill, successively, a bear, a wolf and a fox; each time the life of the peasants improves until, after the third heroic deed, the kolkhoz is established. The conclusion leaves the reader in no doubt as to how the story should be interpreted: 'Thus the poor Chuvash Endri, having killed the bear-Tsar, wolf-landowner and fox-kulak, at last found his happiness'.[59]

Other tales, such as V. Bespalikov's *Three Sons* (1937) and *The Sun* by the Chuvash V. Khramov, celebrate Stalin's role as father and mentor of heroic young people.[60] In Khramov's tale an old kolkhoznik says he will give his blessing to whichever of his three sons reaches the sun; one becomes a pilot, the other a sailor and the third a soldier, seeking the sun by air, sea and land. Finally all three are rewarded by Stalin, and the old man gives his blessing to them all, as 'The brightest of all suns in the world is our Stalin'.[61] Other tales, such as I. Kovalyov's *Icy Hill* and a tale by the old story-teller Ayau from Dagestan, *How the Heroes Subdued Ilmukhanum*, celebrate the exploits of the Arctic pilots, depicting the conquest of icy northern regions by young heroes inspired by Stalin.[62] One aspect of Stalin's early life emphasised in adulatory biographies was his daring escapes from exile. This was dramatised in a Nenets tale from a Siberian kolkhoz, *Stalin and Truth* (1936), in which Stalin is sent to the tundra by the wicked Tsar because he is friendly with Truth; Stalin fraternises with the peoples of the tundra, and because he is 'not a simple man, but a hero' (*bogatyr'*) and 'the gods have invested him with the strength of a bear and the wisdom of a polar falcon' he manages to send a letter to Truth discussing 'how the poor people can live better on earth'. Stalin tells the people to fight for Soviet power, and when it is achieved, their life becomes happier.[63]

The revival of folk genres did not prove to be a particularly successful method of inculcating praise of the leader or of portraying a model of the new man, because, in Katerina Clark's words, 'the crudity of the engrafted folksiness and the transparency of the devices reduced its effectiveness as a repository of myth'.[64] In 1947 critics came out against the folk bards, quoting a phrase in Zhdanov's speech of 1946, 'Russia is not the same', to argue that the policy of encouraging folk epics was misconceived.[65]

One work which presents a striking contrast to the artificially sponsored adulatory songs and tales about Stalin is an ironic song, *Comrade Stalin, You're a Real Big Scholar* (first published abroad in 1964), which circulated in the prison camps and became a genuine folk song of the late Stalin era. The composer subsequently turned out to be Yuz Aleshkovsky, a former convict, who had been published in the USSR only as a children's writer, and who emigrated in 1979.[66] The song parodies various aspects of the 'cult of personality' by juxtaposing them with the hard life of the prisoners in Stalin's camps:

> Comrade Stalin, you're a real big scholar
> You know what's going on in linguistics
> But I'm a simple Soviet convict
> And my comrade is the grey Bryansk wolf.[67]

The singer, incarcerated in the Turukhansk region where Stalin himself had been imprisoned under Nicholas II, calls himself a fool for not being able to escape even once, when Stalin managed to escape from exile six times (this is an ironic reference to the far harsher conditions for prisoners and exiles in the Stalin era than in Tsarist times).

Aleshkovsky's irony is aimed against those party members who remained loyal to the party and Stalin in the camps and even accepted Stalin's ideological justification for the purges:

> What I'm in for, I swear I don't know,
> But the procurators are right, it would seem . . .
> Naturally, I understand all this
> As an intensification of the class struggle.

The song ridicules those 'loyalists', to use Solzhenitsyn's term,[68] who remained convinced that when the all-wise Stalin found out what crimes were being committed in his name by the security organs, he would investigate the cases of party members and set them free. The song tells of a dying Marxist:

> And before he passed away forever,
> He willed you his tobacco pouch and all his words,
> He asked you to get to the bottom of all this here,
> And screamed out quietly: 'Stalin's so clever!'
>
> Live a hundred years, comrade Stalin,
> And though it may be my fate to kick the bucket here,
> I only hope the production of steel can rise
> Per head of population in the country.

A genre which proved particularly effective in inculcating Stalinist values, especially pride in Holy Mother Russia, was the historical epic, or film. Aleksei Tolstoy's *Peter the Great*, published in serial form from 1929 to 1945, a portrait of the ruthless Tsar who transformed Russia from a backward country into a European power, was a skilful attempt to create a parallel with Stalin and an apologia for his tyranny.[69] Similarly, numerous historical films of the 1930s, such as Petrov's *Peter the First*, Pudovkin's *Minin and Pozharsky*, Dovzhenko's *Shchors* (made in response to Stalin's request for a Ukrainian version of *Chapaev*) and Eisenstein's *Alexander Nevsky*, featured a powerful and charismatic leader.[70] Film was Stalin's own favourite art form, and he was fond of quoting Lenin's dictum: 'Cinema for us is the most important of the arts'.[71] Stalin's awareness of the value of films on historical subjects was demonstrated in 1947 when he summoned Eisenstein and instructed him to make a film showing Ivan IV as a 'great and wise ruler'; of all the leaders in Russian history, he claimed, Ivan and Lenin were the only two who had introduced a state monopoly of foreign trade. According to Ehrenburg, Stalin contrasted Ivan favourably with Peter the Great, who did not cut off enough heads.[72] In Part I of *Ivan the Terrible* Eisenstein followed Stalin's instructions, glorifying autocracy and putting into Ivan's mouth what Stalin could not say to anyone: 'O God, am I right in what I do?', to which God seems to answer that he *is* right.

However, if historical works could be used to extol Stalin, they could also be subverted to express criticism of him. Vera Alexandrova, writing in 1943, recognised a similarity between the Russia depicted in the first part of V. Kostylev's trilogy *Ivan the Terrible* (1943–55) and contemporary Soviet reality.[73] Part II of Eisenstein's *Ivan the Terrible* was banned by the Soviet authorities, as it represented a clear attempt to attack Stalin and tyrannical rule. Eisenstein himself in his autobiographical notes compared the 'black forms of the *oprichniki* of Ivan the Terrible' with the 'soulless automatons of the *apparatchiki* of Stalin the terrible'.[74] The film director Mikhail Romm, a witness to the first showing of Part II, saw Ivan's henchman Malyut Skuratov as Beria; and the victim in the film, Vladimir Staritsky, can be interpreted as an image of Eisenstein, the victim in real life.[75]

It was not only hack writers who contributed to the personality cult; some of the best Soviet poets also felt obliged to write poems about Stalin. The better poets, such as Nikolai Zabolotsky, treated this theme obliquely, with greater subtlety than the majority of Soviet writers. Zabolotsky's poem *Gori Symphony* (1936) provides a good description of Stalin's birthplace, the small town of Gori in Georgia, with its trees and encircling mountains.[76] The poet's attention is attracted to a poor dark hut, and he tries to understand how in such a remote place unutterable thoughts first formed in Stalin's head, and how:

> The original structure of his soul
> Was formed by the action of nature.

Most of the poem is a hymn in praise of Georgia, and only the final stanza bows to the prevailing literary climate with a conventional eulogy of the revolution, the birth of the new world and the Five Year Plan. Unfortunately, Zabolotsky's willingness to write a poem in praise of Stalin did not save him from persecution: he spent the years 1938 to 1946 in camps and exile.

Another unconventional work which includes a reference to Stalin is Alexander Tvardovsky's long narrative poem *Muravia Land* (1936), which skilfully combines elements of the *bylina* with the flavour of peasant speech.[77] Rumour spreads through the countryside that Stalin is coming, and he appears like a fairy-tale *bogatyr*' 'on a raven-black horse', 'in a greatcoat, with his pipe'. He looks around, speaks to the people and takes note of conditions. (This is, of course, an idealised picture of Stalin, who rarely travelled into the countryside). The hero Nikita Morgunok tells Stalin everything in his heart: he admits that conditions are improving and agrees to join the kolkhoz one day, but regrets the loss of his own land. Stalin listens in silence as Nikita asks if he can make allowances for him and 'for the time being' leave him his farm. The rest of the poem concerns Nikita's search for the peasants' Utopia where he will be allowed to keep his smallholding; but experience and the advice of a mysterious old man teach him that there is no Muravia Land, and he must join a collective farm. This poem, which demonstrates Tvardovsky's understanding of the psychology of the peasant, perhaps represents the poet's attempt to smooth over his own doubts about collectivisation (his father was deported as a kulak). Tvardovsky was subjected to some criticism for alleged 'peasant anarchism';[78] and indeed, *Muravia Land* is by no means an orthodox embodiment of Stalinist ideology, as at times the author appears sympathetic to Nikita's dream. Nevertheless, the poem was eventually awarded a Stalin Prize.

In order to understand Tvardovsky's real feelings about Stalin and collectivisation it is salutary to contrast *Muravia Land* with his posthumously published poem *For the Right of Memory*,[79] which evokes both the guilt that Tvardovsky was made to feel in the 1930s as 'the son of a kulak', and the guilt he subsequently felt in relation to his father's persecution when he had reassessed the experience of collectivisation.

One of the most tragic aspects of the effect of the personality cult on literature was that the best and most independent poets in the country were obliged to join in the chorus of praise. A brief discussion of some of the darkest pages in the biographies of Pasternak, Mandelstam and Akhmatova (without any intention of passing judgement on their actions) will help to illuminate the impact of politics on literature in Stalin's time.

Pasternak's poetic inspiration declined in the 1930s; he did not himself write 'poems about Stalin', but his decision to translate Georgian poetry as a refuge from the need to create original works meant that it was difficult to avoid references to Stalin in his translations. Some of his translations of the 1920s, for example P. Yashvili's *On the Death of Lenin* (1924) and V. Gaprindashvili's *October Lines* (1929), contained passing references to Stalin;[80] but a new departure occurred in 1934, when Pasternak's translations of two poems dedicated to Stalin by N. Mitsishvili and P. Yashvili became widely known through their publication in the journals *Novy Mir* and *Krasnaya Nov'*.[81] The poems were written at the beginning of 1934 and rapidly translated by Pasternak so that they could be published before the Seventeenth Party Congress (the 'Congress of Victors'). Mitsishvili's *Stalin*, with its grandiose tone and ornate symbolism, is particularly alien to Pasternak's own style. Lazar Fleishman argues that Pasternak's decision to translate these odes cannot be ascribed to bureaucratic compulsion; rather, in 1934 his views did not significantly diverge from those of the Georgian poets. He saw Stalin as a unifying force in the country after the troubled period of the 'Great Turning-Point', and hoped that the development of fascism in Europe would inspire the socialist state to move in the direction of greater civilisation and humanity. Pasternak's decision may also have been inspired by a desire to help his fellow poets in the Georgian 'Blue Horn' group whose work had suffered neglect; and possibly also represented a reaction against Mandelstam's epigram about Stalin, which horrified Pasternak as a 'suicidal' act. Moreover, in 1934 the cult of Stalin was only in its infancy; Pasternak could not have foreseen the extravagant proportions it would reach in later years.[82] These odes are an exception in Pasternak's *oeuvre*; most of his translations, while published in collections containing eulogies of Stalin, are remarkably free from references to Stalin. In general Pasternak deliberately avoided political themes, concentrating on personal or nature lyrics.[83] Nevertheless, these odes to Stalin may have played their part in ensuring Pasternak's survival and cementing his enigmatic personal relationship with Stalin (as witnessed by the famous phone call from Stalin to Pasternak after Mandelstam's first arrest in 1934).

Although Pasternak, like many other people in the USSR, was 'morbidly curious about the recluse in the Kremlin',[84] in his later work he preferred to pass over the subject of Stalin in silence. *Doctor Zhivago* , however, contains a reference to 'pockmarked Caligulas', which may well express Pasternak's considered judgement of Stalin as the latest in a long line of tyrants.[85] It is true, as Neil Cornwell points out, that Pasternak was being particularly cautious if he placed a reference to Stalin in the mouth of Zhivago's uncle Vedenyapin, who was speaking in 1903;[86] but this argument does not invalidate the allusion, since Pasternak frequently displayed caution in his literary activities, and may have been resorting to deliberate camouflage in the hope that *Doctor Zhivago* would be published in the USSR. Isaiah Berlin mentions a theory current among the Soviet intelligentsia that Evgraf, Yuri Zhivago's mysterious half-brother, was intended to represent Stalin – a theory apparently dismissed by Anna Akhmatova.[87] The parallel is valid only in the limited sense that Evgraf is a high official who acts as a *deus ex machina* in Yuri's life, as Stalin did in the lives of such writers as Pasternak, Mandelstam and Bulgakov. Although there have been many other more plausible and complex interpretations of the figure of Evgraf,[88] the theory nevertheless possesses some interest as an example of the highly political interpretations accorded to literary works by the Soviet reading public.

The case of Mandelstam is more tragic. Nadezhda Mandelstam describes how in the winter of 1936–7, foreseeing the impending catastrophe, her husband made an attempt to save himself by writing an *Ode to Stalin*.[89] The artificiality of the whole project was evident from the fact that Mandelstam forced himself to sit down at their table with paper and pencil and waited for words to come, 'like Fedin, or someone of that kind'. Since he had never in his life composed in that manner, the plan was bound to fail; 'his attempt to do violence to himself met stubborn resistance', but the artificially conceived poem about Stalin led to the creation of other poems, antagonistic to the Ode, which formed part of the *Second Voronezh Cycle*. Mandelstam asked his friend Natasha Shtempel to destroy the Ode when they left Voronezh, but some indications of its content can be extrapolated from Nadezhda Mandelstam's memoirs. The word *os'* ('axle') which featured in the ode, perhaps connected with Stalin's first name 'Iosif', led to a scattering of words containing the syllable 'os' throughout the cycle. In the Ode an artist, with tears in his eyes, draws a portrait of the leader; but another poem of 8 February contained the line: 'I do not draw and I do not sing'. A reference to Aeschylus and Prometheus in the Ode led in the other poems to a treatment of the theme of tragedy and martyrdom; and the Caucasus, mentioned as Stalin's birthplace in the Ode, occurs again in the reference to Tbilisi as the place which remembers not the Great Leader but the poor poet with his worn shoes. Nadezhda Mandelstam concludes: 'To write an ode to Stalin it was necessary to get in tune, like a musical instrument, by deliberately giving way to the general hypnosis and putting oneself under the spell of the liturgy which in those days blotted out all human voices. Without this, a real poet could never compose such a thing: he would never have had that kind of ready facility. M. thus spent the beginning of 1937 conducting a grotesque experiment on himself. Working himself up into the state needed to write the 'Ode', he was in effect deliberately upsetting the balance of his own mind. "I now realise that it was an illness", he said later to Akhmatova.'

Although Nadezhda Mandelstam was advised not to speak of the Ode, as if it had never existed, she insists on telling the truth about the double life that she and her husband were forced to live in Stalin's time. She comments bitterly that, unlike other poets who 'wrote their odes in their apartments and country villas and were rewarded for them, M. wrote his with a rope around his neck'. The Ode did not achieve its aim of saving Mandelstam's life, but it may have been instrumental in saving his wife's life and enabling her to preserve his poems.

Another poet who wrote poems to Stalin in similar tragic circumstances was Anna Akhmatova. She had suffered persecution since 1946, when she had been singled out for attack in a speech by Stalin's henchman Zhdanov. She was subsequently expelled from the Union of Writers, and in 1949 her husband Nikolai Punin and her son Lev Gumilyov were arrested. It was in order to save her son's life that she wrote for Stalin's seventieth birthday in December 1949 *In Praise of Peace*, a cycle of poems extolling Stalin, which was sent directly to Aleksei Surkov, Secretary of the Writers' Union, for prompt publication.[90] Akhmatova regarded the cycle as a sacrifice, and expressly requested that it be omitted from her *Collected Works*.[91] Earlier, in a poem of her *Requiem* cycle written in 1939, she had recognised the inner necessity of surrendering to the authorities and begging for forgiveness, despite the futility of the sacrifice:

> For seventeen months I have cried
> I call you home.
> I have thrown myself at the feet of the executioner,
> You are my son and my terror . . .[92]

Akhmatova was aware that she could not write the panegyric to Stalin in any remotely literary style; it is striking in its banality. The poems are a contribution to the peace movement launched by the Soviet Union in 1949–50, which was intended to suggest to world public opinion that America's possession of atomic weapons rather than Soviet policies constituted the major threat to peace. Akhmatova demands 'peace' on Soviet terms, praising the Stockholm peace charter of 1950, a document calling for a ban on the atom bomb which was allegedly signed by 500 million people, and attacking the imperialists for their participation in the Korean War. She praises Stalin in many of the current clichés; he is an eagle, the transformer of nature,

> The true master of life,
> The sovereign of mountains and rivers,

who utters the 'radiant word – peace'.[93] There is a bitter irony in her words:

Legend speaks of a wise man
Who has saved each of us from a terrible death.[94]

Akhmatova's real feelings had been expressed in a poem of the 1930s, *An Imitation of the Armenian*, in which an oriental tyrant is asked:

And was my son to the taste
Of yourself and your children?[95]

In Praise of Peace is one of the most tragic documents of the age, but Akhmatova's sacrifice may have saved her son's life (he was released in 1956). The very artistic poverty of the cycle makes it an ironic work: in Amanda Haight's words, it was 'a joke on the very times themselves when a handful of bad poems by someone who had written the poems of *Requiem* could actually result in saving someone's life'.[96] As Nadezhda Mandelstam says of her friend Akhmatova and her husband: 'Who can blame either her or M.?'.[97]

Prose fiction was the most important genre for the inculcation of Stalinist values; and during the period of the 'personality cult' writers were unanimous in their extravagant eulogies of Stalin. As Katerina Clark has shown, in the mythology of the 1930s sightings of Stalin or meetings between Stalin and young pilots or Stakhanovite workers, which were extensively reported in the press, played the role of 'ritual exchanges between "mentor" and "disciple", between "father" and "son", which conferred greater consciousness' on the young heroes.[98] Such climactic moments were also important for characters in fiction. In P. Pavlenko's *In the East* (1936), for example, the heroine Olga feels great joy when she sees Stalin's 'calm figure' and 'severe' countenance, and listens to 'the voice of our motherland, the simple, clear, infinitely honest, boundlessly kind, unhurried and fatherly voice of Stalin'.[99]

In the 1930s writers of fiction, like historians, fulfilled the function of rewriting history to legitimise the Stalinist succession. One of the most effective promoters of the Stalin cult was Aleksei Tolstoy, who enjoyed a good personal relationship with Stalin and, according to Ilya Ehrenburg, would go to any lengths to achieve 'peace and quiet'.[100] His novel *Bread* (1937), an adulatory account of Stalin's allegedly single-handed defence of

Tsaritsyn in the Civil War, contains some of the clichés with which we are already familiar from poetry and folk epics, and some which became the stock-in-trade of the prose writer for the next decade. The most prominent is Tolstoy's evocation of Stalin's 'calm' voice and manner; as Katerina Clark demonstrates, the epithet *spokoinyi* ('calm, confident') is frequently used in Soviet novels as a sign of complete self-control and firmness in the revolutionary faith.[101] Tolstoy's Stalin first appears as Lenin's close comrade-in-arms, and gives Lenin advice in the 'even, quiet, calm voice in which he conducted all conversations'; when he arrives in Tsaritsyn his face is 'serious and calm', and he greets everyone without distinction 'not too warmly and not too drily'.[102] Stalin's good nature and courage are stressed: his eyes are 'cheerful', and when under fire he merely laughs and says: 'It happens'.[103] It is Stalin who alerts Lenin to the importance of Tsaritsyn; his role as Lenin's equal is emphasised by the orders which are issued in the names of 'Lenin and Stalin'. He tackles his job as organiser of the food supply in south Russia in a business-like manner; he is firm, decisive and knowledgeable, with a 'penetrating gaze'.[104] He stresses the importance of the political preparation of his soldiers and of hard work to produce armaments. Although he does not immediately use his emergency powers, he is ruthless in dealing with enemies: he comes into conflict with the Supreme Military Council headed by Trotsky, and has several officers and specialists shot for counter-revolutionary activities. Tolstoy rewrites history in order to contribute to the mythology surrounding Stalin in the 1930s: Trotsky's role as creator of the Red Army is ignored, and Tolstoy emphasises Stalin's part in revitalising the Red Army by purging its command of saboteurs. Tolstoy also anachronistically projects on to Stalin an interest in aviation: he predicts that one day Soviet people will fly like birds.

During the first, disastrous period of the war, July–December 1941, Stalin's name was notable for its absence from newspapers and war stories. Ehrenburg relates: 'Stalin's name was hardly mentioned; for the first time for many years there were neither portraits nor enthusiastic epithets; the smoke of nearby explosions banished the smoke of incense'.[105] Even Stalin appeared to understand that he needed to take a back seat, since his unpreparedness for war had led to the initial heavy defeats. For a long time Soviet writers kept silent about the first months of the war and began their account with the counter-offensive of December 1941.

After the shock of the invasion had subsided, however, Stalin returned to prominence. Alexander Korneichuk's play *The Front*, published in *Pravda* in August 1942, was commissioned by Stalin himself to improve his image – a striking example of the political use of literature.[106] Korneichuk attempts to exonerate Stalin, laying the blame for the defeats of 1941–2 at the door of generals with old-fashioned ideas and practices. Although Stalin himself does not appear as a character in the play, he is shown to be supremely well-informed and actively concerned with introducing new technology and replacing inefficient commanders with younger, more talented men. Another work of the same year, Leonid Leonov's play *The Invasion* (1942), emphasises the patriotic and near-religious aspects of Stalin's leadership. Before Stalin's speech of November 1941 an old man tells his grandson about a previous meeting at which Stalin was present: 'It was an enormous great hall and there were more than a thousand of us, but it felt empty and cold somehow. Then one man entered, and it felt as though there weren't an empty seat. His presence set us on fire.'[107] Another aspect of Stalin's leadership which was emphasised in wartime fiction was his ability to organise industrial production. A. Karavaeva's *Fires* (1943) also evokes Stalin's speech of November 1941, emphasising his claim that Germany's resources will be more quickly exhausted and that Soviet tanks, although less numerous, are of better quality; Stalin's 'calm' voice with its 'deep trust' in the Soviet people makes a great impression on the listening workers, who vow to produce tanks more rapidly.[108] Works published later in the war, such as Simonov's *Days and Nights* (1944), also concentrated on the inspiration inculcated by Stalin's speeches, perhaps because it was easier to portray Stalin as a national and spiritual leader than as a military strategist.[109] By 1945 adulation of Stalin had become more intense. The climax of V. Kataev's novel *A Son of the Regiment* (1945) is a boy's dream of ascending a marble staircase, at the top of which stands Stalin with his brilliant marshal's star and his 'severe paternal smile'.[110]

After the victory, during the oppressive 'Zhdanov period' in literature until Stalin's death in 1953, the cult flourished with renewed vigour; and writers once again extolled Stalin's military genius. In Vsevolod Ivanov's *At the Capture of Berlin* (1946), Marshal Zhukov asks an artist to give him a sketch of Stalin's face so that he can look at it during the capture of Berlin: 'I always look at Stalin! We conquer through his genius. Always!'.[111] In the conclusion of Ivanov's novel the panegyric rises to hagiographic proportions. Stalin mounts the Mausoleum steps with 'a thoughtful gait, the gait of a thinker and wise soldier, sure of every step' and 'all rapturously applaud Stalin, the father of the people, the happiness of humanity, the greatest military leader in the world .... And everybody can clearly see love written on his face, an inextinguishable love for his people, for their lives, for their happiness, and those in the square, realising his feelings, applaud again and again'.[112]

Nikolai Virta's play *Great Days*, written in 1947 and allegedly edited by Stalin himself, depicts Stalin making all the major decisions about the battle of Stalingrad. Virta includes a theory widely disseminated in the post-war years to explain the events of 1941: the myth that the retreat of the Soviet troops was a deliberate strategy conceived by Stalin to draw the Germans deep into the country prior to the launching of a counter-offensive, a plan allegedly based on the example of the ancient Parthians. Moreover, Virta suggests that already in August 1942 Stalin had devised the precise tactics through which the Red Army's offensive in November would trap the Germans in Stalingrad (Marshal Zhukov, who at the time of the victory at Stalingrad was recognised as the chief planner, is not mentioned). One innovation introduced into Virta's play is the shadowy character of 'Stalin's Friend', whose function is to humanise him. The Friend comments sympathetically on 'Joseph's' grey hair and tiredness, advises him to rest more and not to smoke (although Stalin admits he cannot give it up) and recalls his escapes from exile and the battle near Tsaritsyn (about which Stalin comments modestly: 'I always have to undertake something'). Stalin is cordial and polite with his Friend, inviting him to his dacha to talk about old times; when his comically solicitous secretary Poskryobyshev reminds him of the urgent business that awaits him, Stalin protests wearily: 'Don't I get any free time, even at night?'.[113] Virta's play, although set in the war, reflects the atmosphere of the post-war years: the emphasis laid on Churchill's refusal to open a second front in Europe is redolent of the confrontation of the Cold War period; and Virta implausibly depicts Stalin reflecting in the middle of the war both on post-war car production and the need to make contact with Lysenko about a new type of grain in order to double agricultural production by 1950. Other incongruous elements in Virta's play are Stalin's solicitude and respect for Molotov (notwithstanding the arrest of Molotov's wife in 1948), and an anachronistically friendly reference to the Americans, who are presented as good, if naive people who call Stalin 'Uncle Joe' (a name which never became popular in the USSR). It is not surprising that Virta's play was singled out for satirical treatment by Solzhenitsyn in *The First Circle*.[114]

Another work satirised by Solzhenitsyn is V. Vishnevsky's play *Unforgettable 1919* (1949), which also depicts past events in order to provide lessons for the present. Vishnevsky's portrayal of Stalin's stern treatment of spies in Petrograd in 1919 and his arrest of members of the Military Council, a body headed by Trotsky, is an attempt to justify the renewed campaigns in the late forties against anti-cosmopolitanism and bourgeois national-ism. Stalin's final threat that 'if anyone is to be bloodied' he will make sure that it is 'the bourgeois camp and not the Soviet state' is clearly aimed against the USA.[115] According to Shostakovich, Stalin was particularly fond of the film *Unforgettable 1919*, based on Vishnevsky's play. As he watched his young self riding by on the footboard of an armoured train with a sabre in his hand, he was heard to exclaim, 'How young and handsome Stalin was!'. Shostakovich comments ironically, 'He talked about himself in the third person and gave an opinion on his looks. A positive one'.[116]

In the late 1940s and early 1950s the cult of Stalin reached new heights. In Alexander Kron's *Party Candidate* (1950), the hero, in the middle of a love scene, when asked by the heroine if he has one 'sacred dream' . . . a fantastic dream, an almost impossible one', responds: 'I would like to have a talk with Comrade Stalin'.[117] In A. Gribachev's *Spring in 'Pobeda'* (1948) Stalin's sainthood is established when he personally escorts the party organiser Zernov across the threshold of death, with the words:

'You have struggled not in vain.
You have laboured not in vain.
Your last day is your first step into the commune.
Here comes its dawn.'
Thus, at dawn
  in "Pobeda"
Zernov, the party organiser,
  died.[118]

Since apparently orthodox works such as A. Fadeyev's *The Young Guard* and V. Kataev's *For the Power of the Soviets* came under attack in the late 1940s for underestimating the role of the party in the war, it was inevitable that history would be rewritten to present Stalin as a supreme military genius. Two extreme examples of 'varnishing reality' are the first part of G. Berezko's *Peaceful Town* (1951) and the second part of M. Bubyonnov's *White Birch Tree* (1952), which contain frequent, extravagant depictions of Stalin.[119] Both writers dramatise the myth of Stalin's counter-offensive strategy, suggesting that Stalin's aim in 1941 was to conserve reserves, not to weaken them in defensive fights, and to defeat the enemy outside Moscow. Berezko describes Stalin in a 'large bright room' in the Kremlin, poring over maps with a 'concentrated face' and an 'enormous energy of thought . . . analysing, comparing, predicting, creating'. Stalin's speech on 7 November 1941 is seen as 'a father's blessing'; Stalin, as always, is 'attentive, very serious, very calm', and his omniscience is emphasised: 'He had thought of everything, predicted everything'.[120] Bubyonnov depicts Stalin on the night of 16 November 1941: he is concerned about the forthcoming battle, but confident that Moscow will stand; and he plans an improvement in the war industries in the Urals.[121] Both writers suggest, with hindsight, that Stalin's defensive strategy in 1941 marked the beginning of the Soviet victory.

The hagiography in which Soviet writers indulged during the 'period of the personality cult' now appears absurd, but the main reason for the cult's survival is that it was highly effective. Just as tyrants of the past had solicited flattery and worship in order to retain their power, the personality cult of Stalin, which perhaps corresponded to Russia's deep-rooted autocratic traditions, enabled Stalin to survive unchallenged until his death in 1953.

Aesopian language

Apart from the anonymous composers of folk songs and anec-
dotes, only very few writers explicitly expressed hostility to
Stalin in his lifetime – and, of these, Pilnyak and Mandelstam
perished. After the war the only writer to compose and recite
verses against Stalin while Stalin was still alive was the young
poet Naum Mandel (Korzhavin). One of his poems was:

> There in Moscow in a whirlpool of darkness
> Wrapped in his greatcoat,
> Not understanding Pasternak
> A hard and cruel man stared at the snow.

Korzhavin was exiled, but Evtushenko claims that the very fact
that he did recite his verses openly saved his life, because the
authorities thought him insane.[122] More frequently, although still
very occasionally, writers made derogatory references to Stalin
obliquely, through Aesopian devices, although works containing
such allusions only rarely achieved publication in the USSR.

Mikhail Bulgakov's play *Batumi*, which concerns Stalin's early
life and, particularly, his activities during the strikes and
demonstrations in Batumi in 1902, followed by his imprisonment, exile to Siberia and escape, at first sight appears to be yet
another tragic example of a great writer's sacrifice of his artistic
integrity. The play was conceived in March 1936 under the title
The Pastor, but was put aside until September 1938 when well-
meaning friends from the Moscow Arts Theatre, the literary
consultant P. Markov and the theatrical scholar V. Vilenkin,
suggested that Bulgakov complete the play to coincide with the
celebrations for Stalin's sixtieth birthday in 1939. Bulgakov
finally agreed, and the play was finished on 24 July 1939.
Vilenkin states in his memoirs that the aim of giving the subject
to Bulgakov was that there would be 'no varnishing, no speculations, no incense; the emotional content of the drama could
arise from the truth of the authentic material, if only a dramatist
of Bulgakov's stature took it up'.[123] Bulgakov's decision to write
the play, which gave the author no pleasure, and is not particularly successful, can be ascribed to several factors. Firstly, *The
Pastor* was originally conceived at a time when Bulgakov's play
Molière, which implies a parallel between Molière's relationship

with Louis XIV and Bulgakov's relationship with Stalin, had been subjected to criticism in the press and eventually taken off. It is possible, as Ellendea Proffer suggests, that the first version of the play about Stalin was 'far from icon-painting'.[124] Secondly, Bulgakov's life and works testify to his interest in tyrants. He had a strange personal relationship with Stalin, which began on 18 April 1930 when a letter he had sent to the Soviet government was followed by a telephone call from Stalin offering Bulgakov a choice between emigration and the possibility of working in a consultative capacity in the Soviet theatre. Subsequently Stalin took an interest in Bulgakov's literary career, and in particular, became fascinated by Bulgakov's play *The Days of the Turbins*, (first produced in 1926 and restaged in 1932 at Stalin's personal request), which he went to see fifteen times. Moreover, as an artist Bulgakov was interested in Stalin in the same sense that he was interested in other absolute rulers such as Louis XIV or Nicholas I. Another factor was the strong pressure exerted on Bulgakov by his friends in the Moscow Arts Theatre to write something for the Stalin jubilee. Bulgakov's wife Elena Sergeevna also supported the idea, hoping that it would assist the publication and production of Bulgakov's other works. Personal reasons were, however, perhaps the decisive factor: Bulgakov was ill and knew he was dying, so although he himself had no further need for protection, he hoped the play might secure the future for his widow and her son.

Vilenkin describes the character of Stalin in Bulgakov's play as 'a young, fearless, intelligent revolutionary who had already won authority among the workers, a recent pupil of a theological seminary. Without a halo. With the right to ordinary human feelings, a living, authentic daily life and humour'.[125] This is an apt characterisation: Bulgakov's Stalin is an unimpeachable hero, but he is also a realistic character, unlike the idealised stereotypes who were later to appear in plays by Virta and Vishnevsky.[126] Bulgakov's play was fated to have an unsuccessful outcome: on the very day when Bulgakov and other members of the theatre were going to Batumi to collect more material for the production, he received a telegram in the train informing him that the play had been banned. According to one commentator, Stalin decided that all young people were alike and saw no need for a play about his youth;[127] but the real reason may have been that the contrast between Stalin's youthful democratic ideals portrayed in the play and the USSR of the 1930s was too great for comfort.

Although *Batumi* appears on the surface to follow the pattern of Soviet hagiography, Bulgakov was unable to write a truly servile play. As Lev Loseff demonstrates, the ease with which Bulgakov's Stalin implements his schemes is absurd, and all his enemies, from the police informant to the governor and Tsar Nicholas himself, are ludicrously inept.[128] The primitivism of Bulgakov's style in this work contrasts markedly with the psychological subtlety of his other plays. Moreover, the text itself contains hints that the work can be read on another level of Aesopian parody. As Loseff points out, the rector of the theological seminary from which Stalin is expelled uses phrases which could be construed as critical of Stalin, such as 'wrong-doers', 'crazed people clanging the cymbal of their barren ideas', and 'human society proclaims an anathema on the noxious tempter'.[129] The scene at the end of Act II where Stalin is beaten on stage by his jailers also diverges from conventional depictions of Stalin. Furthermore, as Loseff demonstrates, Bulgakov makes a subtle equation between Stalin and the imbecilic Nicholas II through their use of the word 'miraculous': Nicholas refers to miracle cures and his 'miraculous trained canary'; and Stalin says that his rescue from the icy river during his escape from Siberia, after which he has not coughed once, was 'miraculous'.[130]

Loseff's Aesopian reading of the play can be taken even further. A Moslem worker relates a dream in which he watched the Tsar swimming, and makes a comment which recalls Hans Christian Andersen's tale *The Emperor's New Clothes*, 'But how would he [the Tsar] walk naked if someone stole his uniform?'. Then the Tsar drowns and everyone shouts: ' "The Tsar has drowned! The Tsar has drowned!" And all the people were joyful'.[131] This dream is reminiscent of Stalin's 'miraculous' escape from drowning at the end of the play (although Stalin himself also appears in the worker's dream, perhaps in an attempt to deceive the censor). Furthermore, the prison scenes in the play evoke the imprisonment of many people under Stalin. At one point a prisoner sings:

The Tsar lives in great halls,
He walks and sings;
Here in grey overalls,
The people croak in prison cells.[132]

The Tsarist police report read out in the play which states that Stalin's appearance 'makes no impression' may indicate Bulgakov's own feelings about Stalin's mediocrity; and Stalin's story about the 'black dragon' which 'stole the sun from the whole of humanity' could refer to Stalin's terror of the 1930s. Moreover, the Tsar's trained canary which sings the first line of 'God save the Tsar' could be interpreted as an allegory of the Soviet writer in the 'period of the personality cult'.[133]

In his novel *The Master and Margarita*, written during the period 1928–40, but first published in the USSR posthumously in a censored version in the years 1966–7,[134] Bulgakov chose to approach the figure of Stalin obliquely, through allegory and fantasy. Donald Piper has argued that much in Bulgakov's portrait of the Devil, Woland, suggests Stalin, who was also 'aloof, mysterious, rarely seen in the thirties, having difficulty with the Russian language, destructive when affronted, demanding subservience, impressive in his self-control'.[135] Other scholars dispute Piper's interpretation;[136] and, indeed, it is difficult to sustain, as Woland is not a sufficiently independent force of evil to be an adequate personification of Stalin. He is, rather, a fallen angel who frequently acts as the agent of the 'other department' of light, tempting people, but not compelling them to do evil, and using black magic for beneficent ends.[137] Bulgakov does, however, draw an ironic comparison between the servility of Woland's retinue and the cult of Stalin's personality. The cat Behemoth speaks of the grandeur of Satan's ball, but, after being contradicted by Woland, immediately hastens to agree with his master: 'Of course, messire . . . If you think it wasn't very grand, I immediately find myself agreeing with you'.[138] The Soviet censorship was evidently conscious of this allusion, since the passage was deleted in the version of the novel published in the journal *Moskva* in 1966–7. The censor also heavily cut passages in Chapter 26 containing Pilate's ambiguous conversation with his secret policeman Aphranius during which he explicitly warned against, but implicitly proposed, the murder of Judas.

These passages must have been removed because they would have suggested to Soviet readers Stalin's dealings with his security services, notably in the case of Kirov's assassination in 1934, widely believed to have been committed by the Soviet security police on Stalin's secret instructions.[139]

There is more evidence to suggest that Bulgakov intended a parallel between the Rome of Tiberius and the Moscow of the 1930s. Both societies are permeated by philistine values, spies, denunciations and the power of the secret police; and the eulogies of Tiberius, for example Pilate's insincere toast: 'For us, for thee, Caesar, father of the Romans, most beloved and best of all men!', are reminiscent of the praise of Stalin in the period of the 'personality cult' (although they were also characteristic of contemporary references to Tiberius).[140] Significantly, the phrase 'most beloved and best of all men' was omitted in the journal edition, in order to remove the implied parallel with Stalin. Furthermore, the comment on the nature of political power which Bulgakov puts into the mouth of Yeshua (Jesus), 'Every form of authority means coercion over men and . . . a time will come when there shall be neither Caesars, nor any other rulers'[141] is a general statement which is clearly applicable to Stalin's Russia. Although the interpretations of Piper and others who see *The Master and Margarita* as a 'cryptotext' for Stalin's Russia are highly debatable,[142] it is indisputable both that the Soviet censorship in the 1960s read the novel in an Aesopian fashion, and that some Soviet intellectuals perceived a parallel between Woland and Stalin (although some readers appear to have been disappointed by Part II of the novel which did not seem to bear out this interpretation as clearly as the first part). One prominent Soviet intellectual to support this reading was Andrei Sinyavsky, who compared Woland's relationship with the Master to Stalin's strange relationship with Bulgakov.[143] Although Bulgakov's love of ambiguity and mystification makes it impossible to prove conclusively any definite parallels between either Woland or Tiberius and Stalin, it should be remembered that Bulgakov was fully aware of the subversive nature of his manuscript, suspecting that he would have been shot if the novel had been discovered, and feeling it necessary to burn a draft of the manuscript at the time that he wrote his letter to Stalin and the government in March 1930. Moreover, Bulgakov was a close friend of Zamyatin, and the multiple possible implications of such Aesopian, but not entirely precise parallels with contemporary society as Zamyatin's *We* would have been familiar to him.

As we have seen, one of the most successful forms of anti-Stalinist satire was that conceived on the basis of children's literature. In 1941 Daniil Kharms used the children's magazine *The Siskin* (*Chizh*) to parody stereotyped May-day verses to Stalin. Kharms's *May Song* displays all the hallmarks of the military-patriotic song, with its simple metrical patterns and frequent repetitions:

> We'll get to the reviewing stand
> We'll get there
> We'll get to the reviewing stand
> First thing in the morning
> So that we'll shout the loudest
> Shout the loudest
> So that we'll shout the loudest
> 'Hooray for Stalin!'[144]

As Loseff has shown, the exaggerated urgency of the repetitions and the illogicality of the content are disproportionate even by the usual standards of the 'song about Stalin': the lyric hero longs not to accomplish heroic deeds but merely to shout 'Hooray!', and his faith in the invincibility of the USSR is based only on the belief that Voroshilov will lead the Soviet army into battle 'on a horse'.[145]

The most skilled exponent of the genre of 'fairy tales for adults' was Evgeny Shvarts, whose play *The Dragon* can read on several levels: as a fairy story, a morality play and an Aesopian satire.[146] *The Dragon* was written for the Leningrad Comedy Theatre at the request of the theatre's director, chief set designer and artist Nikolai Akimov; it was begun during the period of the Nazi-Soviet Pact and the first version was completed by November 1943. On the surface the play is an obvious satire against Nazism: the Dragon is related to Attila the Hun; he persecutes gypsies (a reference to Hitler's persecution of gypsies, and, by implication, his much more extensive repression of Jews); his proclivity for sudden invasions, aerial tactics in battle and use of 'poisonous smoke' are reminiscent of the methods of the German armed forces; moreover, the names of the townspeople, such as

Müller and Friedrichsen, as well as the Gothic lettering on the town hall, help to create a Germanic atmosphere. However, Shvarts's use of typically Soviet words, phrases and plot situations suggests that the allegory was also intended to point to Stalin and Stalinism.

Shvarts was clearly not unaware of the possibility of equating the Dragon with Stalin, since his earlier plays *The Naked King* (1935) and *The Shadow* (1940) had established a pattern of introducing elements which could apply equally well to the west or to the USSR. (In particular, *The Naked King*, based on Andersen's story *The Emperor's New Clothes*, could be interpreted as a satire on the 'personality cult'). In *The Dragon* the stage direction in Act I which precedes the Dragon's entrance states: 'At this point a middle-aged, but robust, man, looking younger than his years, enters the room. He is towheaded and has a military bearing. He wears his hair in a crew-cut. On his face is a broad smile. Despite its coarseness, his manner is in general not without a certain appeal'.[147] The portrait of the leading villain is so drawn that it combines traits which could apply equally to the typical Nazi or the typical Soviet leader of the 1930s: the crew-cut hair, military bearing and genial appearance of a father-commander. However, the Soviet slang of the Dragon's opening lines: 'Hello, lads!' ('*Zdorovo, rebyata!*') points the reader in the direction of Soviet, rather than German, reality. Another double-edged reference is made by Charlemagne: 'The only way of getting free of dragons is to have one of your own'.[148]

Shvarts parodies many specifically Soviet situations: for example, the Burgomaster's address to an empty chair, as he appeals to the Dragon to act as the meeting's 'honoured head', is reminiscent of the Soviet ritual of electing an 'honoured presidium' at ceremonial gatherings to demonstrate loyalty to the Politburo; and Heinrich's direction of the townspeople in a rehearsal of 'greetings to the leaders' recalls a time-honoured Soviet custom. The battle scene contains a satire on Soviet wartime information and propaganda: the Burgomaster and Heinrich issue communiqués which try to prove, against the evidence of the citizens' own eyes, that the Dragon is winning the battle, and that all his efforts to evade the invisible Lancelot, including the loss of his three heads, are well-planned military manoeuvres. This is particularly reminiscent of the theory of

Stalin's tactical withdrawal of Soviet troops in 1941. In Act III Shvarts even includes a veiled reference to the Stalin terror: the conversation between the Burgomaster and the jailer contains a pun on the Soviet term *sazhanie*, which means both the 'planting' of seeds and the 'planting' of men in prison.

Shvarts's play met a fate as unsuccessful as that of Bulgakov's *Batumi*. There was one preliminary showing of the play in Moscow in August 1944, in the course of which Akimov was summoned by an official who told him the production was to be discontinued. Akimov later commented: 'There were no motives, and indeed they could not be expressed: a long time later it became clear that some excessively vigilant official of that time had seen in the play what was not in it at all'.[149] This is the only suggestion that the play was banned for any more specific reason than a lack of *ideinost*': the unsuitably trivial treatment of a subject as serious as fascism. *The Dragon* remained banned until after Shvarts's death in 1958; it was performed in Leningrad during the theatrical season of 1962–3, but, despite its great popularity with the audience, was soon taken off (perhaps because the character of the Burgomaster who rules the town after the Dragon's death could now be identified with Khrushchev). Shvarts's play can certainly be interpreted as an anti-Stalin satire, but, as Amanda Metcalf reminds us, it is more than that: 'a play about a tyrant – especially one which uses allegory – can always support as many different meanings as there are tyrants in the world'.[150]

The last phase of Stalinism was an unpromising period for anti-Stalinist satire, but one rare example of a children's story of the 1940s which uses 'Aesopian language' to criticise Stalin was Lev Kassil's *Tale of the Three Master Craftsmen* (1949).[151] Kassil's portrayal of King Vainglorious, whose kingdom is ruled by winds, implicates Stalin and the time-serving sycophants of the 'personality cult'. The tale of the three master craftsmen seized by the King's 'weathercocks' suggests the persecution of talented people and the success of pragmatists and intriguers in Stalin's time.

In the year before Stalin's death *Novy Mir* published Vasily Grossman's *For the Just Cause* (1952), ostensibly a conventional war novel which emphasised Stalin's brilliant strategy in the battle of Stalingrad and juxtaposed a favourable depiction of

Stalin and Molotov with a satirical picture of Hitler and his generals. There were, however, certain passages in the novel, notably the views expressed by an academic, Chepyzhin, which hinted at a parallel between Nazi and Stalinist obscurantism.[152] Grossman's novel aroused Stalin's personal displeasure and was criticised in the press; some of the offending passages were removed from subsequent editions. That a parallel between Nazism and Stalinism was indeed in Grossman's mind has only become evident since the appearance of the sequel, originally entitled *Stalingrad*, but published abroad in 1980 under the title *Life and Fate*.[153] In this novel Chepyzhin's dismissal is presented as a harmful result of Stalin's repressive cultural policy.

Chapter five

The image of Stalin in Soviet literature of the post-Stalin period

Ever since Stalin's death in March 1953, which created, in the words of the Russian *émigré* Yuri Glazov, an 'enormous atmosphere of grief and relief',[1] the dead dictator and the era he represented have continued to dominate the minds of Soviet people. In the post-Stalin period it soon became clear that the task of analysing the past and grasping its full implications would fall not to historians, who were still bureaucratically controlled by the Soviet authorities, but to literature. Since 1953 the image of Stalin has featured prominently in literature published in the USSR, and has been subject to all the revaluations imposed by Khrushchev and his successors. Soviet fiction on the theme of Stalin and Stalinism has been concerned with more than a reassessment of the life of the dictator himself; it has played a major political role in promoting discussions about the legacy of the past and the possible future development of Soviet society. Literary works and the cultural debates they have engendered afford valuable insights into the prolonged and continuing conflict between 'anti-Stalinists' and 'pro-Stalinists' in the USSR. There is a famous saying which still circulates in Moscow: 'Tell me your opinion about our Stalinist past, and I'll know who you are'.

The Khrushchev period 1953–64

The treatment of Stalin in Soviet literature did not change in the immediate post-Stalin period. Stalin's death was marked by an effusion of tributes in prose and verse, written in the style of the 'personality cult' in many of the languages of the USSR, which combined great grief at the leader's death with confidence in his immortality. Aleksei Surkov lamented: 'Death closed those eyes which had looked so far into the future'; and Nikolai Gribachev declared: 'Stalin is dead. Stalin eternally with us. Stalin – life' (an echo of Mayakovsky's famous line 'Lenin lived, Lenin lives, Lenin will live'). A poem by the Yakut poet Sergei Vasiliev (Borogonsky), *Our Sun Stalin is with us for ever*, voices the poet's heartfelt desire:

> Without thinking,
> I would give up my own life
> If only Stalin could remain alive!

Konstantin Simonov claims that 'the similarity of these poems was engendered not by the obligation to write them – it was possible for them not to have been written – but by a deep inner feeling of the enormity of the loss, the enormity of what had happened'.[2]

The tradition of referring to Stalin and Stalinism in Aesopian terms was also continued in Leonov's novel *The Russian Forest*, written in Stalin's time and even allegedly censored by Stalin himself, but not published until 1953, shortly after Stalin's death.[3] Leonov's novel is an exceptional case in which, before de-Stalinisation, an author used symbolism and allusive imagery to paint a negative portrait of Stalin. Leonov manages to exploit the figure of the conventional Stalinist villain to launch a subtle attack on Stalin and Stalinist values, despite the seemingly insuperable pressures of the years when the novel was written. Leonov depicts the unscrupulous professor of forestry Gratsiansky who possesses all the characteristics of a conventional villain of Stalinist fiction: a wealthy careerist, the son of a professor of theology, he once betrayed a Bolshevik friend to the Tsarist secret police and still has connections with counter-revolutionary foreign espionage within the Soviet Union. Gratsiansky fails to make any positive contributions to Russian forestry, but is a master of political invective who slanders his honest rival Vikhrov for alleged ideological deviations, narrowly failing to secure his arrest.

While Gratsiansky can by no means be totally identified with Stalin, certain features of his life – his theological background, activities as a spy, unscrupulous destruction of his opponents and isolation from ordinary people – suggest known or alleged facets of Stalin's own biography. Moreover, as throughout the novel the Russian forest symbolises the Russian land and people, Gratsiansky's insistence that Russian forests are inexhaustible and can be felled ruthlessly in the interests of socialist construction can be interpreted as an allegory of the liquidation of millions of people in Stalin's purges. There are scattered references to Dante throughout the novel, and the recurrent image of ice, culminating in Gratsiansky's apparent suicide in a hole in the ice, is reminiscent of the fate of Dante's Satan, lying eternally paralysed in a lake of ice in the deepest circle of *The Inferno*. Through this oblique parallel between Gratsiansky, Stalin and Satan, Leonov suggests that Stalin is the source of evil in Soviet society.

Although the new party leaders had begun, from 1953, to sanction a policy of gradual de-Stalinisation, not all Soviet writers and editors were bold enough to respond immediately to the changing climate. Konstantin Simonov's poem *The Bleak Anniversary* (written for the anniversary of the Revolution in 1941, the year of the German invasion), which had praised Stalin and expressed confidence that he would ultimately lead the USSR to a victory over Germany, was reissued in 1955, with no alterations.[4] Simonov has recently explained that when he first wrote the poem he believed that Stalin did not know about the purges of the 1930s: 'I put all my soul into the poem, trying to convey everything I felt about Stalin then'. Simonov claims that he wept at Stalin's death, and that it was not until after the Twentieth Congress of 1956 that he gradually learnt the truth. Indeed, so great was his sense of the 'grandiose nature of the loss' the country had suffered that even though, at Beria's instigation, Simonov, as a candidate member of the Central Committee of the Communist Party, had been allowed shortly after Stalin's death to read documents which revealed the disintegration of Stalin's personality, the 'cruelty' and 'half-mad suspiciousness' of Stalin's last years, he nevertheless co-authored an article entitled 'The Writer's Sacred Duty' which argued that the most important task facing Soviet writers was to portray the image of Stalin 'in its greatness and fullness' for the sake of their contemporaries and future generations. This article incurred the wrath of Khrushchev, who threatened to dismiss Simonov from the editorship of *Literaturnaya gazeta* as a 'confirmed Stalinist'.[5]

In the years 1953–6 Simonov's complex feelings about Stalin were undoubtedly shared by many other conformist Soviet writers, uncertain how to approach the subject of Stalin in this interval of transition. Some liberal writers, however, took advantage of the changing climate, attempting to portray Stalin more realistically (although their depictions could still only be cautious and partial). One sign of change was the second edition of Grossman's *For the Just Cause*, published in book form in 1955, which expunged a great deal of material about Stalin's individual part in the war and represented his decisions as those of a 'collective' – either the High Command or the State Defence Committee.[6] Grossman retains only brief ritual references to Stalin's inspiring speeches, particularly his exhortation 'Forward to victory!' during a public appearance in Red Square. Another work of 1955, Sergei Smirnov's play *The Fortress over the Bug*, while not directly attributing mistakes to Stalin, nevertheless raises profound questions about the USSR's lack of preparedness for war in 1941.[7] The signs of a German offensive are ignored as a matter of policy; and Hitler's real intention is alleged to be an attack on England.

Khrushchev's denunciation of Stalin at the Twentieth Congress of 1956 enabled Soviet writers to reassess the Stalin period more frankly, and, in particular, to re-examine their own former acquiescence in the cult of Stalin's personality. One of the most convincing and memorable interpretations of the Stalin cult in Soviet fiction is the depiction of Stalin's funeral in the opening pages of Galina Nikolaeva's novel *Battle on the Way* (1957), which provides a socio-political context for the dispute about industrial management which is to follow.[8] Nikolaeva evokes the enormous impact which the death of a single individual – Stalin – exerted on the minds of millions of people. The enthusiasm of the Soviet people for their dead leader, their very real grief and their uncertainty about the future are graphically conveyed. The occasion is portrayed, in the words of the Stalinist factory director Valgan, as 'a magnificent display of national grief'.[9] The strange phosphorescent light suffusing the scene gives the impression that even the natural world is conscious of the magnitude of the catastrophe. A woman in the crowd expresses the feelings of many Soviet people, who see Stalin as the embodiment of the country's greatness, and cannot even imagine life without him: 'What will happen now? We had got used to thinking that the victory was him! The hydro-electric power stations were him! The forest belts were him! What will we do without him?'. Nikolaeva's hero, the engineer Bakhirev, has become accustomed to the idea that Stalin is the 'embodiment of everything sacred'. Death takes away the grandeur of the Stalin seen in monuments and portraits, and leaves an ordinary mortal 'entirely given to the people'.[10] Although Nikolaeva's main aim is to convey the sorrow and confusion which many Soviet people experienced at their leader's death – feelings which have also been attested to by dissidents such as Sinyavsky and Zinoviev[11] – she does not disguise the contradictory nature of Stalin and Stalinism. The two contrasting aspects of Stalin's rule – grandeur and cruelty – are highlighted on the day of Stalin's funeral, when there is a danger of being crushed in the huge crowds of people who throng through the streets of Moscow. Although the mere mention of this disaster in a novel published in the USSR is itself surprising – it has elsewhere only been mentioned in dissident literature and in Evtushenko's controversial autobiography, published abroad in 1963[12] – Nikolaeva fails to tell the whole truth. Apparently, gangs of young villains pressed into Trubnaya Square and about five hundred women and children were crushed in the crowd.[13]

In the 1950s and early 1960s numerous literary works first published in the Stalin era were reissued with passages formerly containing adulation of Stalin expunged. The 1961 edition of Konstantin Fedin's novel *No Ordinary Summer*, for example, omitted a passage contained in the original version of 1949 which had referred to the great strategic importance of Tsaritsyn during the Civil War, and expressed fulsome praise of 'the new art of revolutionary military leadership' developed by Stalin which had enabled the city to withstand Krasnov's Cossacks and caused it to be renamed Stalingrad.[14]

In the early 1960s new works appeared which contained explicit or implicit attacks on the 'cult of personality'. One notable example was a section of Tvardovsky's poem *Horizon beyond Horizon* published in 1960 which drew an extensive parallel between the cult of Stalin and the worship of a deity.[15] However, dramatic new ground was broken by Simonov's novel

The Living and the Dead (1959), which revealed Stalin's part in
the purges and hasty promotions in the army, analysed people's
feelings towards him and asked how Stalin, the author of the
purges, could be the same man who appeared to have been duped
by Hitler.[16] In particular, Simonov's hero General Serpilin fails
to understand how Stalin, who did so much for the army, could
have allowed the army to be purged; and why, after foretelling the
capitulation at Munich and signing the Nazi-Soviet Pact, he was
not prepared for war. Nevertheless, the view of Stalin presented
in the novel remains ambivalent: some characters believe that
Stalin was not responsible for the initial defeats, and apportion
blame between Stalin and his generals. Simonov has admitted his
own mixed feelings towards Stalin, characterising him as 'a
complex figure . . . great and terrible, terrible and great'.[17]

A similar ambiguity is evident in other works published in the
confused interval between the Twentieth and Twenty-Second
Congresses, before the party had issued a forceful public condemnation of Stalin's crimes. In Vera Ketlinskaya's novel
Otherwise There is No Point in Living (1960),[18] Beria tries to
persuade Stalin to sanction the arrest of two young chemical
engineers for 'wrecking' following an accident at their experi-
mental station; Stalin himself is presented in a more positive
light as a defender of scientific initiative. Ketlinskaya's novel is
an example of what Khrushchev later disparagingly termed 'the
Beria version'[19] – the official fiction whereby Beria became a
convenient scapegoat for Stalin's own crimes. Another work
published in the same period, Alexander Bek's *A Few Days*
(1960), a semi-documentary study of General Panfilov's famous
division during its retreat to Moscow in 1941, also fails to
implicate Stalin directly, but sadly poses the question: 'Why, oh
why are we retreating? Why did the war begin for us so gravely, so
unsuccessfully?'[20]

Even in the Khrushchev period, at the height of de-
Stalinisation, literary dogmatists opposed the limited revelations
of liberal writers, continuing to express a favourable attitude
towards Stalin. An unpublished poem by Feliks Chuev, which
circulated in manuscript among Stalinists, exclaimed:

I never grew tired/of the call
Put Stalin back/on the pedestal![21]

Grigory Konovalov's novel *Sources* (1959) praised the diplomatic brilliance of the Nazi-Soviet Non-Aggression Pact of 1941; while the neo-Stalinist Ukrainian writer Natan Rybak, in his novel *The Time of Hopes and Achievements* (1959), emphasised Stalin's wisdom and statesmanship at the Potsdam Conference of 1945.[22] Rybak suggests that when President Truman announced the testing of the first American atomic bomb at Alamogordo Stalin expressed no surprise at the news, but retained his dignified composure and refused to make concessions to the west.

In the period between the Twenty-Second Congress of 1961, at which Khrushchev denounced Stalin in public, and the fall of Khrushchev in October 1964, only a few works were published in which Stalin appeared as a character, but a steady flow of literature gradually eroded the image of the dead dictator. One notable work was Evgeny Evtushenko's poem *Stalin's Heirs*, published in *Pravda* in 1962, which suggested that the guard around Stalin's coffin should be redoubled, lest he rise again and communicate with his successors who 'seem to suffer these days from heart trouble'.[23] This was a clear reference to the neo-Stalinists still occupying high positions in the party and government after Stalin's death, particularly Khrushchev's opponent in the Presidium, Frol Kozlov, who had just suffered a heart attack. Not surprisingly, Evtushenko's poem, which was out of favour in the Brezhnev era, has again become popular in the Gorbachev period, since it can also be interpreted as an attack on the 'era of stagnation' under Brezhnev.

An even greater sensation was created by Solzhenitsyn's *One Day in the Life of Ivan Denisovich* (1962), the first work published in the USSR to provide a realistic depiction of a labour camp of the Stalin era. Solzhenitsyn's short novel refers only once to Stalin, when a prisoner shouts, 'D'you mean to say you think Old Whiskers will take pity on you? Why, he wouldn't trust his own brother'.[24] Although Stalin had originally been omitted altogether from Solzhenitsyn's work (and this, as Solzhenitsyn comments, was 'hardly an accident'), the allusion was included at the behest of Khrushchev's cultural aide V.S. Lebedev, in order to lay responsibility for the injustices of the camp system exclusively at Stalin's door without implicating Stalin's successors, and hence to make it easier to secure the novel's

publication. The hint in Solzhenitsyn's memoirs that he deliberately left out references to Stalin because he felt that the camp
theme was a timeless one, not a subject merely to be relegated to
the Stalinist past, appears to be contradicted by Solzhenitsyn's
admission in *The Gulag Archipelago* that when he brought his
story to Tvardovsky at *Novy Mir*, 'I, too, genuinely believed that
the story I had brought him was about the past'.[25]

In many works of the early 1960s responsibility for both the
military and civilian purges was directly attributed either to
Stalin or to the system of government and chain of command for
which he was directly responsible. The fullest realistic portrait of
Stalin published in this period is to be found in Simonov's novel
People are Not Born Soldiers (1963–4). Simonov manifests a
genuine fascination with Stalin, and ventures further than most
other Soviet writers in his criticism of the dictator. Simonov's
recently published memoirs reveal that his portrait of Stalin in
this novel was not only based on his long record as a war
correspondent and eminent Soviet writer, which gave him the
opportunity to discuss Stalin informally with people who knew
him closely, but also on many years of personal experience.
Simonov once spent several hours in a meeting with Stalin as a
member of a delegation from the Union of Writers; Stalin once
spoke to him on the telephone about his work; and he attended
several meetings of the Politburo convened to discuss the award
of Stalin Prizes for literature; as a candidate member of the
Central Committee, he attended the Nineteenth Party Congress
of 1952 and the last Central Committee Plenum at which Stalin
spoke; and he took part in the guard of honour at Stalin's
funeral.[26]

In *People are Not Born Soldiers* Simonov uses a combination of
physical description, dialogue and narration of Stalin's thoughts
to undermine some of the clichés of the 'cult' period. In
particular, Stalin's 'calmness' is now not invariably seen as an
asset. On the eve of war Stalin speaks 'very slowly and calmly, as
if he was not in a hurry to go anywhere, although the situation
was grave'. He asks questions 'calmly, but when he looks at you
you have the feeling that he is testing you, that he wants to know
you to the core'. Stalin's face is 'calm' in 1938 when he purges the
army; and when he speaks of punishing the secret police chief
Ezhov his eyes are 'ruthlessly calm' (*bezzhalostno-spokoinye*).

Stalin is described as older and smaller than his image in the portraits, and he has a slight limp; when he is listening he gazes into people's eyes or walks up and down in his soft-soled boots 'like a cat' or a 'tiger'. Stalin's good nature, on which so much emphasis was laid in novels of the Stalin period, is now presented in a different light: his attitude to General Serpilin is 'at the same time arrogant and hospitable'; he laughs when he thinks of Ezhov's execution; and, although he does not condemn people to their face, he has a habit of deciding a man's fate while looking at his retreating back.[27]

Simonov's novel provides a deeper psychological portrait of Stalin than most other works published in the USSR. Simonov emphasises Stalin's indifference to heavy casualties among his own men, his inability to admit that he has made a mistake, his ruthlessness and will-power, and the fear he inspires in his subordinates. Generally suspicious of gifted people and preferring mediocrity, Stalin nevertheless has a respect for certain bold individuals: 'along with the despotic demand for total obedience, which was a rule for him, in his cruel nature, like the obverse side of the same rule, lived the need to meet exceptions'. This 'capricious and unstable trust' in certain resolute people sometimes leads to hasty promotions. Simonov also emphasises Stalin's immense vanity, which manifests itself in a childish readiness to take offence at any criticism of his military prowess: 'With all his inhuman scorn for people he had not lost such a human feature as the capacity to be offended by them'. His vanity is at stake in the diplomatic 'contest of minds' with his allies; and he is infuriated by his powerlessness to make Churchill and Roosevelt do what he wants: 'Sometimes this feeling of impotence, combined with the feeling of loneliness, drove him to cold fury'. Simonov's work is the only novel published in the USSR during the Khrushchev period to imply that Stalin the man needs 'Stalin', the cult figure. He calls himself 'Comrade Stalin' in the third person, and carefully prepares the expression on his face before receiving visitors. He is proud of his ability to 'step over' his memories of the purges, to 'free himself for ever' from his murdered enemies in order to conform to his image of himself as a 'politician able to decide the fate of the revolution, who did not retreat before anything, including his own memories'.[28]

Another writer who took advantage of the more liberal atmosphere after the Twenty-Second Congress, but also provided a balanced assessment of Stalin, was Konstantin Paustovsky, who in *A Book of Wanderings* (1964), the last volume of his autobiography *Story of a Life*, includes two scenes in which Stalin appears – one fictional and based on hearsay, the second factual and autobiographical.[29] Paustovsky's memoir is remarkable for being one of the few works published in the USSR to use humour in its depiction of Stalin. Paustovsky reproduces a comic story told by his friend Bulgakov after a letter Bulgakov had sent to Stalin in the 1930s asking for permission for his works to be published and performed had received no reply. Bulgakov related how every day he sent Stalin long, enigmatic letters signed 'Tarzan', whereupon Stalin, curious and a little anxious, ordered Beria to find their author. When Bulgakov's identity had been discovered Stalin frequently invited him to the Kremlin for a chat, gave him some decent clothes and confided to Bulgakov that he was often lonely: 'You understand, Misha, everyone shouts "He's a genius, a genius". But I haven't even got anyone to have a brandy with'. The sight of Bulgakov's tiredness and depression prompted Stalin to make his famous phone call to the Moscow Arts Theatre instructing them to perform some of Bulgakov's plays. Paustovsky comments that although Bulgakov suffered considerably at Stalin's hands, the benign power of his talent enabled him to create an image of Stalin which was 'human and even to some extent sympathetic'.[30]

Later in his memoirs Paustovsky gives an account of the only time that he himself saw Stalin in person, at a Komsomol Congress in the Kremlin in the 1930s. Paustovsky dispassionately describes the thunderous ovation which greeted Stalin's appearance, and, like other writers of the Khrushchev period, contrasts the reality of Stalin's appearance with the embellished figure in the portraits and photographs: 'This was a stocky little man with a heavy face, reddish hair, a low forehead and a thick moustache'. Paustovsky emphasises the incongruous contrast between the mass adulation of Stalin and the banality of his words, 'Long live Soviet youth!', pronounced in a hoarse voice with a thick Georgian accent. The enigmatic divinity of Stalin's public image is highlighted by the fact that he 'vanished through the wall as mysteriously and as suddenly as he had appeared'.[31]

Paustovsky's account is couched in the detached tone of a man hostile to all fanaticism and baffled by the mass hysteria which makes people in a crowd surrender to a supreme, unchallengeable authority.

The Brezhnev era

The years 1962–4 marked the climax of de-Stalinisation in Soviet literature, but even after Khrushchev's fall the tide was so strong that it could not be halted immediately. Alexander Rozen's *The Last Two Weeks*, published early in 1965, for example, was able to expose the mistaken calculations behind the Nazi-Soviet Pact and Stalin's unpreparedness for war.[32] Rozen depicts the factory director Podrezov, who in the last fortnight before the outbreak of war is arrested as a provocateur for criticising the manufacture of an imported German turbine. Although the German director of the turbine firm has admitted that the turbine is defective, Podrezov's guilt has already been established on political grounds, for Stalin himself has decided that Podrezov's case will serve as an appropriate illustration to his latest 'important document, which will show with the insight of genius that "Germany does not intend to fight the Soviet Union" and will give "provocateurs" their due'.[33] Rozen rejects the notion that Stalin failed to heed the warning signs because he believed Hitler. Through a commissar, Shirokov, he argues that Stalin miscalculated because he believed that it was not rational for Hitler to invade the USSR: 'Don't think that he believes Hitler one little bit . . . . And if, in 20 years time, you are told that he believed Hitler, turn your back and walk away. He doesn't believe Hitler, but he is obviously convinced that the latter cannot and therefore does not want to fight Russia.' Stalin is unable to admit that he is mistaken, because 'He believes only in himself. His prognoses have to come true'.[34]

Rozen also draws a remarkable allegorical portrait of Stalin through the depiction of the warden of an orphanage who exercises unbounded power over his charges, allows no departure from routine, and harbours suspicion of people until they obey him unconditionally. The description of his funeral is particularly evocative: 'It was strange, but almost all the pupils came to the funeral. Perhaps it was to make sure that the old order really was dead. Or perhaps it was to pay their last respects to the regime.'[35] The parallel with Stalin is intensified by the reference to the changes in the rules of the orphanage after Stalin's death.

Few Soviet writers delve deeply into Stalin's psyche in order to provide an explanation of his behaviour in 1941. A striking exception is the 1965 edition of V. Sokolov's novel *The Invasion*, which contains a passage describing the actions and thoughts of Timoshenko, Zhukov and Stalin immediately before and after the outbreak of war.[36] Stalin is described as falling into a state of deep shock at the news of war and failing to believe that Hitler knew of the invasion. When the full realisation dawned on him, 'he cursed in his heart the Soviet ambassador in Berlin, Dekanozov, who had deceived him with soothing reports, and he cursed Molotov who had boasted of an eternal alliance between Germany and Russia. He damned everybody and everything, excepting only himself'. Sokolov suggests that, whenever faced by a setback, Stalin's first reaction was to look for scapegoats. It is highly likely that Marshal Zhukov was Sokolov's informant, because he wrote a foreword to the 1965 edition, and a new passage is inserted in the novel which shows Zhukov in a good light; moreover, much information could only have been provided by Zhukov or an officer close to him.

Frank appraisals of Stalin's wartime leadership such as those of Rozen and Sokolov could only appear during the confused interval between the fall of Khrushchev and Brezhnev's consolidation of power. The climate began to change in May 1965 when Brezhnev made a speech praising Stalin's wartime role as Chairman of the Defence Committee.[37] From 1966 until the death of Chernenko Stalin's wartime record was presented in a more favourable light.

During the period of transition lasting from late 1964 until 1966 some other works not directly concerned with the war, but which also portrayed Stalin in a negative light, were allowed to appear. One such is Yuri Trifonov's *Reflection of a Bonfire*, first published in 1965 and republished in book form in 1966.[38] This is a documentary work devoted to the author's father, Valentin Trifonov, an Old Bolshevik who in 1937 sent a manuscript entitled *Contours of the Coming War* to Stalin. The manuscript received no acknowledgement and the book was never published, since Stalin was one of those 'strange people' who did not believe that war was imminent. Valentin Trifonov was arrested in 1937 at the age of 49, and shot in 1938. *Reflection of a Bonfire* deals with Valentin Trifonov's early life up to 1921, with the aim of correcting the historical record, and, in particular, the false accounts of the Civil War period propagated in the period of the 'personality cult'. when 'both history and the vocation of literature were distorted'.[39] Valentin Trifonov refused to allow his interesting memoirs of the Civil War to be used in one of the cult histories, which depicted Stalin being sent to all the most dangerous sectors of the war, and winning it almost single-handed. In *Reflection of a Bonfire*, as in many of his other works, Yuri Trifonov demonstrates a keen awareness of the importance of memory, of preserving intact both the past lives of individuals and a true record of his country's history.

Trifonov includes in his work a sympathetic memoir of the young Stalin by his former landlady, T.A. Slovatinskaya, who looked after him in 1912 after one of his escapes from exile, and knew him under his revolutionary name 'Vasily'. In Slovatinskaya's account Stalin figures as a model lodger, who 'at first appeared too serious, reserved and shy. It seemed that most of all he feared to trouble or constrain anyone'. His needs were modest: he stayed all day in his room writing, eating bread and drinking beer. He was entrusted with responsibility for the Bolshevik campaign for the elections to the Third Duma, and his landlady faithfully carried out all his instructions for liaison work, carrying packages and taking minutes at meetings. Stalin was re-arrested in 1913 at a charity evening which he had been encouraged to attend by the Social Democrat Duma deputy Roman Malinovsky (who was later exposed as an informer), and Slovatinskaya subsequently sent him food parcels in prison. Thus far Trifonov, like Paustovsky, succeeds in painting quite a favourable picture of Stalin by presenting him through another person's eyes. However, the most controversial point in Trifonov's narrative is the author's own commentary on Slovatinskaya's account. Trifonov states that he is repeating her words 'with a mixed feeling of amazement and bitterness', since although Slovatinskaya's family was subsequently destroyed by Stalin – her son-in-law died and her son and daughter were exiled during the purges – and the memoir was written in 1957, not long before her death, after Stalin had been condemned at the Twentieth Congress, her account contains no reflection of her personal tragedy. Trifonov asks the reason for such continuing veneration of Stalin: 'Why is this? Is it lack of understanding of history, blind faith or a half-century's habit of conspiracy, making her conceal the most terrible pain?'. He expresses the hope that 'some day' this enigma will be solved, but realises that the time is not yet ripe for such controversial issues to be discussed.

Trifonov attempts to disarm potential criticism by admitting that he hesitated before including the memoir of Stalin, which might appear irrelevant to his main theme. He adds: 'But after consideration I decided it was necessary to put it in, because the basic idea was to write the truth, however cruel and strange it might be. And truth will surely come in useful – some day . . . '.[40] Trifonov's passionate meditation on history and truth, inspired by bitter personal experience, reflects both his desire to tell the truth about the Stalin era (a sentiment demonstrated again later in his novel *The House on the Embankment* (1976)), and his awareness of the difficulty of doing so in the USSR after Khrushchev's fall. Trifonov's work may well have encountered some opposition from conservative critics and officials, since it was not republished in his *Collected Works* during the Brezhnev era. In the more liberal atmosphere of the Gorbachev era it once again became acceptable, and was republished in 1988.

Another writer who managed to say more in the Brezhnev period than was officially permitted was the popular guitar poet Bulat Okudzhava, whose song *The Black Tomcat*, published in the USSR in 1966,[41] was widely interpreted as referring to Stalin. Like Stalin immured in the Kremlin until late at night, the tomcat lives in silence and darkness, but rules over the confined doorway as if it were his own estate. He shares certain characteristics with Stalin: whiskers, yellow eyes and the capacity to make people serve him:

> He doesn't nag, he doesn't beg
> His yellow eyes just burn,
> Each one of us brings him something
> And thanks him for the honour.

Okudzhava emphasises the cat's violent nature: he sits

> Clawing the filthy floor
> As if he were clawing throats.

The unhappy house where he lives can be interpreted both as an allegory of Stalin's Russia and of the post-Khrushchev USSR in which the apathetic intelligentsia allow Stalin to be steadily rehabilitated:

> You know, somehow it's no fun
> Living in this house;
> We should put in a light back there—
> We can't be bothered to raise the dough.[42]

The controversial nature of Okudzhava's theme was demonstrated when the editor of the journal *Sel'skaya Molodyozh* was dismissed in 1966 for publishing *The Black Tomcat* and other Okudzhava songs.[43]

This incident was one reflection of the more repressive atmosphere which prevailed in Soviet culture after the trial of the two writers Andrei Sinyavsky and Yuli Daniel in February 1966. The expulsion from the party in July 1967 of the historian Alexander Nekrich, who in his book *22 June 1941*, published in the spring of 1965, had frankly exposed Stalin's unpreparedness for war on the eve of the German invasion,[44] issued a further warning to historians and writers against delving too deeply into the negative aspects of Stalin's rule. It is hardly surprising that after 1967 many writers avoided the issue of Stalin and Stalinism, since the system Stalin had created remained more or less intact, and the dictator himself had been partially rehabilitated – indeed, in 1970 a life-size bust was erected on his previously unadorned grave. Even Mikhail Sholokhov, who can hardly be described as a liberal, had trouble in portraying Stalin in his novel *They fought for the Motherland*. Extracts from Sholokhov's work had appeared in *Pravda* in 1969, but publication of the book was delayed because Sholokhov had included critical references to Stalin's illegal purges, which were cut by the censorship. Konstantin Simonov's fascinating memoir on Stalin, dictated in 1979, which discusses Stalin's close control of literature in the post-war years and presents a devastating analysis of Stalin's responsibility for the German invasion and the initial defeats in 1941, could only be published in the Gorbachev era, after Simonov's death.[45]

The few writers of fiction who did succeed in depicting Stalin in the 1970s and early 1980s concentrate on one particular aspect of his career – his record as a war leader – which is generally seen to be positive. Stalin's wartime role had been reassessed in a series of military memoirs, notably those of Zhukov, Shtemenko and Rokossovsky, published for the twenty-fifth anniversary of VE Day in spring 1969.[46] All paid tribute to Stalin's military skill, although not as extravagantly as in Stalin's lifetime. Since Soviet writers now had access to more reliable information about Stalin's behaviour, they usually made more attempt at factual accuracy than writers of earlier war novels, although their interpretations of events were frequently highly disputable.

Alexander Chakovsky's lengthy semi-documentary epic *Blockade* (1969–75) does not disguise the fact that Stalin was depressed by the unexpected German invasion, and disappeared for a few days to reflect on his miscalculations. However, in Chakovsky's version Stalin soon returns to confer with his generals, fellow party officials and advisers, and organises a heroic defence effort in the first few months of the war. Chakovsky emphasises Stalin's contradictory nature: he possesses 'strength of will', 'huge political experience', 'intelligence' and 'devotion to the cause', and 'with his name was connected the transformation of the Soviet Union into a powerful industrial state'; on the other hand, he has 'faith in his infallibility, suspiciousness and unjustified cruelty – not merely the harshness essential in a conflict with the enemies of the revolution, but, precisely, cruelty, with which he so often damaged his own people'.[47] Yet Chakovsky's portrait is by no means unsympathetic: Stalin is seen to be complex, sometimes mistaken, but always working for the interests of his country. He is subject to attacks of despotic bad temper, but he is also depicted as having learnt his lesson and realised that the success and strength of wartime leadership lies in its collective spirit. Such a view of Stalin can be assumed to have enjoyed official encouragement in the Brezhnev era, as Chakovsky was an influential literary official, the editor of *Literaturnaya gazeta*.

Stalin also features in Chakovsky's later novel *Victory* (1980–2), which gives an account of the Potsdam Conference of 1945 based on documentary sources. Stalin appears as a wise and beneficent leader, whereas Churchill and Truman are portrayed as negative characters who contributed little to the Soviet war effort. At the same time, however, Chakovsky does not subscribe to the myth of Stalin's infallible genius, presenting Stalin as a 'contradictory' character in whose nature good and evil are 'oddly intertwined'. He does, nevertheless, emphasise that in the war and immediate post-war years, when Stalin was the head of a victorious country which had defeated a cruel enemy, the good in Stalin's character came to the fore.[48] Chakovsky uses the past to shed light on the present, drawing a parallel between the Potsdam Conference, which the west allegedly sabotaged for thirty years, and the Helsinki Conference of 1975, where the bad faith of the western powers who approve of interference in the internal affairs of other countries soon becomes apparent. Chakovsky's approach reflects Soviet government policy in the 1970s and early 1980s: while the party leaders did not wish to revive the cult of Stalin (as was shown when Ivan Stadnyuk was criticised for praising Stalin too extravagantly in his novel *War* (1971–4)),[49] the portrayal of a wise, if sometimes erring Stalin presented the least possible threat to the party's dominant position in Soviet society, whereas an evil Stalin might have raised grave doubts about the party's fitness to rule.

By the late 1970s and early 1980s critical analysis of the Stalinist experience had largely been banished from the official press and published fiction, and the praise of Stalin as a great national leader and benefactor was becoming more fulsome in many mass-circulation publications. This was a reflection of neo-Stalinist attitudes prevalent in Soviet society, not only among military and political officials who wished to return to the power and prestige of an earlier era, but also among broader sectors of the population nostalgic for strong leadership, glory abroad and law and order at home. As one Muscovite is alleged to have said in 1978: 'Stalin today is less dead than he was twenty years ago'.[50]

The Gorbachev era

After the death of Chernenko in March 1985 the new leadership under Gorbachev at first did little to promote reappraisal of the Stalinist past, because Stalin's name was linked with preparations to celebrate the fortieth anniversary of the end of the war on 8 May. Before Chernenko died, it had been announced that a film made in the years 1983–4 based on Chakovsky's novel *Victory*, with its favourable portrait of Stalin, would be released in 1985 in connection with the 'Victory day' celebrations. One of the first decisions Gorbachev had to make as General Secretary concerned the release of the film; and he was also under pressure from other groups, especially war veterans, to rehabilitate Stalin. Chernenko was said already to have prepared a draft decree to change the name of Volgograd to Stalingrad in response to petitions from the Volgograd City Council and Veteran Society. Gorbachev chose to compromise: he released *Victory*, but Volgograd was not renamed, to the considerable relief of the Soviet intelligentsia, who regarded this concession as evidence that the new leadership had abandoned any intention of rehabilitating Stalin.[51] In early 1986, however, Gorbachev still maintained his cautious approach, declaring in an interview with the French Communist newspaper *L'Humanité*: 'Stalinism as a concept is an invention of anti-Soviet forces in the west'.[52] Evidently Gorbachev did not at first wish to risk a period of upheaval by further major revaluations of Stalin's role. As Khrushchev discovered, an attack on Stalin might assist the seizure of political power, but not its retention.

Once firmly established in power, Gorbachev's personal commitment to a more truthful assessment of Soviet history and an eradication of the worst excesses of Stalinism has not been in doubt. As a young Komosol official he knew of Khrushchev's 'Secret Speech' to the Twentieth Congress of 1956, and as a delegate at the Twenty-Second Congress of 1961 had voted to remove Stalin's body from the Lenin Mausoleum. From 1986 onwards, Gorbachev has favoured a limited reappraisal of the Stalin era; and the former clear distinction between 'Soviet' and 'dissident' literature on the subject of Stalin and Stalinism has begun to break down. In an informal meeting with the Union of Writers in the Kremlin on 19 July 1986 Gorbachev gave qualified support to a frank treatment of the past: 'If we were to get too involved with the past, we would lose all our energy. We would create internal strife. We have to go forward. We *will* sort out the past. Everything will be put in its place . . . . It must be understood that for us everything lies in the future.'[53]

One significant sign of change occurred in October 1986, wher after a favourable report to Gorbachev by Alexander Yakovlev, head of the Central Committee propaganda department, the party's chief ideologue Egor Ligachev gave permission for the controversial film *Repentance* by the Georgian director Tengiz Abuladze to be shown to a limited audience. It aroused so much interest that it was put on general release on 1 December 1986.[54] Varlam, the main character in the film, wears a pince-nez like Beria, but is a composite figure based on Stalin, Beria, Hitler and Mussolini. Although the film adds little to the satire on dictatorship contained in Chaplin's *The Great Dictator*, the release of Abuladze's film was a momentous event in the USSR, transcending purely artistic considerations. The fact that *Repentance*, which clearly refers to Stalin's purges of the 1930s and the later mass deportations, and asserts the need to confront the past in order to come to terms with it, was allowed to be shown after it had been banned in 1984, demonstrates Gorbachev's willingness to reverse the worst aspects of his predecessors' policies, in cultural as well as economic matters.

By 1987 Gorbachev felt sufficiently confident to take a more prominent, and politically daring, part in the debate about public comment on the Stalin era. In a major speech at the January 1987 Central Committee Plenum he expressed more fundamental criticisms of the Stalin era, referring to the adverse effect of Stalinism on Soviet development and observing that Soviet socialist theory had remained largely fixed 'at the level of the 1930s–1940s' when 'vigorous debates and creative ideas disappeared . . . while authoritarian evaluations and opinions became unquestionable truths'.[55] In February 1987 he told Soviet journalists that there should be no 'blank pages' in the country's history, and that memories of the men who made the 1917 revolution, only to be subsequently purged, should be restored.[56] In an interview of May 1987 with correspondents of the Italian Communist newspaper *L'Unità* Gorbachev argued that it was necessary to learn the lessons of the past in order to aid the task of 'reconstruction' (*perestroika*).[57] Without mentioning either Stalin or Brezhnev by name, he admitted that 'in our history there were difficulties, mistakes hindering the development of socialist democracy, infringements of socialist legality and democratic norms. These are the realities of our historical path. We evaluate them as such'. In his view such 'mistakes' were not merely a result of 'subjective factors', but of the difficult objective circumstances hindering the development of the USSR from its foundation. Gorbachev ventured back even further than

the Stalin era to analyse the causes of these 'mistakes', referring
to the Civil War and intervention, the subsequent economic
blockade and 'cordon sanitaire', 'military provocations and
constant pressure from imperialism', which led to the cruel
conflict with fascism and the period of post-war reconstruction
in 'Cold War' conditions imposed by the west. Gorbachev
expressed a belief in the need to confront the country's problems,
past and present: 'We are convinced that a society which
consciously and actively struggles for its physical and moral
health has no need to hide its ills – this only makes them more
difficult to cure'. Gorbachev claimed that in the new conditions
of *glasnost'* (openness) the role of public opinion would increase,
but that there was no conflict between the intelligentsia and the
party. Formulating in a new guise the old socialist realist concept
of the *partiinost'* (party-mindedness) of literature, Gorbachev
spoke of the duty of the creative artist to support the party's
policy of reorganisation: 'The interests of the intelligentsia and
the aims of the development of Soviet society coincide. The artist
and the party are moving towards a single aim – the renovation
of society on socialist principles'.

Gorbachev's speech demonstrated that Soviet literature was
still, as always, to be closely harnessed to party policy; but party
policy had now changed to favour liberal writers who criticised
the Stalin period and sought to eradicate its legacy. Censure of
Stalin and Stalinism would also implicitly provide support for
Gorbachev's policy of attacking the 'subjectivism', bureaucracy
and inertia of the Brezhnev era. The immediate task of Soviet
publishing houses in the new era has been the publication of the
backlog of literary works censored under Gorbachev's predecessors, in order to contribute to Gorbachev's policies of 'reconstruction', 'openness' (*glasnost'*) and 'democratisation' , so it
may be some time before new works produced in the Gorbachev
era will emerge. However, the newly published works provide
some clues about the reassessment of the Stalin era which is now
permitted.

In 1986 and 1987 some works by major Soviet writers which
were already well known to the Soviet intelligentsia through
samizdat were published posthumously, simply to set the historical record straight. One such is Anna Akhmatova's poetic cycle
Requiem, published in full for the first time in the USSR in

1987.[58] In this tragic work Akhmatova's private grief at the arrest of her son merges with the wider grief she shares with the whole Russian people during the Stalin terror. The critic A. Urban, in a sympathetic review which quotes Akhmatova's famous lines 'I have thrown myself at the feet of the executioner', ruefully admits that 'Ecstasies on account of *Requiem* would now appear belated'.[59] Nevertheless, the publication of this and other works about the Stalin period demonstrates the determination of Soviet editors, supported by the present leadership, to restore historical justice and resurrect the treasures of Soviet culture.

Another heartening sign of a reappraisal of the Stalinist past was the posthumous publication in 1987 of Tvardovsky's last work, the long poem *For the Right of Memory*, written in the years 1966–9, set up in type for *Novy Mir* in 1970, but banned at the time that Tvardovsky himself was dismissed as editor of the journal.[60] In this poem Tvardovsky rethinks his personal experience of collectivisation and the death of his parents as 'kulaks', which had found no reflection in his earlier poem *Muravia Land*.[61] Tvardovsky, like Trifonov and Abuladze, is deeply concerned with the theme of memory, feeling that it is essential to recall the past in order to expiate it. He tells of his guilt at having a 'kulak' father, and of the relief he felt at hearing the words 'A son does not answer for his father' from the lips of Stalin himself – sentiments incomprehensible to young people in the contemporary USSR. Tvardovsky frankly admits his own adulation of Stalin, who was for his entire generation 'the only earthly controller of destinies'. With bitter irony he recalls how young people in the 1930s expressed abject gratitude to 'the father of the peoples' for 'forgiving' their own fathers.

Tvardovsky exposes Stalin's habit of blaming others for the failure of his own policies by attributing excesses to 'some enemy distortion' or 'dizziness with success', a ploy which encouraged people in the mistaken belief that if only Stalin knew the truth, he would correct the abuses committed in his name. In an extended image, Tvardovsky compares Stalin with Jesus, who told his disciples to leave home and follow him in order to live in paradise. He points to the contradiction between the USSR's professed atheism and the cult of Stalin's personality which made people denounce their own fathers, bear false witness, and commit atrocities in the name of the leader.[62] Tvardovsky attacks the falsehood of the cult, which obliged all Soviet people, even members of persecuted nationalities such as the Crimean Tartars, Kalmyk and Ingush, to applaud Stalin for his godlike acts and the harsh sentences which they could not understand. Tvardovsky's main theme is that all Soviet people are responsible for the Stalinist past, and that the judgement of history will continue:

> The children have long ago become fathers
> But we are all answerable
> For the universal father
> And the judgement of the decades continues,
> There is no end in sight.[63]

Tvardovsky clearly states his own political position when he praises Lenin, who disapproved of personality cults. The poet recognises, however, that during the Stalin era people became accustomed to regarding Lenin and Stalin as one. Tvardovsky concludes by bringing his theme up to date, attacking the neo-Stalinists who wish to return to their 'former abundance'. Like Evtushenko in *Stalin's Heirs*, Tvardovsky expresses the fear that Stalin may come to life again:

> He was a god
> He can rise again.[64]

Tvardovsky's Leninist idealism and his view that honest people must confront the past frankly in order to rise above it bring him closely in line with Gorbachev's policy of *glasnost'* and *perestroika*. This was emphasised by the liberal critic Evgeny Sidorov, who claimed that 'The cult of personality of the leader and the consequences of this cult can be finally overcome only in the conditions of wide openness' (*glasnost'*). Sidorov used the publication of Tvardovsky's poem as an opportunity for attacking Gorbachev's ideological opponents in the contemporary USSR who wish to conceal the past and fail to contribute actively to the task of *perestroika*: 'The conscious concealment of historical truth is the worst form of social pessimism, which can inflict a great loss to the ideology and practice of Communist construction'.[65]

At a lively meeting of the Writers' Union in May 1987 the majority of speakers to treat the subject of Stalin and Stalinism, including the new First Secretary of the Union Vladimir Karpov, expressed gratitude for the belated appearance of such long-awaited works as Abuladze's *Repentance*, Tvardovsky's *For the Right of Memory* and Akhmatova's *Requiem*.[66] However, one speaker, Sergei Vikulov, questioned whether such works ought to be published in monthly journals addressed to the mass reader, or whether it would be better if they were to appear only in book form, in limited editions aimed at lovers of literature and book collectors. He expressed the view that journals should publish works concerned with the contemporary world, and that dwelling on the past might confuse the reader and harm the task of 'reconstruction'. Some conservative critics went as far as to condemn the 'literary necrophilia' involved in delving into the past; but a succinct response to this criticism was provided by the eminent literary scholar Academician D. Likhachev, who in a telegram addressed to the Writers' Plenum asserted: 'The past does not die. It is necessary to publish in journals of mass circulation works that were not published in the past .... The most important thing in literature now is repentance'.[67]

In the years 1986 and 1987 some previously censored prose works were also published, not only in response to the need to restore historical justice, but also as a contribution to Gorbachev's drive for 'reconstruction' and greater economic efficiency. This was particularly evident in the case of the posthumous publication in 1986 by the journal *Znamya* of Alexander Bek's novel *The New Appointment*, which had previously only been published in the west.[68] In his introduction the editor of the journal, the liberal writer Grigory Baklanov, emphasises the contemporary nature of Bek's documentary novel, which he sees as 'a report on the time in which he himself lived, before his contemporaries, his conscience and the future'. He argues that Bek's main protagonist Onisimov can be regarded as a type of Stalinist official created by an age in which 'there was so much triumph and so much tragedy'. Citing a character in the novel, Academician Chelyshev, who tells Onisimov to 'climb in spirit out of those times', Baklanov points to the close connection between the belated appearance of Bek's novel and Gorbachev's new policy: 'In days when a revolutionary reorganisation of the whole of society is occurring, when our society "is climbing in spirit out of those times", this novel sounds exceptionally contemporary'.[69]

Another previously censored novel which eventually appeared in 1987 was Dudintsev's novel *White Robes*, which discusses the problems of Soviet biologists persecuted by Lysenko and his supporters in the late Stalin period.[70] Dudintsev allegedly spent thirty years writing this novel, and it was published after a ban of over twenty years, since as early as 1964 Dudintsev mentioned that he had almost finished a novel about biologists.[71] Dudintsev explicitly links the power of the Lysenkoites with Stalin's patronage. He depicts the rapid rise and malign influence of the 'people's academician' Kasyan Demyanovich Ryadno (a character obviously modelled on Trofim Denisovich Lysenko) who gains Stalin's confidence and becomes an 'idol' himself. Ivan Strigalyov, a brilliant scientist who has created a new hybrid potato following the laws of classical genetics, declares: 'If Stalin himself had told me that in the interests of the state and people it was necessary to cancel this work of ours and destroy this potato ... But I was virtually told this ... virtually in Stalin's name ... I would not not destroy it and would be ready for anything. Such is life! And if I live – I will be right once again!'.[72] Although Strigalyov's important discovery enhances the international reputation of Soviet genetics, he is rewarded by a long term in prison, where he eventually dies. His tragic fate is closely based on that of the famous geneticist Academician Nikolai Vavilov, who died in prison in 1940.

The critic Vladimir Shaposhnikov has emphasized the contemporary nature of Dudintsev's theme. He contends that Dudintsev is not merely concerned with historical justice, with adding another 'touch to the portrait' of the personality cult, but that his main aim in providing an accurate account of the sombre events of the past is to indicate the 'sources, roots, origins of many of our present shortcomings, troubles, stagnant phenomena'.[73] Thus, as in the case of Bek's *The New Appointment*, the belated appearance of Dudintsev's novel is justified by its alleged relevance to the attack on bureaucracy in the Gorbachev era.

Most of the previously banned or withheld literary works initially published under Gorbachev did not venture much further than the works published during the most liberal periods of Khrushchev's rule. The works of Bek and Dudintsev are fairly mild examples of *samizdat* which endorse a Leninist, or democratic socialist viewpoint close to that of the present leadership. However, a new note is struck by another previously banned work, Mikhail Shatrov's play *The Peace of Brest-Litovsk*, which graphically demonstrates how under Gorbachev literature can be used to signal a change of policy.[74]

Shatrov's play, begun in 1962 and finally published in 1987, illustrates another aspect of Gorbachev's policy of *glasnost'*: the reinterpretation of Soviet history in order to shed light on the problems of the present. It demonstrates the correctness of Lenin's policy which led to the signing of the Treaty of Brest-Litovsk in 1918, and features not only Lenin and Stalin, but also former 'unpersons' such as Trotsky, Bukharin and Zinoviev.

Shatrov emphasises Stalin's harshness and rudeness: he constantly boasts of being 'self-taught', has a dismissive attitude to the liberal humanist Gorky, and attacks the 'spinelessness' of his colleague Bukharin. Envy is shown to be one of Stalin's chief motivating forces: Bukharin comments acutely, 'Koba can't live if he hasn't got something that someone else has'.[75] Shatrov is one of the few Soviet writers to draw a comic picture of Stalin. In one scene Stalin challenges Bukharin to a hand-walking competition, admitting frankly: 'I am envious of everyone who knows more or who can do more than me'. Stalin and Bukharin walk off stage on their hands, and when the competitors return, a telling exchange occurs: Stalin is asked, 'Who won?', but he refuses to reply, commenting, 'Let historians answer that question', whereupon Lenin remarks, 'They'll lie, all the same'.[76] The implication is that the full truth has not yet been told in the USSR about Stalin's conflict with Bukharin, which led to Bukharin's trial and execution in 1938.

Shatrov also undermines the myth that Stalin was Lenin's best disciple and natural successor. In the discussion about whether to sign a peace treaty with the Germans, Stalin follows Lenin's policy, stating, 'I believe in you'.[77] However, Lenin expresses disapproval of this attitude, remarking that he does not want to be believed in, but to be understood. One of Shatrov's main aims is to demonstrate the different approaches to the party on the part of Lenin and Stalin. Stalin is accused by the Soviet President, Yakov Sverdlov, of regarding the party as a 'closed order of crusaders with its hierarchy, discipline, morality and philosophy'.[78] Lenin has a much more tolerant approach to intra-party disputes than Stalin, who argues that the decision of Lenin's opponents Bukharin, Uritsky and other Left Communists to resign from their Central Committee posts is tantamount to a resignation from the party. Lenin, however, firmly states, 'Leaving the Central Committee does not mean leaving the party'.[79]

The publication and staging of Shatrov's play in the USSR showed that the reassessment of Stalin's role which had been taking place since Gorbachev's accession had also made it possible to consider a revaluation of the contribution to Soviet history of other Bolshevik leaders such as Trotsky, Bukharin and Zinoviev. Although Shatrov emphasised the wisdom of Lenin's policy and the mistaken calculations behind both Bukharin's belief in a revolutionary war and Trotsky's advocacy of the agitator's formula 'No peace, no war', the appearance of Bukharin and Trotsky as characters on the stage who were more than mere caricatures was a signal that the role of Stalin's opponents and victims in history was no longer a taboo subject. In his speech on the seventieth anniversary of the Revolution in November 1987 Gorbachev took up this theme, condemning Trotsky's deviation from the party line in terms which render his rehabilitation highly improbable.[80] However, Gorbachev did pledge himself to revive the process of rehabilitating innocent victims of Stalin's purges begun twenty years earlier by the Pospelov Commission, appointed by Khrushchev. Two new commissions have been established, one to sift the documents which will enable the courts to revoke false sentences, the other to empower the party to restore those falsely condemned to posthumous membership of the party. The work of these commissions bore fruit by February 1988, when it was announced that Bukharin, Rykov, Radek and Pyatakov were to be rehabilitated; subsequently Zinoviev and Kamenev were also rehabilitated.

By May 1987 another bitter ideological dispute was raging in the press about how much, under the new policy of *glasnost'*, the public should be told about Stalin's purges in which millions perished. The reformist weekly *Moscow News* published an article by the controversial historian Yuri Afanasyev demanding a full reassessment of Stalin's role, since, he claimed, Soviet textbooks distorted history and passed over sensitive issues in silence.[81] Five letters were subsequently published both attacking and defending Afanasyev's views. An assistant professor, Anatoly Borisov, alleged that Afanasyev was 'playing into the hands of bourgeois historiography', whereas Yuri Lisovsky supported the principle that 'to carry out the reconstruction in real earnest, there is a need to tell the whole truth about our country's past'.[82] The deep emotional divisions evident in the public debate about Stalin's legacy reflect the current conflict in Soviet society over the wider implications of Gorbachev's policy of economic and moral renewal.

An important contribution to this debate, and by far the boldest of the works of prose fiction newly made available to the Soviet public, was Anatoly Rybakov's *Children of the Arbat* (1987), completed in 1966 and twice announced for publication (Part I by *Novy Mir* in 1966; Part II by *Oktyabr'* in 1978), but suppressed for twenty years.[83] Rybakov's novel, set in the period between September 1933 and December 1934, depicts Soviet society in the interval between the First Five Year Plan and the beginning of the Great Purges. Rybakov's work takes a step no Soviet author has been able to take before, since it does not merely refer to the persecution and wrongful arrests which occurred in Stalin's time, but also gives a frank account of how people were sent to the camps, and by whom. No other work hitherto published in the USSR has so openly named and described Stalin and his lieutenants who managed the systematic terror. Moreover, Rybakov's willingness to explore the period before 1934 and, in particular, to give a sympathetic treatment of the NEP period, as well as his decision to depict the secret police officials Yagoda and Ezhov and allude to many former leaders disgraced in the 1920s and 1930s – Bukharin, Enukidze, Kamenev, Lominadze, Rudzutak, Zinoviev – venture beyond the topics permitted in Khrushchev's time. Since Gorbachev's approval must have been required for the novel's publication, its appearance suggested that the current leadership was contemplating a more radical reappraisal of Soviet history than ever before in order to prepare the way for far-reaching economic and political reforms.

Rybakov himself chose not to circulate his work in *samizdat* or to send it abroad for publication, since he felt strongly that he wanted it to come out in Russia: 'I wanted my people to have it'.[84] His novel aroused such great interest that readers queued up to obtain successive issues of the journal *Druzhba narodov*, in which it was published in instalments in 1987; and readers subsequently wishing to obtain the journal in libraries were obliged to add their names to long waiting lists.[85] Rybakov himself has linked his exposure of past abuses with the future development of his country: 'This is a book that raises the most pointed questions for our whole country. In the 1930s, Stalin built up industry in this country, but he did it by force. He deprived people of the opportunity to think independently, to think freely. He deprived them of initiative. We have to free ourselves of this psychological legacy so the country can move forward and be what it should be'.[86]

In an interview Rybakov related that he first conceived the idea of a novel about his Moscow contemporaries in the 1930s during the late 1940s and early 1950s, but the conception only took shape after the Twentieth Congress of 1956. Initially Stalin did not figure in the work, but first one scene with him was written, then another, and he gradually came to occupy an ever greater place in the novel. Rybakov realised that 'without him – the main figure – the picture of the epoch would not be recreated in its full scope'.[87] Rybakov was conscious of the historical importance of his enterprise, not only at the time of writing, but also at the time of publication, since more than thirty years after Stalin's death no systematic biographical or historical work about Stalin had appeared in the USSR. Rybakov's main sources for the depiction of Stalin were Stalin's own speeches (including Stalin's speeches to the Seventeenth Party Congress and to the conference on the reconstruction of Moscow), his writings, notably *Questions of Leninism* and *The Short Course of the History of the Party*, party documents, newspaper reports, books 'where they existed',[88] numerous tales about Stalin by people who knew him, as well as rumours and gossip current in the USSR and Rybakov's own impressions. It is also probable that he was familiar with some works on Stalin published in the west, since Stalin's meditations on Robespierre and the Convention correspond closely to the chapter entitled 'The Great Deserter' in Abdurakhman Avtorkhanov's *The Secret of Stalin's Death*, and the characterisation of Machiavelli as 'old-fashioned' is reminiscent of a passage in Trotsky's *Stalin*.[89] Although Rybakov insists on the right of the fiction writer to invent, he claims that he 'has tried to be as historically accurate as possible', priding himself that 'not one action of Stalin in the novel is invented, they are all historically based'.[90] However, he admits that in his reconstruction of Stalin's monologues he proceeded first from Stalin's actions, and then imagined the motivation behind them. In Rybakov's opinion, such imaginative reconstructions of a historical character's thoughts are justified if they are seen to correspond to the character's personality and actions.

Children of the Arbat presents a realistic portrait of Stalin at the time of the Seventeenth Party Congress of January–February 1934, and traces in detail events leading up to the murder on 1 December 1934 of Sergei Kirov, head of the Leningrad Party organisation, in which Stalin is clearly (if not explicitly) implicated. Rybakov's depiction of Stalin is more comprehensive, and contains a deeper analysis of Stalin's psychology, than Bek's *The New Appointment*, or indeed any other work hitherto published in the USSR. Rybakov's penetrating analysis of Stalin's history and character, and, in particular, his evocation of the tortuous reasoning involved in the fabricated purge cases of the 1930s, are matched in only a few works of fiction published outside the USSR, for example Solzhenitsyn's *The First Circle*. However, in contrast with Solzhenitsyn's novel, where Stalin appears only in a few chapters, Stalin figures as a major protagonist throughout *Children of the Arbat*. Moreover, Rybakov's Stalin differs considerably not only from the idealised portraits of the 'cult' period, but also from the mild half-truths published in the Khrushchev period and the black, satirical portraits in *émigré* fiction. Rybakov has stated that he tried to describe Stalin 'objectively': 'I put aside my personal antipathy for the man, and I tried to understand him from within, how he appeared to himself. I tried to show him from all sides, his philosophy of power, of one-man rule, his ruthlessness'.[91]

In *Children of the Arbat* the appearance of Stalin is carefully prepared, so that the reader gradually builds up a composite picture of the dictator. Stalin is first discussed by other characters, then introduced through 'external characterisation', first in a short scene of action and dialogue, then as a remote figure standing on the Lenin Mausoleum. Gradually the reader learns more about Stalin's past and psychology through the perceptions of his subordinate, the factory director Ryazanov, and Stalin's former friend, the Old Bolshevik and ex-diplomat Budyagin. Only at the end of the first part of the novel do we gain access to Stalin's inmost thoughts, through a masterly evocation of Stalin's interior monologue.

Stalin is first mentioned in a discussion between two of the main protagonists, the student and Komsomol member Sasha Pankratov (a character based on the author), and his uncle Mark Ryazanov, a prominent industrial manager in the Urals, who bears a close resemblance to Abram Zavenyagin, a Bolshevik activist in the Ryazan region during the Civil War who from 1931 to 1937 was plant director at Magnitogorsk.[92] This scene introduces one theme which is developed throughout the novel: the contrast between Stalin, the real man, and Stalin, the cult figure. Sasha remarks that Stalin is small in stature, although he appears tall on the rostrum; and expresses distaste for Stalin's statement at his fiftieth birthday celebrations that 'the party bore me in its own image and likeness'. His uncle, however, interprets this more favourably, as meaning that Stalin is aware that the congratulations apply to the party, not to himself personally. Sasha then asks the startling question, 'Is it true that Lenin wrote that Stalin is rude and disloyal?'. This shows that Sasha is familiar with the postscript to Lenin's famous *Letter to the Congress*, dictated in January 1923 shortly before his death, which stated 'Stalin is too rude, and this fault . . . becomes unbearable in the office of General Secretary. Therefore, I propose to the comrades to find a way to remove Stalin from that position and appoint to it another man . . . more patient, more loyal, more polite and more attentive to comrades, less capricious, etc.'. This letter and other documents which together became known as Lenin's *Testament* were suppressed in May 1924, but were made available to the delegates at the closed session of the Twentieth Party Congress of 1956, at which Khrushchev gave his 'Secret Speech' denouncing Stalin. The *Letter to the Congress* subsequently remained unpublished in the USSR and had never previously been mentioned in literature. The allusion to this document alone demonstrates the extent of the change which has occurred in cultural policy since the accession of Gorbachev. Sasha's uncle expresses surprise at his nephew's familiarity with this secret document, but argues that it refers only to Stalin's 'personal qualities'; the 'political line' is the most important thing. Sasha responds with the awkward question: 'Can you separate them?', an issue explored throughout the novel. Sasha clearly expresses his own position: 'I am also for Stalin. But I would like fewer eulogies – they grate on the ear'.[93] Through the autobiographical character of Sasha, Rybakov illustrates the ambivalent feelings towards Stalin characteristic of many Soviet people in Stalin's time. Although he voices doubts about Stalin in private, Sasha enthusiastically joins in the general public acclaim, shouting 'Stalin! Stalin!' along with his comrades during a demonstration in Red Square.

When Stalin first appears in person, in a short technical interview with Ryazanov, Rybakov provides a realistic physical description of the dictator similar to that in Simonov's *People are Not Born Soldiers*, published in the Khrushchev era. No attempt is made to conceal any of Stalin's unattractive features or physical defects, such as his small stature, greying hair, pockmarked face, strong Georgian accent and withered arm. Like other writers, Rybakov devotes particular attention to Stalin's pale, slanting Asiatic eyes with their 'penetrating, testing gaze' which can become 'yellow, heavy, tigerish' when referring to an alleged 'wrecker'. Rybakov affords a balanced assessment of Stalin's approach to industrialisation. Stalin's demand that a new blast furnace in Ryazanov's factory be brought into production by the Seventeenth Congress illustrates his tendency to sacrifice economic planning to political expediency. However, Stalin is shown to be amenable to reason: when Ryazanov explains the difficulties involved, Stalin, after a searching question: 'So the Central Committee are technical adventurers?', modifies his original deadline, declaring, somewhat disingenuously: "We do not need Communists who promise anything you like. We need those who speak the truth', Stalin's acquiescence in Ryazanov's reasonable demand reflects the new, realistic approach to the formulation of the Second Five Year Plan after the spectacular, unrealistic tempos of the First.

Through his depiction of Ryazanov, Rybakov provides a convincing exploration of the ambivalent feelings of anxiety and veneration felt by many of Stalin's subordinates. Although he feels a certain 'awkwardness and anxiety' in Stalin's presence, Ryazanov excuses Stalin's ruthlessness on the grounds of the magnitude of his historical task: 'The unparalleled construction which he directed demanded an iron will . . . This will was cruel. What could be done? Historical transformations are not achieved by compassion'.[94] Stalin's ability to create disciples in his own image is suggested by Ryazanov's growing firmness and unapproachability: 'If he had not had Stalin's iron will above him, he would not have been able to show his own'. The formation of the psychology of the Stalinist 'New Man' is further illustrated by Ryazanov's readiness to accept the mass dispossession of the peasantry, and even the arrest of his own nephew. Like many Soviet people in Stalin's time, he justifies repression by reference to the 'merciless laws of history': 'A new history is being created. And everything old collapses with pain and losses'.[95] For Ryazanov, the industrialisation of the country is a revolution which justifies the sacrifice of individuals.

Rybakov ventures further than other Soviet writers in demonstrating that Stalin's terror began before the murder of Kirov in 1934, the date ascribed to it in Khrushchev's 'Secret Speech'. Already before the Seventeenth Congress of 1934, party and Komsomol members were being arrested. The fate of Sasha Pankratov closely mirrors the experience of Rybakov himself, who was arrested in 1933 and sent to exile in Siberia for three years. As the novel develops, we are gradually initiated into the ramifications of the case fabricated by the secret police on Stalin's orders. Sasha is merely one small link in a vast chain designed first to implicate V. V. Lominadze, a member of the Central Committee who opposed Stalin's policy towards China in 1927 and had been expelled from the party in 1930 for obtaining support from various local party secretaries for an attempt to limit Stalin's powers (Lominadze, who committed suicide in 1935, was later named as a conspirator in the Zinoviev and Bukharin trials), and ultimately to incriminate Ordzhonikidze and Kirov, two popular members of the Politburo whom Stalin regards as potential rivals. The incongruity of Stalin's excessive suspiciousness is highlighted by a depiction of the Seventeenth Congress, the so-called 'Congress of Victors', at which Stalin receives a prolonged ovation, and he himself praises the 'unusual ideological, political and organisational unity of the ranks of our party' now that the former 'anti-Leninist groupings' have been defeated.[96]

Rybakov evokes Stalin's inner monologue in order to analyse what he has called Stalin's 'philosophy of power'. After gaining the leadership of the party and the country Stalin believes that he is uniquely qualified to rule, mainly because he alone understands how to govern Russians. Stalin has no faith in the Russian people; rather he sees himself as continuing the tradition of powerful Russian Tsars like Ivan the Terrible and Peter the Great, who ruled through the inspiration of awe and terror. He regards dictatorial power as essential in order to control people's base instincts, but, like other autocratic rulers before him, such as Caesar or Napoleon, he also feels the need for supreme power to be 'regally grand', so that people will bow down before it. Using a chain of tortuous reasoning, Stalin argues that he alone is the true representative of the party which made the revolution; collective leadership is a myth, and only leaders are important in history: 'The history of mankind is the history of class warfare. But the Leader appears as the spokesman of the class, and therefore the history of mankind is the history of its leaders and rulers'.[97]

Stalin, who is a supreme egoist, is fully conscious of the value of the personality cult, and does his best to promote it. In his opinion, Machiavelli's ideas are now old-fashioned; power can be maintained only if the leader inspires love as well as fear. He refers to himself in the third person, and in capital letters like a god: 'Now HE rules these people. They believe in him like a god, and one can only believe in a god blindly, without caution. They call him father; people respect only a heavy, severe, but firm and reliable fatherly hand.'[98]

Stalin, whose own sole concern is the seizure and maintenance of supreme power, is convinced that all his associates are potential rivals for power. He is insecure to the point of paranoia, and utterly ruthless towards his enemies or potential enemies: 'all his opponents – past, present and future – must be destroyed and will be destroyed'.[99] He suspects defeated oppositionists, especially Zinoviev and Kamenev, of intriguing to return to power; and his colleagues in the Politburo (with the exception of Molotov and Kaganovich) of wanting to limit his power or get rid of him altogether. It is clear that he is preparing an attack on Kirov and Ordzhonikidze: he believes that Kirov's tolerance of former oppositionists in the Leningrad Party organisation is either an example of extreme naïveté or part of a scheme to build up an independent power base; and he mistrusts Ordzhonikidze's predilection for introducing into the Central Committee technical specialists whose influence and power are increasing. Rybakov provides a plausible explanation for Stalin's recourse to terror against his own party cadres. Stalin contends that 'the Russian people hate noblemen', but have always supported strong Tsars like Ivan the Terrible and Peter the Great who destroyed the boyars and service gentry.[100] Stalin casts himself in the role of autocratic Tsar, and party officials in the role of 'new landlords' whom the Russian people despise. Stalin uses terror as a means of preventing the party bureaucrats from forming contacts and interest groups which might threaten his supreme power.

Stalin justifies terror by the necessity to make the one socialist country in the world sufficiently powerful to withstand attack in time of war, or, in peacetime, sufficiently powerful to be feared by her enemies. He regards enormous human and material sacrifices as an inevitable concomitant of the rapid transformation of a peasant country into an industrial power. His philosophy is the simple theory that the end justifies the means: 'A great aim demands great energy, the great energy of a backward people is achieved only through great cruelty'. Stalin has already achieved one revolution – the destruction of the kulaks during collectivisation – which has cost millions of lives. The people's fear must be maintained by the theory of permanent class struggle, and even if there are millions more victims, Stalin is firmly convinced that 'History will forgive Comrade Stalin for this'.[101]

Rybakov delves more deeply into Stalin's past than any other writer (with the possible exception of Solzhenitsyn) in order to analyse his psychology. The picture of Stalin's childhood which Rybakov paints differs considerably from most western biographies of Stalin, suggesting that Rybakov may have based his account more on rumour than on hard evidence. In contrast to western scholars such as Tucker, who argues that Stalin loved his mother and was brutally treated by his father, Rybakov suggests that Stalin loved his father, a gentle but ineffectual man, but hated his dominant mother. From an early age, Stalin harboured pain at his father's weakness, and also at all the humiliations he himself had suffered, particularly over the false rumours of his illegitimacy. His suspicion that people are all liars is confirmed when he receives a report of his father's death in a drunken fight, which he does not believe. His unhappy experiences lead to an extreme desire for self-assertion, a need to avenge all the petty insults and imagined slights he has suffered in his life. He sees not love of humanity, but the desire for vengeance and self-assertion, as the hallmark of the true revolutionary. This view forms his character and ideas, leading him to adopt a revolutionary outlook in order to defend the poor and downtrodden, but later deforms his character, leading him to erect a bastion of fear between himself and his people.

Another important childhood influence was the theological seminary, which shaped not only Stalin's catechistic style of argument (faithfully reproduced by Rybakov), but also his belief in supreme power as 'OMNISCIENT, ALL-KNOWING and OMNIPOTENT'.[102] Stalin's early experience of ruined churches in Georgia, which 'struck him with their resonant emptiness, their remote mystery', later influences his predilection for monumental architecture. He wishes to achieve immortality by rebuilding Moscow in a classical style, so that it will become a 'grandiose monument to HIS epoch'.[103]

Stalin's past is also evoked by Budyagin, an Old Bolshevik who was Stalin's companion in exile in Tsarist times, subsequently a diplomat who falls into Stalin's disfavour. Budyagin analyses Stalin's personal faults which became more pronounced in the 1930s: his capriciousness, inability to take a joke, quickness to take offence, propensity for bearing grudges and inability to forgive. In a remark which helps to explain the psychology behind the purges, Budyagin comments: 'Stalin never took a step towards reconciliation – for him an ideological opponent became a personal enemy'. Another of Stalin's major defects indicated by Rybakov's Budyagin (and which had previously only been mentioned by such dissident writers as Solzhenitsyn and Maksimov) is his dogmatism, one-sidedness, absolute conviction that he is right – a habit allegedly inherited from his years in the seminary. The penetrating analysis of Stalin's historical role provided by Budyagin is also unique in Soviet fiction. During the revolution and Civil War Stalin's will-power and energy were useful; his negative qualities, which Budyagin characterises as 'disloyalty, rudeness and aspiration to autocracy', were tolerable at that time, as revolution demands extreme measures. However, these defects became dangerous during the period of the New Economic Policy, an 'era of construction'; Lenin was correct to warn in his *Testament* of Stalin's possession of unlimited, all-embracing power. Budyagin realises that Stalin measures loyalty to the party by the extent of loyalty to himself, and that significant changes are likely to occur after the Seventeenth Congress: 'Having asserted his exclusiveness at the Congress, Stalin will now assert his uniqueness'.[104]

During an interview with Budyagin, it becomes obvious that another of Stalin's major failings as ruler of the USSR in the 1930s is his mistaken analysis of foreign policy. Stalin does not know Europe, and scorns Russians who have lived in Europe as intellectuals and *émigrés*. He considers that the main enemies of the USSR are England, France and Japan, and regards the USSR, USA and Germany as natural allies. The ex-diplomat Budyagin sees the possible catastrophe that may ensue from Stalin's total underestimation of German might. Another of Stalin's failings as leader of a 'dictatorship of the proletariat' is his inability to deal with the working class. Budyagin relates that Stalin felt intimidated by an encounter with some English dockers during the Fifth Congress of the Russian Social Democratic and Labour Party held in London in 1907. As a young man Stalin was acutely sensitive to anything indicating lack of courage or physical weakness, and this sensitivity gave rise to morbid suspiciousness. Already in exile he had expounded to Budyagin his belief that 'Rudeness must be met with even greater rudeness – people take it for strength'. With age, Stalin has become even more inflexible; Budyagin understands that his attempt at changing Stalin's views on foreign policy is doomed to failure, because 'now, more than ever, he is convinced of his infallibility'.[105]

Rybakov's extensive depiction of Stalin enables him to provide a rounded picture of the dictator, exploring many facets of Stalin's character, everyday life and interests which have been ignored or merely touched upon by other writers: for example Stalin's fascination with the cinema, particularly with Charlie

Chaplin films, his love of Georgian music, his liking for good food and drink, his interest in gardening, his attitude towards his doctor and dentist, and his relationship with many individuals – Old Bolsheviks, current colleagues and secret police officials like Yagoda, Ezhov and Beria.

Rybakov devotes considerable attention to Stalin's desire to rewrite history, presenting it as another example of his need for self-assertion. Stalin wishes to establish new criteria for the analysis of historical events in order to ensure a correct interpretation of his own epoch. In contrast to the Marxist historian Pokrovsky and his school, Stalin believes that the role of personality, and particularly of leaders, in history should be emphasized. History must demonstrate that Stalin is the true successor of Lenin and the sole interpreter of Lenin's ideas; it is necessary for Stalin to rewrite his own past in order to prove that he 'always stood side by side with Lenin'.[106] The memoirs of Lenin's wife Krupskaya and a pamphlet by Stalin's childhood friend Avel Enukidze, *Our Illegal Printing Shops in the Caucasus*, must be refuted because they imply that Stalin played only a minor role in the underground movement before the revolution, whereas Stalin now wishes to prove that his contribution was vitally important, second only to that of Lenin. When Stalin contemplates his own past, the frontiers between reality and legend become blurred. Although Kirov refuses to participate in the dubious exercise of distorting the history of the revolutionary movement in the Caucasus, the implication is that Beria is waiting in the wings to fulfil this role. (Beria attacked Enukidze's pamphlet in his work *On the History of the Bolshevik Organisations in Transcaucasia*, which was highly flattering to Stalin, and Enukidze himself was shot without trial in 1937).

Throughout the novel Rybakov is careful to draw a clear distinction between Stalin and Lenin. Through the mouth of the Old Bolshevik Budyagin, Rybakov makes a remarkable analysis of both NEP and the relationship between Lenin and Stalin which is elsewhere only found in dissident literature. Although Lenin envisaged that NEP should be introduced 'seriously and for a long time', Stalin claimed to be following Lenin's policy when he liquidated NEP. Stalin came into conflict with Lenin on several issues, such as Lenin's slogan of 'nationalisation of land' and his lack of understanding of military matters. Stalin was, however, well aware of Lenin's prestige in the party, and therefore strove to present himself as Lenin's like-minded disciple and natural successor. In a phrase which recalls the views of the historian Roy Medvedev, Budyagin states that 'instead of socialist democracy, towards which Lenin was striving, Stalin created a completely different system'.[107]

Stalin's opposition to Lenin is also clearly demonstrated through Stalin's own interior monologue. Stalin criticises Lenin's view that NEP had been introduced 'seriously and for a long time' and that collectivisation was impossible until the peasantry had attained the correct level of culture to choose it voluntarily. Stalin takes the opposite view: 'first collectivisation, then culture'. Moreover, he rejects Lenin's support for democratic rule in the party; he regards what Lenin called a 'bureaucratic distortion' as 'the only possible form of rule'.[108] Stalin favours rule through bureaucracy, as long as the bureaucracy does not try to interpose itself between the leader and the people, and remains a mere instrument of his rule.

Rybakov introduces certain issues which are particularly dear to him personally, as a writer and Jewish intellectual. He shows that, unlike Lenin, who relied on the intelligentsia to make the revolution, and was close to Gorky, Stalin scorns the intelligentsia and wishes to make them subservient to the party. He employs Zhdanov to establish the Union of Soviet Writers which will render docile a group of people who 'always aspired to spiritual leadership of the people'.[109] Stalin, who himself wrote poetry in his youth, is not ignorant of literature, but interprets great writers of the past in a purely political manner, and has a pragmatic, instrumental attitude towards talented writers of his own time, such as Gorky and Mayakovsky. He wishes his own epoch to be immortalised in literature, but is scathing of proletarian poets and *émigré* writers such as Bunin (one suspects here a connection between the thoughts attributed to Stalin and Rybakov's own view of *émigré* writers).

As a Jewish writer, the author of *Heavy Sand* (1979) a novel about the persecution of Jews during the Nazi invasion, Rybakov is particularly interested in Stalin's Russian nationalism and anti-Semitism. He implies that Stalin, a Georgian, while ostensibly attacking Great Russian chauvinism, is conscious of the dominance of the Russian people, who alone, he believes, have historical significance: 'For the Russian people he must be Russian, as the Corsican Napoleon Bonaparte was French for the French'.[110] Stalin is hostile to the Jews, because, with the exception of Kaganovich, they are unable to submit to a leader. The Jewish religion, unlike Christianity, Islam and Buddhism, does not recognize a God incarnate in human form; hence Jews cannot accept the idea of a god-like leader. They regard democracy as a chance to argue; Jewish intellectuals such as Trotsky, Zinoviev and Kamenev mistakenly wish to set their personal opinions against the opinion of the majority.

Rybakov's novel is also remarkable in that it attempts to analyse Stalin's relationship with his colleagues in the Politburo in the 1930s. Stalin characterizes his lieutenants in turn: the reliable executives Molotov and Kaganovich; the oldest and youngest members of the Politburo, Kalinin and Andreev, who vote with the majority; and his unreliable colleagues Kirov, Ordzhonikidze, Kossior, Kuibyshev and Rudzutak (all of whom subsequently perished). Stalin's old friendship with Ordzhonikidze is of no consequence now; he sees Ordzhonikidze's desire to express an independent opinion as an attack on the party, since 'The leader has no like-minded people, the leader has comrades-in-arms'.[111] However, it is Kirov whom Stalin suspects of being the leader of the opposition to him. Rybakov graphically evokes the intricacies of the alleged opposition intrigue, as it appears to Stalin's paranoid imagination. His hatred of Kirov is connected with his suspicion of Leningrad, the seat of the old Russian intelligentsia, the former power base of his opponent Zinoviev and the home of his former wife Nadya, who committed suicide because of her opposition to collectivisation. Rybakov shows that Stalin lives a solitary life of suspicion and mistrust: 'You could not trust anyone – even your wife'.[112] He plays his colleagues in the Politburo off against each other and often bypasses them altogether, coming to rely more and more on his private secretariat and secret police officials: Yagoda, who is closely bound to Stalin by the dictator's threat of publishing documents purporting to implicate his as a former collaborator of the Tsarist secret police; and Yagoda's deadly rival Ezhov, a solitary, amoral man willing to destroy every 'mutual protection society' in the party apparat. The thoughts which Rybakov attributes to Kirov perhaps summarise the author's own viewpoint: 'As he had strengthened his position, Stalin had become all the more intolerant, capricious, had woven secret intrigues, played leaders of the party off against each other, had made the security organs the chief weapon of leadership . . . . Stalin wanted to rule with the help of terror and only terror – this was necessary for the strengthening of his personal power'.[113]

Rybakov's novel represents a major contribution to the public debate about formerly sensitive issues connected with Stalin and Stalinism which is still continuing in the USSR. Rybakov asks whether NEP should have lasted longer, as Lenin originally intended, and whether collectivisation was doomed to failure because the peasantry were not sufficiently educated to work the system properly. This reflects the general revaluation of the NEP period which is proceeding in the USSR in connection with Gorbachev's plans for economic reform, and culminated in the introduction of the New Economic Mechanism at the July 1987 Plenum of the Central Committee. Rybakov suggests that Stalin's rudeness and megalomaniac belief in his own infallibility rendered him unsuited to be leader in a period of economic reconstruction, and that Stalin's personality was largely responsible for the introduction of a regime totally different from that established by Lenin. This view corresponds to that of Gorbachev, who sees himself in the tradition of democratic socialism established by Lenin. It is also reminiscent of the views of the historian and former dissident Roy Medvedev, and even bears some resemblance to Trotsky's analysis of Stalin's betrayal of the revolution. Rybakov describes in detail Stalin's fabrication of a purge case against his supposed enemies, and, through the character of Ordzhonikidze, suggests that comradely disagreements within the party might have been handled differently. This implies support for the more liberal policies introduced by Gorbachev, and, indirectly, raises the question of the possibility of rehabilitating former oppositionists, such as Bukharin, Zinoviev, even Trotsky. Rybakov's emphasis on Stalin's particular mistrust of the Leningrad party apparatus may be an oblique attempt to explain the genesis of the 'Leningrad affair' of 1949, which still remains obscure (Malenkov's possible complicity, which was hinted at in the Khrushchev period, is not suggested). Stalin's attack on Kirov's democratic style of leadership, particularly his habit of walking through the streets of Leningrad to meet ordinary people, implies the author's support for Gorbachev's similar style (he has been compared to Kirov), and suggests that those who oppose it are neo-Stalinists.

To a Soviet audience, Rybakov's frank novel represents a major revaluation of Soviet history. However, as John Barber points out, although *Children of the Arbat* explores many historical questions formerly barred to Soviet writers, it does not add a great deal to western historians' understanding of the period 1933–4.[114] Inevitably, like most historical novelists, Rybakov oversimplifies historical events. In the first place, he presents Stalin as the sole initiator of repressive actions. Neither Molotov nor Kaganovich appears in the novel, and Ezhov merely takes notes from Stalin's dictation. Secondly, there is little real discussion of policy issues, and during the only two debates which occur in the novel – on technological development and foreign policy – Stalin's views are somewhat misrepresented. Thirdly, Rybakov sometimes omits known facts, such as the opposition to Stalin among delegates to the Seventeenth Party Congress. Possibly Rybakov chose not to include the rumour that many delegates wished Kirov to succeed Stalin as General Secretary, since this would have provided some basis for Stalin's paranoia. Fourthly, as the Soviet critic Alexander Latsis points out, Rybakov sometimes uses the freedom of the novelist to invent certain episodes, such as the alleged meeting between Kirov and Ordzhonikidze in Moscow in November 1934. At the time, apparently, Ordzhonikidze was ill and recuperating far away in the Caucasus; he and Kirov did not meet in the last three months of Kirov's life.[115] Thus, as John Barber convincingly shows, *Children of the Arbat* has serious limitations as an analysis of historical events in the USSR during the years 1933–4. Rybakov seeks to ascribe the Great Purges solely to Stalin and his immediate aides, without any reference to internal conflict (for example, the presence of a militant faction within the leadership, or active collaborators) or other, wider factors such as external threat, Soviet ideology, culture or the political system.

Shortly after the appearance of the final instalment of Rybakov's novel, the magazine *Ogonyok*, under its bold editor Vitaly Korotych, published a series of letters which Rybakov had received since 1966 from prominent literary and artistic figures who had read his novel in *samizdat*, demanding that the truth about Stalin be made public. In particular, a letter by Okudzhava took de-Stalinisation one step further even than *Children of the Arbat* itself. Rybakov's novel is mainly concerned with members of the Party and Komsomol who suffered in the purges, but Okudzhava referred explicitly to the widespread nature of the civilian purges in the 1930s, and suggested that they might have cost the country as much, if not more than its human losses in two world wars. Okudzhava did not infringe the next taboo, over the estimated total of those who perished in the purges or vanished. Nevertheless, he warned, 'The more prudish about them we are, the more we hide them, the more we will be confused and estranged from each other'.[116] The publication of these letters in *Ogonyok* coincided with the first public rehabilitation since Gorbachev's accession of Nikolai Muralov, a close colleague of Lenin who was shot in 1937.

Rybakov's novel has subsequently aroused a great deal of comment both in the USSR and the west. Most correspondents to the Soviet press praised the novel for its truthfulness, and regarded it as a major contribution to Gorbachev's policy of *glasnost'*, but some dissenting voices were raised asking why it was necessary to 'muddy the water' and even threatening to denounce Rybakov to the KGB.[117] In the Russian *émigré* paper *Russkaya Mysl'* Natalya Kuznetsova, in an article entitled 'Repentance or Veneration?', attacked Rybakov from a diametrically opposed point of view.[118] Her most fundamental criticisms were aimed at the general approach of the novel. Writing from a position similar to that of Solzhenitsyn, she accused Rybakov of adopting a Leninist, pro-party point of view, and, in particular, criticised him for suggesting that Stalin's political line was basically correct, whereas his methods were wrong. Kuznetsova has correctly identified Rybakov's stance, but instead of remarking on the frankness of his work in comparison with previous Soviet novels, she underestimates its boldness and impact. Her criticism is fundamentally misdirected, for it is unreasonable to expect any novel published in the USSR to deviate greatly from the current party line. The view of the narrator in *Children of the Arbat* (which no doubt reflects the author's own opinion), corresponds, not surprisingly, to that expressed by Gorbachev in many speeches throughout 1987. Kuznetsova's complaint that Rybakov's novel does not go any further than Khrushchev's criticisms of Stalin in 1956 and 1961 is somewhat unfair, because Rybakov gives the New Economic Policy a favourable mention and refers to oppositionist Communists whom Stalin defeated before 1934, such as Riutin, Smirnov, Tolmachev and Eismont, as well as to many intellectual Marxists whom Stalin opposed, such as Lunacharsky, Pokrovsky, Rozhkov, Goldenberg, Bogdanov, Krasin, Nogin, Lomov and Rykov, whose names had largely been forgotten in the USSR. Moreover, Rybakov alludes to 'millions' of victims of collectivisation and potential 'millions' to be killed in the future. It is true that there is no reference in Rybakov's novel to the purges in the army, which Khrushchev discussed in public in 1961, but Marshal Tukhashevsky's name has been mentioned in the press in letters about Rybakov's novel, and he may well feature in one of the subsequent volumes of Rybakov's trilogy, which are apparently entitled *1935 and Other Years* and *1944*.[119]

Kuznetsova's second criticism, that Rybakov fails to implicate Stalin directly in the murder of Kirov, is also unjustified. Rybakov was concerned with historical accuracy, and felt that he did not have enough historical evidence to prove Stalin's guilt conclusively, but many hints are dropped about Stalin's probable complicity.[120] By the end of the novel Stalin's personal envoy Zaporozhets has been sent to Leningrad to reorganise the NKVD, where he acts independently of Kirov's colleague, the former police chief Feliks Medved, and makes contact with Nikolaev, Kirov's future assassin. The passing reference in Rybakov's novel to Hitler's 'Night of the Long Knives', which Kuznetsova unequivocally considers to have exerted an influence on Stalin, can be regarded as another broad hint of Stalin's complicity, but no definite connection between the two events can be established.

Kuznetsova's more detailed criticisms of Rybakov's artistic technique do possess some validity. She complains that too much of Rybakov's novel is based on Stalin's own written words; we are *told*, rather than *shown*, Stalin's behaviour, except in rare cases such as the scene with the dentist, when Stalin's dislike of people doing anything behind his back illustrates his paranoia. However, there are many other such details (for example, Stalin's secretary Poskryobyshev is aware of Stalin's dislike of open or slammed doors), and the reader is given the perspective of many different points of view on Stalin. Criticism of Rybakov's rather flat, realist style is also to some extent justified; unlike more sophisticated *émigré* writers such as Sinyavsky and Voinovich, Rybakov makes no use of techniques like caricature, surrealism and fantasy, which, in Kuznetsova's opinion, would more effectively evoke Stalin's subconscious thoughts and tortured psychology and the enormity of his actions. There is room for debate about the most effective method of portraying a historical tyrant, but, as Solzhenitsyn also discovered, realism is the most useful method for the writer who wishes not only to depict Stalin's character, but also to subject Stalin's life and historical role to detailed analysis.

As the Soviet critic A. Turkov points out, the appearance of Rybakov's *Children of the Arbat* was an important event in the USSR, because this was one occasion when literature was able to make invaluable use of its own resources in order to overtake its 'neighbours', history and biography.[121] Rybakov has declared that 'We must tell the whole truth about that epoch'.[122] In the first part of his trilogy he has told more of the truth than any other author published in the USSR, although not the 'whole truth'. It remains to be seen whether in the next two volumes of his trilogy even more of the truth will be told. As Turkov remarked, *Children of the Arbat* has by no means exhausted discussion of the theme of Stalin and Stalinism in the USSR, and it is to be hoped that these issues will now be investigated in greater detail by historians. Literary portraits of Stalin published in the USSR, while varying greatly in the degree of historical accuracy they embody, are in the last resort only fictional, and are no substitute for historical or biographical studies of Stalin. Literature may create new myths or clashing interpretations which can only be resolved by historical scholarship.

Nevertheless, as John Barber argues, Rybakov's novel may prove to be of great historical value, because in raising some crucial questions about Stalinism and the origins of the Terror before a mass audience, he has challenged historians to produce alternative, deeper analyses of this difficult period. Such a revaluation of Soviet history will no doubt eventually be re-flected in the revised *History of the Communist Party of the Soviet Union* and in the biography of Stalin by Colonel General Dmitri Volkogonov which began to be serialised in 1988.[123]

Initially, however, Soviet historians displayed a certain reticence about the need to reassess the Stalinist past. Academician Yuri Poliakov complained, 'It's fair enough for writers to present a certain picture of that time, but an historian needs documentation – and our archives, frankly, have been in quite a mess'.[124]

By the summer of 1987 there were signs that Gorbachev too was becoming rather more circumspect in his approach to revelations about the past. Two weeks after the Central Committee Plenum of July 1987 which announced the introduction of the New Economic Mechanism, Gorbachev put the brakes on the policy of de-Stalinisation, warning his over-enthusiastic followers against 'one-sided notions and sentiments' in the current reappraisal of Stalin's role in Soviet history. Although he explicitly stated, 'We can never and should never forgive or justify what happened in 1937–8. Never', Gorbachev attempted to restore the balance, claiming, 'Those events do not belittle everything done by the party and the people'. It is possible that Gorbachev was coming under increasing pressure from the conservatives in the Politburo and Central Committee; in any case, he did not wish the vigorous criticism of Stalin which was becoming fashionable in the USSR to upset the careful preparations for the celebration in November 1987 of the seventieth anniversary of the Bolshevik Revolution.

Gorbachev's anniversary speech steered a careful middle course on the question of Stalin.[125] On the one hand, he attacked the cruel excesses of collectivisation and the purges as 'real crimes stemming from an abuse of power', and claimed that 'the guilt of Stalin and his immediate entourage before the party and the people for the wholesale repressive measures and acts of lawlessness is enormous and unforgivable'. He countered the frequent objection that Stalin did not know of these abuses, admitting that documents existed which conclusively proved that Stalin had known all about the repressions and illegalities. On the other hand, Gorbachev characterised Stalin as 'an extremely contradictory personality' whose gross errors and abuses had to be weighed up against his 'incontestable contribution to the struggle for socialism'. Gorbachev claimed that in the 1920s Stalin had pursued the accepted line of the Leninist centre of the party; although collectivisation had been carried out with excessive cruelty, the policy itself had been essential to develop a modern agriculture and to release manpower for industry. The rapid industrialisation of the country undertaken in the 1930s had ensured the victory over Nazi Germany. However, the victory was not to be seen as Stalin's personal victory, but as the triumph of the Russian people and the ordinary Red Army soldier.

For all its forthright condemnation of Stalin, Gorbachev's speech was also notable for its omissions. He stated only that 'many thousands of people inside and outside the party had been subjected to wholesale repressive measures', failing to admit that millions had been falsely condemned. Moreover, he made no reference to the execution of Marshal Tukhashevsky and the purges in the Red Army on the eve of war. Clearly, Gorbachev's speech had failed to satisfy Soviet liberals, since the very next day *Moscow News* published a letter from Academician Andrei Sakharov arguing that Gorbachev had not gone far enough in attacking Stalin. Nevertheless, Gorbachev's balanced, though partial, analysis of Stalin and Stalinism continued to be official Soviet policy at the Extraordinary Party Conference in June 1988, although the enduring commitment of the present leadership to the redressing of past wrongs was again demonstrated by its acceptance of an appeal for a monument to the victims of Stalinism. 'Memorial', an unofficial organisation established to raise funds both for a monument and an institute devoted to study and research into the past, has invited Solzhenitsyn, Sakharov and Roy Medvedev to become members.

Another important literary work which has helped Soviet society publicly to come to terms with its Stalinist past is Mikhail Shatrov's play *Onward . . . onward . . . onward!*, published in January 1988, which goes even further in its investigation of Soviet history than Shatrov's earlier play *The Peace of Brest-Litovsk*.[126] The play is subtitled 'The author's version of events which occurred on 24 October 1917 and significantly later'. Shatrov depicts Lenin waiting impatiently in his refuge on the eve of the Bolshevik Revolution, and twenty-two other major figures of the revolution, including the right-wing generals Kornilov and Denikin, the head of the Provisional Government Alexander Kerensky, the Menshevik Martov and the Left Socialist Revolutionary Maria Spiridonovna, as well as Stalin and his victims Bukharin, Kamenev, Zinoviev and Trotsky. The author justifies his belief in the importance of personality in history through the mouth of his character Sverdlov: 'How much in life and in a revolution in particular depends on those who are on the captain's bridge'. The main theme of the play is an investigation of why and how the Bolshevik Revolution of 1917, with its high ideals, degenerated into Stalinism. Each of Shatrov's characters explains his views and actions with the benefit of hindsight.

Trotsky is presented as a self-important maverick figure who is, nevertheless, acknowledged to have played a major part in the revolution and the consolidation of Bolshevik power. He accuses Stalin of murdering him 'without even the appearance of a trial', whereupon Stalin retorts that he cannot have his hands tied by 'bourgeois morality', and that Trotsky's assassin 'executed the sentence of a proletarian court'. Trotsky and Stalin are shown to be poles apart in their political views, but alike in their 'scorn for people, for the masses'.

Shatrov explores the question of why Lenin's successors did not fulfil his wish of removing Stalin from the position of General Secretary. Trotsky, Kamenev, Zinoviev and Bukharin, the major figures of the post-Lenin Politburo, are shown to have subordinated the interests of the party to their own factional intrigues. Bukharin admits: 'We were the victims of a behind the scenes bureaucratic struggle'. Lenin acknowledges his own moral responsibility for what happened after his death, admitting: 'I understood too late ... the system which allowed one man to concentrate unlimited power in his hands ought to have been changed'. Shatrov exposes Stalin's attempt to rewrite history to prove that he 'was always close to Lenin'. On the contrary, he suggests, the repressions of the 1930s, with their 'millions of senseless victims', were a result of the loss of those moral principles which always guided Lenin's political actions. Shatrov presents a rather too favourable interpretation of Lenin's ideas and conduct, but Soviet writers of the Gorbachev era who wish to attack Stalinism have no option but to elevate a worthy Leninist ideal which may serve as an inspiration for contemporary Soviet people.

Shatrov allows Stalin to justify his methods and to present a plausible case for his claim that he learnt many lessons from Lenin. Stalin maintains that Lenin acted in an authoritarian manner in moments of crisis, as at the Tenth Congress of 1921 when he passed a resolution on party unity designed to stifle opposition, which subsequently helped Stalin to defeat his opponents in the party. During the 'Great Turning-Point' of 1929, Stalin declares, he was merely applying the methods Lenin used in the Civil War. However, Lenin indignantly refutes this argument: 'To make methods and means adopted exclusively in the conditions of open civil war into universal methods of building socialism is a most grave crime against socialism'. Stalin also argues that history will justify him, because he made the Soviet state into a great power, and won the war against Hitler: 'We live in Russia, the land of the tsars . . . it will be impossible to remove me from the popular memory'.

Stalin's exchanges with Bukharin are relevant to contemporary debates in the Gorbachev era about the future path of Soviet development. Bukharin condemns Stalin's police state; his forcible collectivisation policy, which was much easier than 'working out flexible prices, rational taxes and good agronomy'; and his encouragement of war by purging the Red Army and Navy and condemning foreign social democrats as fascists. Bukharin wins the author's sympathy, as his ideas are presented as closer to Lenin's. The last letter which Bukharin wrote before being shot in 1938, appealing for the party to justify him posthumously, which had already appeared in the Soviet press, is reproduced in Shatrov's play. Shatrov's Bukharin advocates a policy similar to that of Gorbachev: 'humane socialism' and 'a complicated combination of personal, group, mass, public and state initiatives, a striking pluralism of intellectual life'. Nevertheless, Shatrov does not underestimate the difficulties facing Gorbachev in his policy of pressing 'onward', following the principles advocated by Lenin, not the methods adopted by Stalin. The author hints at the continuing presence of many neo-Stalinists in contemporary Soviet society through Stalin's remark: 'Many people will defend me in defending themselves'.

Shatrov's play did not please the conservatives in Soviet society: Victor Afanasyev, the editor of *Pravda*, condemned it as 'irresponsible'.[127] However, although Shatrov, like most writers, dramatists and film-makers who have treated the subject of Stalin, overemphasises the personal element in the great issues of Soviet history which he confronts, his play, like Rybakov's *Children of the Arbat*, is a bold attempt to present the Soviet people with a new version of their past. Shatrov has issued a challenge to professional historians who, if they disagree with his interpretations, must labour to produce another, more accurate version of Soviet history which will satisfy the party leaders and the Soviet public in the age of *glasnost'* and *perestroika*.

The literary 'thaw' of 1986–8 has been directly sanctioned by the party leadership, suggesting that Gorbachev takes the view that it is necessary for a country to understand its past in order to build a better future. However, it is not clear how much further the current reappraisal of the Stalin era will extend. The year 1988 has seen the publication after sixty-two years of Pilnyak's *Tale of the Unextinguished Moon*, and the appearance of some major works previously banned in the USSR, such as Zamyatin's *We* and Pasternak's *Doctor Zhivago*, as well as novels containing hostile portraits of Stalin, for example Grossman's *Life and Fate* and Yuri Dombrovsky's *The Faculty of Unnecessary Things* (see pp. 115–19).[128] The case of Grossman's novel is particularly astonishing, because when it was confiscated by the KGB in 1961, Aleksei Surkov, then Chairman of the Writers' Union, claimed that it might be published in the USSR, but 'only in 250 years'.[129] Although at first only banned works by famous dead writers received permission for publication in the USSR, Vladimir Voinovich's satirical novel *The Life and Extraordinary Adventures of Private Ivan Chonkin* has been announced for publication in 1989, and it now seems conceivable that other works containing portraits of Stalin by writers obliged to emigrate who have hitherto been classed as 'dissident' (see pp. 108–34) will eventually achieve publication. A new and fascinating stage of de-Stalinisation will be reached if Solzhenitsyn one day accepts Gorbachev's invitation to visit the USSR and signs a contract for the publication of his works, including *The Gulag Archipelago*. Even if this momentous event, which once seemed totally inconceivable, finally occurs, it will be yet another demonstration of Gorbachev's instrumental attitude towards the past. Like other Soviet leaders before him, Gorbachev believes that the past should be dwelt on not for its own sake, not merely to set the historical record straight, but in order to draw valuable lessons about the origins of negative phenomena in contemporary Soviet society, and hence to overcome them in the future.

Chapter six

Portraits of Stalin in western and dissident literature

Western literature

Some writers of political novels working outside the USSR have also felt the need to come to terms with Stalin and the totalitarian system he embodied, both in his lifetime and after his death. Most fictional works dealing with Stalin published in the west in Stalin's lifetime sprang directly from the personal experience of the authors. They were either the creation of Russian *émigrés.* or of European socialist intellectuals who had at one time been sympathetic to communism, but had subsequently become disillusioned, and were eager to communicate their altered perceptions to the frequently ill-informed western public.

Into the latter category fall Arthur Koestler and George Orwell, in whose novels *Darkness at Noon* and *1984* Stalin (or some composite dictator-figure ultimately responsible for everything) appears as a shadowy, abstract figure. Both are highly concentrated works; neither Orwell nor Koestler distracts from the dilemma of his central character by presenting the dictator and his thoughts. The dictator in Koestler's *Darkness at Noon* (1940) is called 'No. 1', like the central character in Pilnyak's *Tale of the Unextinguished Moon*. Since Koestler had a good knowledge of Russian, and lived for a time in Moscow as a foreign correspondent, it is highly likely that he was familiar with Pilnyak's work. Koestler's No. 1 possesses only one distinctive physical feature: like Stalin, he smokes a pipe. Apart from this, he is a remote figure, presented through the eyes of the oppositionist Communist Rubashov (a composite character based on Bukharin and other victims of the Moscow purge trials, some of whom Koestler knew personally) as a cynical, ruthless, unfathomable dictator who has betrayed the Revolution, but nevertheless may, like his namesake in Pilnyak's story, be the instrument of History. It is the sense of his historical mission which gives No. 1 'faith in himself, tough, slow, sullen and unshakeable'; for party members critical of him 'the horror which No. 1 emanated above all consisted in the possibility that he was in the right'.[1]

If Orwell's *Animal Farm* (1943) represented a powerful allegory of the rise to power of Stalin and the new-style, brutal party he led, with its ruthless liquidation of the Old Bolsheviks,[2] *1984* (first published in 1949), which may originally have been planned together with *Animal Farm* as part of a trilogy, evokes the party in power and the intellectual implications of totalitarianism. In Orwell's totalitarian society of the future the uncontested leader Big Brother looks down from posters and the omnipresent telescreen, 'black-haired, black-moustachio'd, full of power and mysterious calm'. (It is interesting that Orwell uses the word 'calm', typical of Soviet portraits of Stalin in the 'cult' period.) Big Brother, like Stalin, is the object of a 'cult of personality' designed to inspire his subjects with love as well as fear. The protagonist and former rebel Winston, after he has been brainwashed, sees Big Brother as 'the colossus that bestrode the world! The rock against which the hordes of Asia dashed themselves in vain!'. At the end of the novel, the victory of the state over the individual is complete: 'He loved Big Brother'.[3] Orwell was influenced by Zamyatin, but unlike *We*, *1984* is not so much an anti-utopian fantasy or a prophecy, but an extension of certain disturbing aspects of the contemporary world of 1948 forward into the future. Although Orwell saw close connections between Nazism and Stalinism, it is more likely that Big Brother, with his black moustache, was modelled on Stalin rather than on Hitler, since the work was published some time after Hitler's death. It is a measure of the transformation which has taken place in Soviet cultural life under Gorbachev that Zamyatin's *We*, Orwell's *Animal Farm* and Koestler's *Darkness at Noon* have all been published for the first time in the USSR in 1988, and *1984* has been announced for publication in 1989.

Another writer who was concerned with Stalin and the problem of totalitarianism was Vladimir Nabokov, who emigrated soon after the Revolution. It is necessary to be cautious in ascribing any political intention to Nabokov's work, since in the preface to his novel *Bend Sinister* (1947) he scoffs at 'literature of social comment', insists that he has no satirical or didactic purpose, claims that the influence of the epoch on his book has been 'negligible', and singles out Orwell as the sort of mediocre novelist whose clichés he himself has taken pains to avoid.[4] Elsewhere, however, Nabokov himself has repudiated his own somewhat disingenuous denial of the political significance of his writings. He has argued that *Invitation to a Beheading* depicts a 'Communazist state' which persecutes a rebel by putting him in prison;[5] and has described both this novel and *Bend Sinister* as 'absolutely final indictments of Russian and German totalitarianism'.[6] In an introductory note to the 1975 edition of his story *Tyrants Destroyed* (written in 1938), Nabokov states: 'Hitler, Lenin and Stalin dispute my tyrant's throne in this story – and meet again in *Bend Sinister*, 1947, with a fifth toad. The destruction is thus complete'.[7] Undoubtedly, therefore, some of Nabokov's works are meant to be interpreted as an indictment of totalitarianism, and specifically of Stalin.

Nabokov's vision of dictatorship is a comic one: he contends that 'Tyrants and torturers will never manage to hide their comic stumbles behind their cosmic acrobatics';[8] and he regards tyrants as 'the clowns of history'.[9] Nabokov claims that the villain in *Tyrants Destroyed*, his most detailed study of the tyrant as 'clown of history', is a composite character, but the allusions to Stalin in this story are more numerous and explicit than the passing references to the dictator's baldness (which recalls Lenin) and his 'dark zoological ideas' which, like Hitler's views on the master-race, have caught the imagination of his 'fatherland'. The narrator voices Nabokov's own opinion of Stalin and other dictators: 'When a limited, coarse, little-educated man – at first glance a third-rate fanatic – in reality a pigheaded, brutal and gloomy vulgarian full of morbid ambition – when such a man dresses up in godly garb, one feels like apologising to the gods'.[10] Many features of Nabokov's tyrant are reminiscent of Stalin: his encouragement of a fantastic personality cult; the mystery surrounding his youth; his occasional moods of 'nasty, jagged joviality'; his mistrust of 'the machinations of mysterious enemies'; his intellectual mediocrity; and his decision to transform a 'wild-flowery country into a vast kitchen garden, where special care is lavished on turnips, cabbages and beets'. His comment after interviewing an old widow who has succeeded in growing an eighty-pound turnip: 'Now that's genuine poetry for you. Here's something the poet fellows ought to learn from',[11] reflects both Stalin's support for Lysenkoite agrobiology and the low level of his cultural interests. Nabokov believes in the artist's power to destroy tyranny by making it appear ridiculous: 'I see that, in my efforts to make him terrifying, I have only made him ridiculous, thereby destroying him'.[12]

The tyrants in Nabokov's later novels are also stupid, brutal leaders. Paduk in *Bend Sinister* is a more obviously composite figure who has no explicit connection with Stalin (however, the propaganda produced by Paduk's regime contains Russian words and echoes of the Stalin Constitution of 1936). In a letter to Edmund Wilson in 1945, just before starting work on the novel, Nabokov suggested that Stalin in the press photographs of the Yalta Conference was 'not the real Stalin, but one of his many duplicates'.[13] This idea is amplified in *Bend Sinister*, where Paduk undergoes a beautification session with a mortician: his eyes 'sprang open again' after being closed and his speech is jerky.[14] Through this image of the dictator as dummy, Nabokov suggests that tyrants are fools and incompetents vastly inferior to the intellectuals they disdain.

Stalin is more explicitly portrayed in the novels of the Trotskyist Victor Serge, a Russian *émigré* whose works display the influence of his friend Pilnyak. In Serge's *The Case of Comrade Tulaev* (1948) 'the Chief', another pipe-smoker, is addressed as 'Iosif'; while in *Midnight in the Century* (1939) 'the Secretary-General' makes a brief appearance under Stalin's own full name and patronymic 'Iosif Vissarionovich'. Stalin appears as only an episodic character in both Serge's novels, although everything is done in his name: in *Midnight in the Century* he is called 'the living keystone of the edifice'. In this novel he is satirically presented as a ruthless dictator who is morbidly suspicious of his closest colleagues and sees potential traitors everywhere. One of the few sentences he utters is addressed to the secret police chief Yagoda: 'The Right and the Left will be stirring in little corners. Lock 'em up, eh, lock 'em up. And keep me informed of everything'.[15]

In the preface to his later novel *The Case of Comrade Tulaev*, Serge calls his work 'literary fiction' and warns the reader not to confuse 'the truth created by the novelist ... with that of the historian or the chronicler'.[16] Nevertheless, although Serge contends that it would be a mistake to attempt to establish a precise relationship between his novel and real people and historical events, the circumstances he describes bear an extremely close resemblance to the murder of Kirov and the unleashing of Stalin's terror. In contrast with the caricatured portrait in *Midnight in the Century*, Serge in *The Case of Comrade Tulaev* paints a realistic portrait of 'the Chief', who appears in two interviews with his former comrade, the Old Bolshevik Kondratiev, and once in a Politburo meeting. There is little attempt to provide a detailed analysis of the historical background or the psychological motivation of 'the Chief', but quite a sympathetic picture emerges of an isolated man at the summit of power who is convinced that he is surrounded by treachery. Iosif is depicted in what might be considered an atypical situation – an act of mercy. He pardons Kondratiev who makes a personal appeal to him. The interviews have great psychological intensity: Kondratiev is afraid, but, as an old comrade, is the only person who can tell the 'Chief' some home truths. The meetings are the occasion for a confrontation of political ideas rather than a psychological portrait of the Chief. While Serge makes some attempt to analyse the psychological and political position of a man who holds supreme power, he implies that the terror machine has escaped from the Chief's control, and that an individual cannot be considered entirely responsible for all that is done in his name.

One of the most comic portraits of Stalin by an *émigré* writer is contained in *The Red Monarch*, a novel by Yuri Krotkov, a Soviet playwright and film maker who defected to the west in 1963, which David Puttnam later turned into a successful film. Although not particularly well written, the novel nevertheless possesses considerable documentary interest, because the author was brought up in Georgia and became familiar with a circle of Georgian intellectuals and top-ranking party officials in Moscow who told him 'many interesting and unique things about Stalin, which no ordinary Soviet citizen could know'. The fascinating chapter 'Two Stalins' is based on the testimony of the Georgian actor Gelovani who played Stalin in many films and met the dictator personally. Krotkov includes many scenes of pure farce, such as an absurd meeting between Stalin and Mao Tse-Tung;

but some incidents which appear ludicrous have a basis in fact: for example, the humorous scene in which Stalin censures Molotov in a Politburo meeting for allowing the Soviet basketball team to lose recalls Stalin's decision in 1952 to disband the Central Army football team after the Soviet national team had lost to Yugoslavia at the Helsinki Olympic Games. As well as ridiculing Stalin, Krotkov is also careful to humanise him, emphasising that he spared certain old comrades from the camps, loved his mother, wife and daughter and was racked by self-doubt and fear of death. Krotkov's aim is to bring Stalin to life 'the way he was, or rather the way he appeared and appears now to me: good and bad, great and ordinary, principled and unprincipled, a man moved by deep-rooted contradictions'.[17]

Stalin has continued to fascinate western writers, who use his image to explore the nature of the Soviet regime and the implications of totalitarianism. He features, for example, in Robert Bolt's dramatic reconstruction of the Russian Revolution, *State of Revolution*, and David Pownall's play *Master Class*, which deals with Stalin's persecution of the composers Prokofiev and Shostakovich in the 'Zhdanov era'.

Dissident Russian literature

Hostile portraits of Stalin produced in the post-Stalin era by Soviet writers whose works were published first in the west hold considerable interest for both the literary scholar and the historian. It was only in *samizdat* and *tamizdat* fiction that the negative sides of Stalin's character began to be explored in detail. Portraits of Stalin in dissident fiction are divided into three main categories: the realistic, the allegorical, and the comic or grotesque. There is a further distinction between those portraits which are concerned with an analysis of Stalin and Stalinism as historical phenomena, and those designed to draw parallels with the contemporary USSR. Moreover, a whole new genre arose in the post-Stalin period – guitar poetry – which had among its themes an investigation of Stalin and the Stalinist past.

Guitar poetry

Guitar poetry, which rose to prominence in the USSR in the 1950s and 1960s,[18] was an intimate medium for the frank expression of the singer's inmost thoughts to a small audience, a means of bypassing the scrutiny of editor and censor. Later the songs of Bulat Okudzhava, Vladimir Vysotsky and Alexander Galich became highly popular and were widely disseminated in *magnitizdat* (uncensored tape recordings). As we have seen, Okudzhava evoked Stalin in an allegorical manner through the image of the black tomcat; Vysotsky and Galich, in works published outside the USSR, treated the subject of Stalin more explicitly in order to reassess and exorcise the past.

In Vysotsky's poem *Stoke me the Bath-house Smokeless*, published abroad in 1977, a former labour-camp inmate remembers his past and tries to put it behind him.[19] The tattoo of Stalin which he bears on his chest (common even for political prisoners) testifies to his youthful faith in Stalin. Through labour in Siberia his faith is gradually eroded:

> How much belief and timber was felled . . .
> For my selfless belief
> How many years I rested in paradise
> I exchanged my foolish stupidity
> For a dull hopeless life.

Throughout years of hard labour in quarry or swamp he and his fellow prisoners retained their faith in Stalin, hoping that he would sort out their cases and set them free:

> We tattooed his profile closer to our hearts
> So that he would hear how our hearts were broken.

With hindsight these lines are full of bitter irony, since Stalin himself was responsible for breaking the prisoners' hearts and remained indifferent to their sufferings. Eventually the singer realises that his labour was in vain:

> The thoughts have started knocking under my skull.
> It turns out I was condemned by Them for nothing!

The lines:

> So with my birch twigs I'll whip myself
> For the inheritance of those gloomy times

express the singer's desire to punish himself for his former 'stupidity' and 'faith' in Stalin. Gerald Smith's translation:

> So with my birch twig I'll whip out
> The inheritance of those gloomy times[20]

suggests that the poet wishes to exorcise and forget the past, which may indeed be another implication of the lines; but the whole despairing tone of the poem, with its emphasis on 'doubt' and 'madness', suggests that it may not be easy to eradicate the legacy of the past. Smith testifies to the 'personal charge' which Vysotsky put into this song, which he howled out in a hoarse voice, and to its great impact on Russian audiences: 'it seemed to take them by the throats and confront them with the tormenting question that they sometimes formulate for themselves as "What did we struggle for?" and to demand a despairing answer'.[21] Vysotsky's poem received unofficial publication in the USSR in 1979 in the journal *Metropol'*, a collection of hitherto unpublished Soviet writings compiled by liberal writers such as Vasily Aksyonov, Andrei Bitov, Fazil Iskander and others, which was printed in eight copies, but swiftly suppressed.[22] Vysotsky died in 1980 at the age of 42; but since Gorbachev's accession his work has once again become widely known and publicised in the USSR. In 1987 he was posthumously awarded the USSR State Prize.

Galich's song cycle *The Doomed Generation* (1972) is also concerned with those Soviet people who have experienced the Stalin terror and cannot get its effect out of their systems.[23] His *Poem about Stalin*, divided into six chapters which Galich sometimes sang as independent songs, represented an attempt to analyse both the tyrant himself and the effect of his policies.[24] The epigraph 'Ahead is Jesus Christ', taken from the last line of Alexander Blok's famous poem *The Twelve*, indicates that Galich, like Blok, is drawing parallels between biblical figures and historical events, but with ironic intent. The first chapter presents a grotesque version of the Nativity, in which Stalin, with his 'pockmarked face' and 'evil smile', leans over the crib of his rival, the baby Jesus:

> So this is the one, that same
> Pathetic orphan of the earth
> Who will vie with me
> In blood and hosannas . . . .

Galich's vision of a competition between Stalin and Jesus evokes both the quasi-religious nature of the 'personality cult' and the pretensions of both Stalinism and Christianity to be total world systems demanding the complete obedience of the individual. Like Bulgakov and Pasternak, Galich draws a parallel between Rome in Christ's time and the USSR in the 1930s: the three Wise Men are beaten up, 'heads fly' as a result of their denunciations,

And this
Was a very weighty sign
That new times had come.

Chapter 2 consists entirely of a monologue by Stalin, which is one of the most powerful evocations in Russian literature of the unmitigated evil of Stalin's personality. Stalin crudely attacks the Jews as a 'band of rascals and thieves', and mocks Christ as 'not a creator, but a victim of the elements', who, since he was 'weak-hearted and a bit simple', was a butt for Barabbas's jokes and abandoned by his followers in his hour of need. Stalin ridicules the pitiful results of Christ's teaching after two thousand years, and is determined not to repeat his predecessor's mistakes:

You are not the son of God, but the son of man,
If you could exclaim: 'Thou shalt not kill! . . .
Not one blasphemer will be found in the world
Who would lift a lance against me!
If I should die – which might happen –
My kingdom will be eternal!

However, in Chapter 3 Stalin's pretensions to 'mangodhood' are shown to have failed. He is dying alone, tormented by pain, loneliness and insomnia; he tries to summon the ghost of his former friend, Sergo Ordzhonikidze, who committed suicide, to sing him his favourite Georgian song, but he does not come; and Stalin is still convinced that his suspicions of Ordzhonikidze and all his other murdered associates were well founded. Galich demonstrates that God's power is greater than Stalin's: a church bell rings and Stalin tries to pray, but cannot remember the Lord's Prayer; he dies, begging for forgiveness and salvation.

The rest of the poem is concerned with the consequences of Stalinism. In Chapter 3, 'Conversation at Night in a Restaurant

Car', a survivor of the camps drunkenly relates how one day the camp commandant told the convicts that at the recent Party Congress the question of the 'Father and Genius' had been discussed:

> It turns out that the Father
> Wasn't a father, but a bastard . . . .

Galich evokes the joy with which the convicts hew down a great statue of Stalin, but also, through the image of the camp survivor beset by demons, suggests the confusion and disorientation caused by Khrushchev's dethronement of Stalin. Galich's own conclusion is that the person most to be feared is the one who says 'I know what is necessary' and 'Everyone who follows me will have heaven on earth as a reward'. The poet states categorically:

> Drive him away! Don't trust him!
> He's telling stories! He doesn't know what's necessary!

In other poems of the *Doomed Generation* series Galich makes it clear that he believes that Soviet people were responsible for their own history, and actively connived at their own oppression. His poem *The Night Watch*, for example, presents a nightmare vision in which thousands of discarded statues of Stalin come to life. The implication is that there has been little change since Stalin's time, and that Stalinism could easily be revived.[25] The refrain:

> The drums will beat
> Beat, beat, beat!

echoes Stalin's famous order to the security organs during the investigation of the 'Doctors' Plot', as related by Khrushchev in his 'Secret Speech': 'Beat, beat and beat again!'.[26]

Realistic portraits of Stalin

In the post-Stalin period some Soviet writers who had suffered in the Stalin era, several of them former prisoners, became fascinated by the figure of Stalin and wished to present their own, more convincing portraits of the dictator to contrast with the cautious, partial depictions permitted in literature published in the Soviet Union. By the 1950s the portrayal of Stalin in fiction had become an established tradition: realist writers hostile to Stalin merely stood the tradition on its head, portraying Stalin in a style which did not conform to the doctrine of 'socialist realism', but was closer to the 'critical realism' of nineteenth-century Russian literature. Solzhenitsyn, in *The First Circle*, was the first dissident Soviet writer to attempt an extensive realistic depiction of Stalin; and he was followed by four other writers whose works on Stalin were published first in the west – Alexander Bek, Yuri Dombrovsky, Vasily Grossman and Vladimir Maksimov. As we have seen, the realistic portraits of Stalin drawn by Bek and Rybakov in the 1960s eventually achieved publication in the USSR after Gorbachev's accession; and the novels by Grossman and Dombrovsky, both of whom are dead, were published in 1988. (There is as yet no sign of the works of Maksimov, a living *émigré* and religious believer, achieving publication in the USSR.) All these writers are united in their hostility to Stalin and their desire to portray him in a convincing manner, but each writer has an individual approach to his subject and is concerned with different aspects of Stalin's life and character.

Bek's novel *The New Appointment*, written in the Khrushchev period and first published abroad in 1971, was a fairly mild example of *samizdat* which did not go much further than the revelations in Khrushchev's 'Secret Speech' of 1956.[27] Nevertheless, it was remarkable for the realistic portrait of Stalin it contained. The novel was accepted for publication by *Novy Mir* in 1964 and set up in type before eventually being banned by the censorship. Bek's work could not be published in the USSR in the Brezhnev period, because the figure of Onisimov, a minister who is slavishly dependent on Stalin and dies of a heart attack because he is unable to adjust to the climate of the post-Stalin era, a character based on Tevosyan, Stalin's Minister of Ferrous Metallurgy, aroused the ire both of Tevosyan's widow and of Kosygin, the Chairman of the Council of Ministers.[28] Stalin appears as an episodic figure and is described entirely from the outside, through action and dialogue, as in Lukács's classical model of the depiction of historical characters. Like Simonov and other writers of the post-Stalin era, Bek draws a contrast between Stalin the cult figure, and Stalin the ordinary man, emphasising his small stature, his pock-marked face and the grey hairs in his hair and moustache. He depicts Stalin walking up and down in his military uniform and soft boots, stopping to think, light his pipe or to gaze intently at his interlocutor. Stalin's movements are 'slow and imperious. A man could hold himself in this way only if he knew that no one would hurry him, no one would break his silence'.[29] Bek depicts Stalin in action, suggesting that the 'nervous tension' with which he discusses tank production is a positive quality: 'This nervousness became self-discipline, it sharpened his mind'.[30]

Bek mentions the purges in the Donbass in 1937 which swept away most of the relatives and associates of Ordzhonikidze, the Minister of Heavy Industry, with whom Stalin was at one time on friendly terms. Bek does not dwell on Stalin's cruelty; but his despotic power over his subordinates is emphasised when Stalin asks Onisimov, who witnessed a quarrel conducted in Georgian between Stalin and Ordzhonikidze shortly before Ordzhonikidze's suicide: 'Who do you agree with, Comrade Sergo or me?'.[31] Onisimov protests that he does not understand a word of Georgian, but when Stalin repeats the question Onisimov realises his life is in the balance, and slavishly expresses his unquestioning loyalty to Stalin.

Bek draws a contrast between Stalin's conduct in the pre-war years and at the end of his life. In his seventies he has become unsociable and no longer holds large meetings, but invites certain trusted associates to report to him individually. His demeanour is majestic, because 'It seemed that behind his back invisibly soared the great deeds of the epoch which was now called nothing other than the Stalin era'.[32] At the end of his life he still forces his people to accomplish 'unprecedented tasks' and achieve a new. fantastic advance in industry. However, Bek emphasises Stalin's technical incompetence: at a meeting in the Kremlin Stalin issues ill-informed technical instructions, insisting on the use of electricity, rather than coal, to power blast furnaces in Eastern Siberia – a project which later proves disastrous. Stalin's irritability and capriciousness are stressed: the use of electricity in metallurgy is seen as another 'enthusiasm, another of the Boss's hobby-horses'.[33] Stalin admires his own high-sounding phrases, such as 'It is the steel of Communism' and 'Is anything significant born without birth-pangs?', even if they are inappropriate to the technical question under discussion.[34] Bek under-mines the Stalinist view that will-power is sufficient to change the world: 'Stalin, accustomed to everyone and everything obeying him, was now annoyed that technology did not wish to obey him'.[35]

Bek's portrait of Stalin, while not dwelling on the dictator's negative qualities, produces such an impression of authenticity that Gerald Smith, in a book published in 1984, characterised Bek's portrait as 'the most convincing picture of Stalin that has hitherto appeared'.[36] However, Bek does not delve very deeply into Stalin's psychology, and his portrait, although the most interesting of all those to have appeared in the USSR before the publication of Rybakov's *Children of the Arbat*, merely under-lines some of the themes which had been officially acceptable during the Khrushchev period: the debunking of the myth of Stalin as a scientific genius, Stalin's responsibility for the suicide of Ordzhonikidze, and the implication that Beria was Stalin's evil genius.

Yuri Dombrovsky's semi-autobiographical novel *The Faculty of Unnecessary Things* (1978), written in Moscow in the years 1964–75, represents an attempt by a former prisoner to make sense of his own experiences during the Stalin era. The figure of Stalin first appears in a dream to the archaeologist hero Zybin on the eve of his arrest, and explains to him the philosophy behind the mass terror, which Zybin likens to the ideas of Saint-Just during the French Revolution: 'In order to build a bridge years of work and several thousand people are necessary, but in order to blow it up an hour and a dozen people are sufficient. We are get-ting to that dozen'.[37] Stalin is subsequently depicted in a realistic manner, as a complex human being. Dombrovsky evokes his liking for his garden and Georgian wine, and his relations with his associates: he values Molotov, although he is not close to him, and he regrets the death of Ordzhonikidze, who was once a good worker, but allowed conditions in the Urals to deteriorate. An inner voice asks if all those former associates whom he killed, such as Avel Enukidze, his wife's godfather, were really bad people; the secret of Stalin's success, however, is that the concepts of good and evil are irrelevant to him: 'Nothing applies here, no human feeling, no behest of the heart. He had conquered because he had known from his youth that they did not apply.

And he had freed himself from all doubts once and for all'.[38] He cannot take anything on faith where people are concerned: everyone has betrayed him, including his friend Ordzhonikidze and even his wife.

Dombrovsky attempts to humanise Stalin, providing a realistic account of his childhood and youth which is closer to western biographical accounts than that presented in Rybakov's *Children of the Arbat*. Dombrovsky evokes Stalin's drunken bully of a father, his affection for his mother, who defends him under interrogation, his sense of his own self-importance, and the feeling of 'constant suspiciousness' inculcated by his need to evade the Tsarist secret police.[39] The author also uses Stalin's meditation to make an interesting analysis of the psychological impact of different registers of language. Stalin appreciates the bureaucratic language of the police report about him produced by the Ministry of Internal Affairs in 1904, which reminds him of the death lists sent to him by Ezhov. The use of official jargon like 'the first category' for the death penalty stifles all fear and masks the reality behind the words. Such language is ideal for memoranda which are only read by two or three people, but Stalin is aware of the necessity for elaborate rhetoric, such as 'the enemy of the people, the Judas Trotsky' in documents for public consumption.[40] Dombrovsky depicts an atypical incident in Stalin's life: the release of an old prisoner, Georgy Kalandashvili, who once gave the young Stalin fifty roubles, a fur coat and boots to help him in his exile in Siberia. Stalin justifies the payment of this long-standing debt by the theory that prisoners will work better if occasional releases are permitted. Dombrovsky compares the young Stalin, who appeared 'lively, simple, sociable', with the present dictator; but he also distinguishes between Stalin the man, who made an 'ordinary impression' on the Tsarist police, with his pock-marked face, missing tooth and deformed left foot on which the second and third toes had grown together (regarded as the sign of the Antichrist), and Stalin, the hero of the cult.[41]

Another writer to paint a realistic portrait of Stalin was Vasily Grossman, whose novel *Life and Fate* (1980), the sequel to *For the Just Cause*, had one of the most surprising histories of any work by a Soviet writer.[42] Completed in 1960, it was confiscated by the KGB in 1961 and presumed lost after Grossman's death in

1964 until a microfilm was smuggled out of the USSR by the author's friend Vladimir Voinovich when he emigrated in 1980. It may have been copied after its 'arrest' by the relative of an official in the KGB or the party who had some interest in literature. In *Life and Fate* Grossman attacks various aspects of the 'personality cult'. The rewriting of history is condemned by one of Grossman's heroes, the nuclear physicist Shtrum, who takes exception to the claims by historians and fiction writers that Stalin overshadowed Lenin, and that Lenin needed to ask Stalin's advice over vital military matters such as the defence of Tsaritsyn, the invasion of Poland and the Kronstadt Revolt. Grossman demonstrates that many genuine scientists suffered persecution in Stalin's time, although lip-service was paid to the encouragement of science. In certain exceptional circumstances, however, Stalin's personal intervention could save the lives of specialists useful to the state: Shtrum is under threat of arrest for 'cosmopolitanism' until he receives a personal phone call from Stalin telling him that he is working in an 'interesting direction' and wishing him success in his work.[43] Grossman also attacks the myth of Stalin's brilliance as a military leader during the Second World War. He refutes the notion that Stalin's strategy at Stalingrad was an example of 'genius', since 'the definition of genius can only be applied to people who introduce into life new ideas, those which relate to the core and not to the shell'; in his opinion no really new ideas have been introduced into military strategy since the time of Alexander the Great.[44]

For the most part Grossman depicts Stalin from the outside, but his thoughts are sometimes conveyed: for example, Grossman draws a contrast between the depression which Stalin experienced at the outbreak of war and the renewed vigour he feels at Stalingrad. In 1941 Stalin was in despair, and 'sometimes wanted to cede the responsibility to Rykov, Kamenev and Bukharin who had perished in 1937; let them lead the army and the country'. He imagined all the victims of collectivisation and those who died in the camps marching behind Hitler's tanks to exact retribution: 'He, better than anyone, knew that it is not only history which judges the defeated'. At this difficult time he was anxiously aware that his greatness was conditional on victory: 'his greatness, his genius did not exist in themselves, independent of the greatness of the state and its armed forces.

The books he had written, his scholarly works, his philosophy were significant, became a subject of study and admiration for millions of people only when the state was victorious'.[45] In the hour of victory, however, Stalin's mood changes completely: he knows that 'victors are not judged' and feels that he has triumphed not only over the enemy, but also over his own past. His victims no longer trouble his conscience, and he basks in sweet daydreams about his family, feeling now that 'his super-human strength does not depend on great divisions and the might of the state'.[46]

Grossman is less interested in investigating Stalin's psychology than in making a political and philosophical analysis of the Stalinist system. Grossman suggests that Stalin, through his policies of forced industrialisation, collectivisation, the purges and the promotion of new cadres, abandoned the former ideals of the Russian Social Democratic and Labour Party in favour of a new system which he defined as 'socialism in one country'. The victory at Stalingrad enabled him to 'declare openly the ideology of state nationalism', which in the post-war period led to the persecution of 'cosmopolitans' and 'bourgeois nationalists'. Grossman conveys Stalin's great power by listing all the decisions he had to make, including such positive achievements as the strengthening of the Soviet state through great industrial and scientific advances, the liberation of occupied France and Belgium and the liquidation of the Nazi concentration camps, as well as negative actions such as the imprisonment of Soviet prisoners-of-war, the deportation of the Crimean Tartars and the execution of Jewish actors, writers and doctors. The juxtaposition of scenes between Hitler and his entourage with scenes between Stalin and his generals is clearly designed to suggest that the Nazi concentration camps are the equivalent of the Gulag; and Grossman, who is himself Jewish, explicitly presents Stalin as Hitler's successor as the scourge of European Jewry. Although Stalin wields more power than any dictator in Russian history, Grossman introduces a new perspective on this power through the meditation of Krymov, who wonders after his arrest if the 'Great Stalin', 'the man of iron will' is not the most powerless of all, 'a slave of time and circumstances, the submissive, obedient servant of the present day'. Unlike his victims, Stalin is unable to understand that man is not merely a 'physical nonentity', but also a spiritual being.[47]

With the exception of Solzhenitsyn and Rybakov, Maksimov is the Soviet writer who has provided the most extensive portrait of Stalin, in *The Ark for the Unbidden* (1979).[48] Like Solzhenitsyn, Maksimov attempts to demythologise Stalin, but his portrait is less of a caricature than Solzhenitsyn's; he tries to provide a more objective, realistic depiction of Stalin without excessive political polemic or dogmatic moralising. Maksimov is concerned only with Stalin at a particular point in his career (the immediate aftermath of war in 1945) and does not try to give an analysis of his entire biography or explain his rise to power. Maksimov's Stalin is preoccupied with certain specific historical issues: the annexation of the Kurile Islands from Japan and the interrogation of General Krasnov, who led a Russian army against the USSR. However, Maksimov also includes imaginary incidents: the hero, Lieutenant Zolotaryov, goes to Stalin's cinema in the Kremlin; Stalin watches Krasnov's interrogation from behind a screen, and visits an old Georgian comrade with Beria. Maksimov alludes to certain unproven rumours about Stalin, such as his illegitimacy and alleged collaboration with the Tsarist secret police. In general, Maksimov is more concerned with the potentially possible, the psychologically plausible, than with historical accuracy. The portrait of Stalin is fairly conventional in literary terms, containing little variation of points of view and avoiding obvious irony and satire. Geoffrey Hosking has aptly called Maksimov an 'inverted socialist realist' who arrives at different conclusions from orthodox Soviet writers, but 'has taken over in all essentials the Socialist Realist aesthetic'.[49] Maksimov takes pains to draw an understated portrait which presents Stalin as an ordinary person, not a monster, although the very matter-of-factness with which Stalin signs death lists is horrifying. Maksimov is concerned with conveying the 'banality of evil' rather than its spectacular aspects, and the emphasis on Stalin's illness and old age evokes a certain pity for him as an ailing human being.

Maksimov's portrait of Stalin does not contain such an obvious metaphysical dimension as Solzhenitsyn's, although it fits into the general metaphysical system of all Maksimov's literary work which seeks to analyse the fate of Russia in the twentieth century from a Christian standpoint. Maksimov constantly emphasises the baseness and falsehood of men who wield power, violating everything their subjects hold sacred. Stalin made the choice between Good and Evil long ago and his soul is already lost; he has made a pact with the Church, which Maksimov regards as having sold out to the Antichrist. The main theme of the novel is Stalin's relationship with his people, suggested by the image of Moses in the desert. Stalin and his people are inseparable, and he is the head of a machine which functions by 'the inertia of fear' (the phrase is taken from the title of a book by the dissident scientist Valentin Turchin which provides a cybernetic analysis of Soviet society).[50] In Maksimov's earlier novel *Quarantine* (1973) Stalin had appeared in allegorical guise as the 'quiet seminarist' who, despite all the evil he had caused, would still be granted forgiveness and salvation by God.[51] In *The Ark for the Unbidden* it is not clear whether Stalin himself will find redemption, but there is some hope for the collective redemption of Russian society through those who have survived the prison camps – the inhabitants of the symbolic 'ark' of the title (an image first used in Solzhenitsyn's *First Circle*)[52] – who face the future in a spirit of reconciliation. The image of Stalinism as the Flood sent by God as an ordeal to try the Russian people suggests that to some extent Stalin is merely the instrument of God's judgement on the nation, and that, as Ayleen Teskey has suggested, 'Neither he nor the nation can be finally condemned for his actions'.[53] The novel ends with a quotation from Genesis evoking God's decision to spare mankind further vengeance: 'And the Lord smelled a sweet savour; and the Lord said in his heart, I will not again curse the ground any more for man's sake; for the imagination of man's heart is evil from his youth; neither will I again smite any more every thing living, as I have done'.[54]

Allegory and fantasy

Some Soviet writers felt that realism was an inadequate medium for portraying the larger-than-life figure of Stalin. Just as Stalin had been elevated into a fantasy figure through the 'personality cult', so authors hostile to Stalin felt the need to approach his hyperbolic figure through allegory and fantasy. In his essay *What is Socialist Realism*? Abram Tertz (Andrei Sinyavsky) spoke of the irretrievable damage that the death of Stalin inflicted on 'the religious and aesthetic system' of the USSR, since 'Stalin was specially created for the hyperbole which awaited him. Enigmatic, all-seeing, all-powerful, he was a living monument to our epoch and lacked only one quality to become a god – immortality'. Sinyavsky expressed the hope that 'a phantasmagorical art with hypotheses instead of an aim and the grotesque instead of realistic description' would arise to replace Stalinist 'socialist realism'.[55] He followed his own injunction in his novel *The Trial Begins* (1960), which uses an extended image to convey the helplessness and confusion into which the Soviet people sank after Stalin's death because of their slavish dependence on the dictator: 'The Master was dead . . . The town seemed empty as a desert. You felt like sitting on your haunches, lifting up your head and howling like a homeless dog!'.[56] (The same parallel is taken even further in Georgy Vladimov's *Faithful Ruslan* (1975), the fable of a prison camp dog who loses his *raison d'être* after Stalin's death when the camp which he had loyally served is closed.)[57]

The allegorical tradition was continued by Vasily Aksyonov in his story *The Steel Bird*, which attracted great interest when it was read in the Prose Section of the Union of Writers in 1966, but has never been published in the USSR.[58] The title is taken from a military song of the 1930s:

Where the infantry can't pass
Nor armoured train race by
Nor heavy tank crawl through
The steel bird will fly.[59]

The phrase 'steel bird' was also used in many poems of the 1930s to evoke the feats of Soviet aviation, inspired by Stalin. In this story Aksyonov describes a pathetic and mysterious character, Popenkov, who obtains permission to live in the lift of a block of flats, then in the hall; the other residents gradually become accustomed to his presence and begin to accept him; and eventually his power increases until he is transformed into a steel bird which speaks a strange language and oppresses the whole house. Some Soviet intellectuals regarded Popenkov as an image of Stalin; and this interpretation has been supported by such western critics as Daniel Rancour-Laferrière, who states categorically: 'Aksenov's smelly, unclean steel bird is an essentially analised picture of Stalin'. John Johnson, however, contends that 'Popenkov is not Stalin, as some would guess, but in the tradition of Stalin'.[60] These views need not be mutually exclusive, since Aksyonov's steel bird is at the same time Stalin and more than Stalin. The image is relevant to Stalin, but could also encompass all totalitarian societies, including Nazi Germany (which Aksyonov attacked more explicitly in his story *On the Square and Beyond the River* (1966), in which a metallic bird's plunge in a lake symbolises the death of Hitler).[61] Aksyonov's main theme is that human beings must avoid accepting and becoming used to their oppression. The figure of Stalin is evoked by the bird's 'yellow eyes'; the repeated epithet 'steel' which suggests Stalin's pseudonym, 'man of steel'; Popenkov's exhortation to people to work hard and make sacrifices; his desire to step into the boots of Peter the Great; and his triumphant song, which boasts of how he has gobbled up Peter the Great, Yuri Dolmatovsky, a thousand years of Russian history and the Warsaw ghetto. Although Popenkov attends Stalin's funeral and subsequently establishes his own 'cult of personality', this could be mere camouflage introduced by Aksyonov in the hope that his work could be published in the USSR.

Popenkov is also an allegory of any dictator whose eyes express 'the ancient dream and longing of Tamerlane'.[62] There are steel birds everywhere, but Popenkov is their head, the master of history: 'There will not be a past, there will not be a future, and I've already eaten the present'.[63] Another of Aksyonov's concerns is the wider theme of the oppression of modern man by technology and politics. The repeated theme of the *cornet-à-pistons*:

Reason gave us steel wing-like arms
And instead of a heart, a flaming motor,[64]

suggests that progress has been judged only by scientific and technological achievements, and that man's emotions and spirituality have been neglected by his political oppressors.

In *Good Night* (1984), a semi-autobiographical novel written since his emigration, Sinyavsky evokes Stalin's ghost, following his own earlier injunction to Soviet writers to create a 'phantasmagorical art'.[65] Sinyavsky's interest in the theme of Stalin's 'life after death' was first demonstrated by his ironic statement in *What is Socialist Realism?*: 'Oh, if only we had been cleverer and surrounded his death with miracles! If we had announced on the radio that he had not died, but ascended to heaven and was looking at us from there, keeping mum into his mystic whiskers. His imperishable ashes could have cured the paralysed and the possessed. And children, going to bed, could have prayed out of their windows at the shining winter stars of the Heavenly Kremlin . . .'.[66] The spirit depicted in *Good Night*, however, is far from such a beatified image of Stalin. On the contrary, it is an 'indignant spirit' which comes to visit the telepathic Alla, a former prisoner, in the free settlement at Vorkuta two or three days after Stalin's death, but before the Politburo has officially announced the news. Like the sinners in the Apocalypse, Stalin's ghost is faced with a second, final death unless his sins can be redeemed. It is not clear whether he has chosen Alla as his saviour because she is exceptionally sensitive or because she is a 'pure personification of the victim'.[67]

The 'moustachio'd one' does not appear as himself, but as a transparent column of gaseous cold. Sinyavsky emphasises the coldness and loneliness of Stalin's existence: it is as if 'he had shut himself up in his frozen solitude'. Stalin's ghost angrily demands that Alla 'pay his debts', then communicates the phrase 'my sins', using an 'alphabetical Morse code' based on the initial letters of the names of some of his victims. Alla at first responds: 'I owe you nothing! . . . You owe everybody!',[68] whereupon Stalin, angry at his dependence on this woman whom he failed to liquidate in time, nevertheless humiliates himself sufficiently to beg: 'Forgive me!'. When Alla initially refuses her forgiveness, Stalin tries to persuade her in his customary manner through an appeal to patriotism and party loyalty: 'that's not the Soviet way, not the state way – not Lenin's way, not Stalin's way'. Sinyavsky satirises Soviet euphemisms about the 'mistakes' committed in the purges through his evocation of Stalin's lame excuses for the imprisonment of Alla and her husband: 'Well, there were, we understand, individual excesses, local deviations. With you personally . . . It was not humane'.[69] Stalin's most persuasive argument is that Alla is a Christian, and therefore should love and forgive her enemies. Alla eventually passes the 'examination in righteousness': she replies that God has not given her the power to forgive on behalf of all Stalin's prisoners, but she forgives him on her own account, and tells him to visit all of his victims in turn, both living and dead, in order to ask the forgiveness of each one personally. The narrator remarks that such a task will last all eternity, and parodies the Soviet concept of rehabilitation: 'Where, to what wild regions did he go, he who had emerged from the darkness, to attain rehabilitation?'.[70]

In the novel Sinyavsky explains the significance of his use of fantasy. The modern fairy tale is heir to an ancient tradition: it is a tale which starts off prosaically, in the real world, then shifts into fantasy, but through its combination of reality and fantasy 'gives order and solid foundation to everything' and helps us to 'understand our surroundings as something truly worthy of life, great and intelligent'. In particular, Alla's tales help to illuminate Soviet reality, which is itself irrational: 'The miraculous happens to bring an explanation into our environment, where everything, in the true sense, is devoid of logic, without hope, repulsive and incomprehensible'.[71]

Another reason why Sinyavsky needs to use fantasy in his depiction of Stalin is his attempt to liberate himself from his childhood faith. At one point the narrator (who is closely based on Sinyavsky himself) breaks off the account of Alla's tale to admit: 'I'm afraid to write about him [Stalin]'.[72] Stalin still has so much power over him that his pulse races and his hand refuses to write. The awe which Sinyavsky felt towards Stalin is also evoked through the vision of Stalin which the narrator, like Dombrovsky's Zybin, sees on the night before his arrest. Stalin is sitting in the narrator's house at a long table covered with food and wine, waiting for him. Although at the time of writing many years have passed since Stalin's death, the narrator still feels the dictator's great power: 'My God, I am no longer master of my own house, and now he can do whatever he wants with me, . . . with my wife who is turning pale by the door . . . they can do everything'.[73] In *Good Night* Sinyavsky uses the genre of the fairy tale as a means of overcoming his former fear of Stalin and of telling some poetic truth about Stalin's crimes.

Comic portraits of Stalin

Solzhenitsyn's *The First Circle* was the first work of the post-Stalin period to attempt a comic portrait of Stalin. Since the appearance of the first version of Solzhenitsyn's novel, however, other writers, notably Anatoly Gladilin, Vladimir Voinovich, Fazil Iskander, Alexander Zinoviev and Yuz Aleshkovsky, have published works which portray Stalin in a comic manner. Comedy is always an excellent means of deflating pomposity; hence it proves to be a useful medium for debunking the myth of Stalin's genius and infallibility.

In his fantastic tale *Rehearsal on Friday* (1978), published abroad since his emigration, Anatoly Gladilin combines comedy with fantasy in order to shed light on contemporary Soviet society.[74] Stalin creates havoc in Brezhnev's USSR when he returns to life after lying frozen for twenty-one years until he can be cured of a hitherto incurable disease. Gladilin depicts the consternation of party and industrial officials who fear a return to the personality cult, purges and hard-line methods of running the economy, but also suggests that, although Soviet society has become more sophisticated since Stalin's time, there are many people in authority who are prepared to return to Stalinist values. However, Gladilin's story ends with an ironic twist: using an argument current in Stalin's time, the Politburo refuses to readmit Stalin because his daughter Svetlana has defected to America. Stalin's reaction to this rejection – 'They've got wise!' – suggests that Soviet society has not changed in any fundamental sense since Stalin's time.[75] The difference is merely one of degree: Gladilin's Stalin (like Khrushchev in reality) is not arrested, but confined to a country estate to live out the rest of his days in retirement.

In the first part of Voinovich's *The Life and Extraordinary Adventures of Private Ivan Chonkin* (1976)[76] Stalin does not appear as an actual character, although, as Violetta Iverni says, he 'exists invisibly as an indefinable, menacing presence'.[77] Direct satirical references to Stalin occur in some twenty places in the novel. In particular, Voinovich ridicules the personality cult of Stalin: the obligatory references to Stalin in official letters, the mandatory toast to him at banquets, the fear inspired by the very mention of his name. The *émigré* critic Yuri Maltsev has argued that *Chonkin* is not a satirical work, because satire must be black, motivated by anger and hatred.[78] This argument is unconvincing, however, for satire need not necessarily be black; it can possess many different tones, including the good-humoured tone of Voinovich's novel. The innocence of Voinovich's hero, the simple soldier Chonkin, acts as a catalyst which exposes the absurdity of the entire Stalinist system. He is devoted to his Great Leader and wants to do his duty by him; but, although he *believes* in Stalin, he simply cannot comprehend the double-think of Soviet ideology. Chonkin muses on Stalin's famous 'Brothers and sisters' speech on the outbreak of war, and tries in vain to find a logical explanation for some of Stalin's puzzling phrases which defy literal interpretation, such as 'enemy forces having found themselves graves on the fields of battle'.[79]

Voinovich introduces dream sequences which possess significance for the interpretation of Stalin and Stalinism. Chonkin's dreams fulfil several functions. In the first place, they tell him more about reality than his waking perceptions: for example, he feels great fear when Stalin appears to him in a dream as a vengeful leader ordering him to be shot. In the second place, the improbability, even absurdity which, in Chonkin's consciousness, surrounds the whole concept of 'Stalin', justifies the inclusion of dream sequences in which the image of Stalin is taken to fantastic extremes. The horrified reaction of the political commissar to Chonkin's question about whether Stalin has two wives inspires a dream in which the commissar – a beetle – explains that Stalin is a woman and cannot have wives. Voinovich's technique of combining animal and human elements reaches its climax in a grotesque dream in which Stalin is served on a platter as a roast with vegetables. Voinovich regards Soviet reality under Stalin and the idealisation of the dictator himself as so abnormal that he has to portray this reality as ridiculous, fantastic or absurd. In an interview of 1981 Voinovich himself expressed this view, regarding his work as a continuation of the tradition of 'fantastic realism' exemplified by Gogol and Bulgakov: 'I am part of that stream, but it is not realism that is fantastical; it is real life that is fantastical'.[80]

Voinovich's depiction of Stalin is expanded in Part Two of *Chonkin, The Pretender to the Throne* (1979),[81] in which Stalin and Beria both appear as comic characters. Not all Voinovich's comic touches are pure invention; some details of Stalin's life, such as his underground dacha with its study identical to the one in the Kremlin, are authentic, but ludicrous enough to be fictional. Voinovich also includes elements of folklore: he depicts Stalin plotting the German invasion on a globe, following

Khrushchev's accusation in the 'Secret Speech' (a claim which was later denied). Certain facets of Stalin's character are taken to comic extremes: for example, his dabbling in linguistics is ridiculed through a scene in which he takes a great interest in the derivation of the name 'Chonkin'. His mistrust of Beria is demonstrated by the extensive search which Beria has to undergo before entering his dacha; and Beria's sycophancy towards his master is suggested in exaggerated form when Beria fawns at Stalin's feet like a dog. Voinovich, like Grossman, suggests a parallel between Stalin and Hitler, who appears briefly as a grotesque figure who terrorises and is flattered by his closest associate Himmler. The author makes an interesting general comment applicable to both Stalin and Hitler: 'Like every dictator, Hitler was not only cruel, he was sentimental. While planning the extinction of various peoples, he wanted those very people, Jews, gypsies, Poles, Russians, to love him as their liberator'.[82]

Both Voinovich's story *A Circle of Friends* (written in 1967) and Iskander's *Sandro of Chegem* (first published in full abroad in 1979) describe a known aspect of Stalin's life: his long drunken banquets with other members of the Politburo. Neither author makes any attempt at historical authenticity; they both depict these dinners as scenes of pure comic fiction which, nevertheless, provide interesting insights into Stalin's character. Both are concerned to show, like Nabokov, that great villains are also 'the clowns of history'.

The subtitle of Voinovich's story is 'A not particularly reliable tale concerning a certain historic get-together', and a humorous note is struck at the end, when Voinovich claims: 'This story is solely the product of the author's fantasy. Any resemblance of any of the characters to actual people is purely coincidental'.[83] Stalin, who appears under his revolutionary name, 'Koba', is portrayed as a clown who gladly discards his props – his moustache and pipe – when he is alone. He is a consummate actor who pretends to be asleep while his subordinates are talking. When he himself is not in his room he places a dummy in his own likeness at his lighted window in the Kremlin to make people think that he never sleeps, but is always working on their behalf. In this way Voinovich suggests that Stalin is a sham, a figure of fun rather than a devil. As in *The Pretender to the*

Throne, Voinovich uses to great effect certain details based on Russian oral lore about Stalin's life. Some known elements of Stalin's biography are used merely to enhance the comic portrait: for example, the collection of records which Stalin marks 'Good, average, wonderful, rubbish';[84] his propensity for cutting pictures out of magazines; and his habit of spitting at people. Other details based on oral tradition have a satirical purpose: for example, Stalin's morbid suspiciousness is suggested by his fear of being poisoned by his cooks, and by the description of his underground bunker reached through a safe in his official study. The embarrassing occasion on which Stalin forced Khrushchev to dance the Ukrainian gopak – an incident graphically described in Khrushchev's memoirs[85] – is evoked to illustrate Stalin's scorn for his 'courtiers' and sycophants. Voinovich also includes humorous fictional elements to reinforce satirical points: the comic interplay between Stalin's lieutenants who are all jockeying for position; Stalin's suggestion that the brontosaurus should be reintroduced in order to increase the production of meat and milk (a reference to his predilection for Lysenko's agricultural 'miracles'); the suggestion that Stalin slept for ten days when the German invasion was declared and when he woke claimed that news of war was a 'provocation'. The targets of Voinovich's satire are similar to those in *Chonkin*: the 'cult of personality'; Stalin's attitude to the national question; his anti-Semitism and his war record.

Neil Cornwell has suggested that the title of Voinovich's story, *A Circle of Friends*, implies either a parallel with or a parody of Solzhenitsyn's *The First Circle*.[86] Voinovich may well have had Solzhenitsyn's work in mind, as he has drawn a sharp contrast between his method and that of Solzhenitsyn: 'Solzhenitsyn's character is such that he *must* teach somebody every day. I don't have such a character. I don't want to teach anybody or give advice to anybody . . . I am a describer. I'm not a teacher like Tolstoy or Solzhenitsyn'.[87] Unlike Solzhenitsyn's Stalin who never confronts himself directly, Voinovich's Stalin speaks frankly to himself. He confesses that he killed millions of people, ruined Soviet agriculture and created a reign of terror to enhance his own personal power. Because of this the people hate him and, since he has always demanded lies, there is now no one to tell him the truth. The climax of Voinovich's portrait is highly comic, but makes a serious point. Stalin comes to realise that his morbid suspicion of enemies is futile, and eventually shoots at his own reflection in a mirror, saying: 'You like it when everyone fears you like the plague. But you, the creator of an empire of fear, aren't you the most frightened person in it?...Just look to yourself – you are the number-one enemy of the people, the number-one counter-Kobaist'.[88]

In *Sandro of Chegem*, which exposes the destruction of the Abkhazian nation's ancient civilisation through colonisation and collectivisation by Russian imperialists, Iskander makes use of some of the same devices as Voinovich to produce a portrait of Stalin notable for its good-humoured comedy rather than its aggressive satire. Nevertheless, the comedy is inevitably black, because, however absurd the actions of Stalin and his cronies are, they wield enormous power. Stalin, at a banquet given by the First Secretary of the Abkhazian Communist Party, Nestor Lakoba, is seen through the innocent and fascinated eyes of Sandro, a dancer in a troupe of folk dancers who perform in front of him, and whom he sees as 'flourishing delegates of his nationalities policy'.[89] The scene is entirely fictional, although Iskander follows the accounts of similar dinners in the memoirs of Khrushchev and Djilas,[90] showing that everyone at Stalin's table can eat what he likes, but that people are not permitted to refuse drink. Stalin takes malicious pleasure in taunting his cronies, forcing Beria's wife to dance against her will; telling Voroshilov that Lakoba is a better shot than him; and burning Kalinin's fingers when he offers him a match, feeling 'Why shouldn't he suffer too, like me?'.[91] Stalin's mood changes very rapidly, and the threat of his displeasure constantly hangs over everyone. At one minute he is prepared to kiss Kalinin, then, when Kalinin moves away, he immediately thinks, with morbid suspiciousness, 'So he is with them, and not with me'.[92] Another occasion for black comedy is the plight of the wretched party secretary who shouts 'Long live Comrade Stalin!' at an unsuitable moment, and finds everyone shrinking away from him when Stalin's angry gaze alights on him. The guests at the table listen closely to and eagerly interpret Stalin's every word; the Abkhazians are concerned at his phrase 'You in the Caucasus', because they fear it means that Stalin now feels himself to be a Russian, no longer a Georgian. Iskander emphasises Stalin's liking for cruel games: he enjoys Lakoba's trick of shooting at eggs balanced on the head of a terrified cook. In just the same casual way he tells Beria to dispose of the innocent brother of the Old Bolshevik Tsulukidze whom he cannot touch because he was introduced into the party by Lenin. Stalin feels that it will be useful to break up family ties in the Caucasus; he tells Beria: 'Let him regret all his life that he ruined his family'.[93]

Iskander also uses verbal humour to telling effect. When Lakoba relates that Stalin paid promptly for some apricots he was sent – a story designed to display Stalin's supposed modesty – Stalin responds sanctimoniously: 'It was not you and I who planted them; the people planted them'. Everyone repeats the phrase '*Narod sazhal*', which means not only 'The people planted them', but also 'He imprisoned the people'.[94] Unlike Voinovich, Iskander does not use dream sequences, but evokes a daydream induced by Stalin's favourite Georgian song, which allows him to escape from reality and obtain temporary relief from his burden of eternal vigilance. He sees his life as a sad example of the exigencies of Fate and History: 'the sorrowful necessity of taking his place in this procession'. He imagines an alternative life in which he is known as Djugashvili, the man who refused to become Stalin and rule the whole of Russia, because he was aware that 'There would be a lot of trouble. And it would be necessary to shed a lot of blood. He was sorry for the peasants. He would have to unite them all'.[95] He imagines this hypothetical other self telling the peasants to eat their bread and drink their wine in peace, thus winning the blessings of his fellow Georgians. Iskander may well have been influenced by Solzhenitsyn (or by Dostoevsky's 'Legend of the Grand Inquisitor'), since his Stalin, like the Stalin of *The First Circle*, regards himself as a martyr who has sacrificed his own happiness to serve his people. His dream breaks off as he remembers his mother who committed some unspecified offence against him – a possible reference to the unproven rumour that Stalin was illegitimate. Iskander's Stalin, like Solzhenitsyn's, is a lonely figure: he feels that 'Power is the impossibility of loving anyone'.[96] Although the author usually remains absent from his narrative, he does intervene at one point (somewhat unnecessarily) to emphasise the moral that anyone can choose to be, or not to be an executioner. Humanity involves the overcoming of vileness; vileness – the overcoming of humanity.

The banquet scene is put into darker perspective later in the novel when we learn that Beria has been executed and that Lakoba, whom Stalin had called his 'best friend', has suffered in the purges: his son has been killed and his wife tortured. Iskander's hero, however, has won Stalin's favour and managed to survive. Sandro tells a comic story of how, when he was acting as Stalin's guide on a fishing trip, Stalin took a fancy to him and gave him a present of a dry pair of longjohns after he had got wet catching fish for him. Sandro sees this as Stalin's way of saying: 'Live in peace; I won't touch you . . .'.[97] Iskander takes Sandro's role as a representative of his people to a comic extreme, conveying Sandro's conviction that he alone has saved the Abkhazian nation from being deported, as the Crimean Tartars, Volga Germans, Chechen, Ingush and other peoples were after the war.

The comic portraits of Stalin by Voinovich and Iskander are highly effective: while making no claims to historical authenticity, they skilfully blend humour, fantasy and satire to tell some significant truths about Stalin and his system. A more profane form of humour is used to expose the Stalin cult by two writers published only in the west – Alexander Zinoviev and Yuz Aleshkovsky. They refer explicitly to the large scale of Stalin's crimes and employ anality and eroticism to assist the aggressive work of satire.

In Zinoviev's *Yawning Heights* (1976), a powerful satire on the Soviet system, Stalin appears as 'the Boss', who inflicted a 'general thrashing' on his subjects and after his death was denounced by Hog (Khrushchev). The Boss's customary title was 'the super-genius, the most brilliant genius of all the brilliant geniuses', although he was 'the most mediocre of mediocre men'.[98] Zinoviev satirises the Stalin cult, presenting it as the glorification of the leader's penis, with which, according to legend, he strikes all his enemies: 'Songs were written in honour of the Boss's prick, towns were named after it, processions were held to glorify it. At the corner where Boss Street (now Leader Street) met Boss Avenue (now Leader Avenue), a public urinal was erected in honour of the Boss's prick. On its walls Artist, winner of all the prizes and bearer of all titles, drew a large image of the Boss's prick in full working order, with all the leading statesmen of Europe and America sitting astride it'.[99] Zinoviev portrays the Boss as a comic figure with an uneducated accent and a propensity for meddling in subjects about which he knew little, such as linguistics and the arts, but also as a 'true tribal chief' who 'felt intuitively that the main thing was to control men's minds'.[100] Zinoviev does not disguise the 'mass repressions' and 'atrocious crimes' committed under Stalin; the character Bawler, possibly modelled on Zinoviev himself, undertakes a systematic study of 'repression in the period of the Boss' and contributes to the mass of materials used by Truth-Teller (Solzhenitsyn) in the compilation of his Book (*The Gulag Archipelago*).

Yuz Aleshkovsky, a self-taught former convict who emigrated in 1979, also approaches the subject of Stalin through comedy and the grotesque. Since for him Soviet reality is absurd and fantastic, comedy and fantasy are the appropriate means of conveying a faithful picture of reality. Aleshkovsky's *Kangaroo* (written in the USSR in the years 1974–5), an absurd tale of a man accused of the bestial rape and murder of the oldest kangaroo in Moscow Zoo 'in the night from 14 July 1789 to 5 January 1905', is designed to expose the irrationality of the purge trials.[101] Stalin himself is presented not only as a cruel, capricious despot who decides on a sudden whim to execute an old man's son or to deport the Crimean Tartars, but also as a figure of fun. During the Yalta Conference, when Stalin outwits Churchill and Roosevelt, he is subjected to constant insults from his left leg, which addresses him in a parody of the eulogies of the 'personality cult': 'Arsehole of all times! Shit of all peoples!'.[102] His importunate leg, which perhaps represents his inner voice, suggests that he should transform his life, give up 'stinking Marxism-Leninism', return the land to the peasants and live out the rest of his life as a human being.

In his later novel *Hand* (1980),[103] written in the form of a monologue by one of Stalin's executioners who finally asks his interlocutor to shoot him, Aleshkovsky attempts, through his comic treatment of Stalin, to present a deeper psychological and metaphysical analysis of Stalin's character. Aleshkovsky's famous camp song *Comrade Stalin, You're a Real Big Scholar* (discussed above, pp. 31–2) had demonstrated his satirical approach to the 'cult of personality'. Similarly, in his novel he irreverently debunks the Stalin myth through an anecdote about a doctor who holds Stalin's penis in his hand. The doctor calls it 'brilliant' and 'historic', but finds it difficult to express his feelings in words, since an adequate tribute would require an epic poet of the stature of Dzhambul Dzhabaev.[104]

The narrator relates the grotesque tale of his first meeting with Stalin. On this occasion he killed with his bare hands a large dog which was about to spring at Stalin, which earnt him the nickname 'Hand'. Subsequently he is taken under Stalin's wing and ensconced in a small room in the Kremlin where he can listen to Stalin's conversations. A code is established whereby if Stalin mentions the word 'dog', his visitor is a dead man. With black humour, the narrator relates how Stalin asks Bukharin 'What kind of puppy do you advise me to keep?',[105] enquires of Marshal Tukhashevsky whether his wife would appreciate the gift of a Maltese lapdog, and asks Zinoviev and Kamenev when there will be a monument to 'man's best friend' outside the Pavlov Institute. This 'dog theme' is absurd, but its very absurdity emphasises the irrational nature of the purges.

Hatred and fear are seen as the mainsprings of Stalin's conduct. Stalin 'hated the Marxist idea and Lenin personally. . . . He hated the idea, because he did not believe in it, but he served it'. The cult of personality is a result of self-hatred; Stalin's need for constant adulation springs from his own insecurity. He personifies 'the idea', in which he does not believe, 'in odes, films, monographs, paintings, sculptures', just because it is better that he should play this role rather than someone else, such as Molotov.[106] Stalin's persecution mania is born of hatred and fear; he cannot imagine that people can hate him less than he hates them, so he must check everyone and liquidate all 'potential conspirators'. His inferiority complex begets sadism: 'There was not a man in history hysterically praised by a vast propaganda machine to a greater degree than Stalin, but there was nowhere for him to escape to from the consciousness of his insignificance, the ruin of his personal life and hence the immense self-hatred which he projected on to others'.[107] Aleshkovsky emphasises that Stalin's defeat of his enemies has brought him no peace of mind.

Stalin's loathing of Lenin is demonstrated by his descent into Lenin's mausoleum, not to pray to his mentor, as people imagine, but to gloat over his dead enemy. He hates to be called 'the Lenin of today'; rather, he is 'the Djugashvili of yesterday', since he is convinced that Djugashvili, his youthful self, was buried through

Lenin's fault, and that he himself was subsequently forced to move from the 'living path' of revolution to the 'deadly clutches of state service'.[108] Like Voinovich, Aleshkovsky emphasises the anti-Soviet nature of Stalinism. Stalin tells Hand that he is 'even more anti-Soviet than . . .'; the sentence is left unfinished, but the clear implication is that Stalin himself is anti-Soviet.[109]

Aleshkovsky's metaphysical analysis of Stalinism displays the influence of Dostoevsky's *The Devils*. He implies that Stalin's Russia is in the grip of the satanic force of reason, which, as in Dostoevsky's works, takes the soul away from God and leads it towards death. The Stalin terror is explicable by the fact that the devil is in control of the world and has made a pact with the party: the party is given unlimited power, and the devil gains 'slogans, ideology, aims'.[110] This arrangement suits Stalin, who cannot abandon the 'party religion' for fear that he himself might be toppled. Aleshkovsky suggests that Stalin's victims are themselves agents of the devil, since they believe in Lenin and socialism. Moreover, these 'living corpses' are inculcated with love of their murderer, Stalin, a sentiment which goes against logic and must, therefore, be inspired by the devil. His victims' love of death takes the cunning form of the ideals of socialism and communism, which lead to a conflict with God and hence to the ultimate destruction of the world. Aleshkovsky's view of Stalin is eventually elucidated when Stalin wishes to escape from the power of the devil, but finds he cannot, since the devil is inside himself.

Since Bek's *The New Appointment*, Grossman's *Life and Fate*, Dombrovsky's *The Faculty of Unnecessary Things* and the previously censored chapters of Iskander's *Sandro from Chegem* have all been published in the USSR, and Voinovich's *Chonkin* has been announced for publication in 1989, it is quite possible that other works discussed in this chapter may eventually appear in the USSR if the more liberal conditions of the Gorbachev era continue to prevail. The present Soviet leadership has attempted to attract back to the USSR certain well-known *émigré* writers and artists, such as Solzhenitsyn and Aksyonov, and any writer who chose to return might well see his collected works published one day. However, it is probable that the works of Aleshkovsky and Zinoviev would be too profane for Soviet tastes, and religious writers such as Maksimov and Sinyavsky are unlikely to be tolerated even in the era of *perestroika*.

Chapter seven

Solzhenitsyn's 'new' portrait of Stalin: fact or fiction?

The First Circle was not the first of Solzhenitsyn's works to mention Stalin: his influence permeated some of Solzhenitsyn's early plays. In *The Republic of Labour*, for example (formerly *The Love-Girl and the Innocent*), the camp is overshadowed by a large portrait of Stalin and a poster proclaiming Stalin's words: 'Work has become, from the burden it was under capitalism, a matter of honour, fame, prowess and heroism', an ironic comment on the reality of the labour camp.[1] The Stalinist atmosphere was more clearly evoked in *The Captives* (formerly *Decembrists without December*), in which the SMERSH headquarters at Brodnitz, on the Prussian border (the place where Solzhenitsyn was taken after his arrest) is full of huge statues and portraits of Stalin; in one highly symbolic scene a heavy statue of Stalin crashes to the ground.[2] In these early works, however, Stalin figured only as a sombre, menacing presence in the background; the 1968 edition of *The First Circle* was the first work in which Solzhenitsyn attempted to come seriously to grips with the character of Stalin.

Most critical studies of Solzhenitsyn's portrait of Stalin have hitherto been based on the 87-chapter version of *The First Circle*, published in 1968.[3] Indeed, relatively few critical responses to the revised, 96-chapter edition of the novel published in Solzhenitsyn's *Collected Works* in 1978 have as yet appeared.[4] The only study entirely devoted to the 'Stalin chapters' in *Circle-96* is a psychoanalytical approach to Solzhenitsyn's Stalin by Daniel Rancour-Laferrière, who does not attempt to compare the different versions of the novel or to relate fiction to history, stating explicitly: 'Any correspondences between this character and the historical Joseph Stalin are merely coincidental for my purposes (though they could hardly have been coincidental from Solzhenitsyn's personal viewpoint)'.[5] There has hitherto been no attempt to subject Solzhenitsyn's view of Stalin to serious historical examination (in contrast with the attention aroused among scholars by Solzhenitsyn's portrait of Lenin and other historical characters in *The Red Wheel*, the epic which Solzhenitsyn is currently writing).[6] It is hoped that the following chapter will remedy the omission. Its aim is to analyse the historical and philosophical treatment of the figure of Stalin in *Circle-96*, and to consider what light a comparison between the two portraits sheds on Solzhenitsyn's literary and political evolution.

In the 1978 version of *The First Circle*, which, according to Solzhenitsyn, restores the novel to its original, uncensored form, the portrait of Stalin maintains its pivotal position as the centre from which all moral and political evil flows. It is still contained in a block of chapters in the middle of Part I of the novel (Chapters 19–23). Most of the material in the 1968 version of the character study has been retained, with a few additions and minor alterations. The major addition is a new, 25-page chapter, 'Etyud o velikoi zhizni' ('Study of a Great Life') which presents an imaginative reconstruction of Stalin's complete biography. As Georges Nivat has pointed out, the main difference between the five 'Stalin chapters' in *Circle-96* and the four in *Circle-87* is simply one of quantity. The text of 1968 was a contraction of the original manuscript rather than a major reinterpretation, and the restoration in *Circle-96* of the dictator's monologue in its entirety renders Stalin's character, and everything he represents, of greater importance to the novel as a whole.[7]

Careful attention has been devoted to the structure of the 'Stalin chapters': their order has been changed, and the new biographical chapter has been inserted between chapters dealing with Stalin's life in the present. The first Stalin chapter, 'The Birthday Hero' (the new Chapter 19), like the old Chapter 18 of the same title, describes Stalin's study and evokes his reflections on matters of current concern to him: his seventieth-birthday celebrations and the recently published *Short Biography* of himself. The new material includes a description of the pattern of Stalin's working day, and his long, drunken banquets with his lieutenants in the Politburo,[8] as well as his meditations on how to bind young people even more tightly to the kolkhoz system. Stalin's reconsideration of his whole life in the new Chapter 20 renders the 'Stalin chapters' rather less realistic and more tenuously connected with the rest of the novel, but adds a much deeper historical and political dimension to the work as a whole. The author attempts to suggest that Stalin's self-analysis springs directly out of his illness, loneliness and insomnia, but mere verisimilitude matters little to Solzhenitsyn: it is improbable that Stalin ever reflected on his past life in the way that Solzhenitsyn describes, but the events he mentions all form part of his historical record. The chapter ends with Stalin's ruminations on his present troubles: his enmity with Tito and the trial of the Hungarian leader Traicho Kostov. This leads naturally to Chapter 21, 'Give us back the death penalty!' which contains Stalin's conversation with the MGB minister Abakumov about the arrangements for new purges. After this demonstration of Stalin's real power, Chapter 22, 'The Emperor of the Earth', evokes Stalin's meditations on the theoretical basis of his power, and his rivalry with God. At the end of the chapter he suddenly remembers the order for a secret telephone which he has placed with the convicts in the special prison of Marfino[9] – the formal link connecting the 'Stalin chapters' with the rest of the novel. The final chapter, 'Language as a Tool of Production', which portrays Stalin writing his notorious article on linguistics, published in *Pravda* in 1950, contains some new material, but is basically the same as in the original version. The exposure of Stalin's academic pretensions and the theme of Stalin's subversion of language are still important,[10] but secondary to the much more detailed historical and metaphysical interpretation of Stalin's character. The chapter ends with a nightmare vision of the future: Stalin's megalomaniac fantasy of a third world war and a Soviet invasion of western Europe. The portrait of Stalin reaches a natural conclusion as the dictator at last falls asleep.

The principal reasons which Solzhenitsyn has given since his deportation for the reissue of his works are freedom from censorship and mistakes in *samizdat* reprints. He has now told the full story of the genesis of *The First Circle*, and of the Stalin chapters in particular.[11] The original version of the novel, which contained ninety-six chapters, was begun in 1955 in Kok-Terek,

South Kazakhstan, where Solzhenitsyn was exiled, and completed in Miltsevo, in the Vladimir Region of Central Russia, in 1957. The manuscript was written in minuscule handwriting on thin onion-skin paper with no margins, and Solzhenitsyn believed, at the time, that he would have faced death if the authorities had found it. Subsequently, in 1958, when he was teaching in Ryazan, he revised the manuscript twice, but all three of these first versions were later destroyed for reasons of security. From January 1962, while *One Day in the Life of Ivan Denisovich* was under discussion at *Novy Mir*, Solzhenitsyn spent four months reworking the text and producing a fourth, then definitive version of *Circle-96*. The first chapter of this variant described Innokenty Volodin, a Soviet diplomat, telephoning to warn the American Embassy in Moscow that important technological secrets of the production of the atomic bomb were about to be handed over in New York to the Soviet agent Georgy Koval (presumably by the Rosenbergs). In the autumn of 1963 Solzhenitsyn gave four chapters to Tvardovsky, the chief editor of *Novy Mir*, who rejected the novel for publication, because, like *One Day in the Life of Ivan Denisovich*, it also dealt with a prison camp theme, a subject now out of favour after Khrushchev's renewal of repressive measures against Soviet writers as a result of his notorious visit to the Manège art exhibition in December 1962.[12] In 1964 Solzhenitsyn prepared a fifth version in eighty-seven chapters specifically for *Novy Mir*, which Tvardovsky read at the author's dacha at Easter of that year. Hoping that the novel could be published in the USSR, Solzhenitsyn cut out some of the chapters which he knew to be 'politically unacceptable' and 'smoothed over' many other sensitive passages in the rest of the novel. He changed the controversial 'atomic theme' to a much less dangerous one: the depiction of Innokenty's warning to a professor of medicine against handing a sample of a new drug to a foreign colleague. During the 'thaw' years of 1954, 1956 and 1961–2 references to the notorious 'Doctors' Plot' of 1953 and to the persecution of Soviet scientists and specialists in Stalin's time for real or alleged contacts with foreigners and foreign ideas had become an acceptable and fairly common target for criticism in Soviet fiction.[13]

Tvardovsky was excited by Solzhenitsyn's novel and found it politically daring, although his general interpretation of the work, 'The novel's standpoint is that of the Party . . . it contains no condemnation of the October Revolution', was ironically received by the author.[14] In particular, Tvardovsky demanded that Solzhenitsyn should cut out the long biographical chapter on Stalin. His objections were based on considerations of historical authenticity: he argued that Solzhenitsyn's view that Stalin collaborated with the Tsarist secret police was impossible to prove, and that he could not be sure of the details of life in a Georgian theological seminary in the 1890s, or of Stalin's private life. Solzhenitsyn was, however, gratified by Tvardovsky's general approval of the Stalin chapters: 'His general remarks about the Stalin chapters were sound, though: they could be left out, but their absence might be seen as proof that the author had "taken fright", that he had "been afraid he couldn't manage the theme" '.[15] Although Tvardovsky asked Solzhenitsyn to rewrite the Stalin chapters, he generally approved of the novel and was prepared to take great pains to get it published. In the course of two weeks Solzhenitsyn reworked the Stalin chapters and sent the novel to *Novy Mir*. During a discussion in the *Novy Mir* offices in June 1964 Tvardovsky and his colleagues expressed their full awareness of the danger involved in publishing the novel. Tvardovsky still considered that the details of Stalin's private life 'invited attack', and wanted Solzhenitsyn to 'modify the harsher "anti-Stalinist touches" ' of the novel. The liberal critic Lakshin agreed with Tvardovsky that the Stalin chapters were essential to the work, but asserted that 'the didactic passages were like jagged rocks breaking the smooth surface of the novel'. Although Tvardovsky retorted that such polemical passages were a characteristic feature of Solzhenitsyn's style, a more cautious editor, Alexander Dementiev, complained that 'The propaganda passages sometimes border on pamphleteering'.[16] Dementiev felt that the Stalin chapters should be cut to one, and that the novel as a whole went far beyond the official denunciation of the 'personality cult', and even posed the fundamental question: why was the revolution ever made? At the time Solzhenitsyn concealed his true intentions, defending himself by protesting that his novel was aimed only against the 'personality cult', not against Soviet society or Communist ideas in general. In his memoirs, however, and in the 1978 version of *The First Circle*, Solzhenitsyn has subsequently made it plain that his intention was indeed to raise these more fundamental questions about the Soviet system.[17]

Despite considerable opposition, Tvardovsky eventually secured the agreement of the *Novy Mir* editorial board to try to publish Solzhenitsyn's novel. He gave the manuscript to Khrushchev's aide on cultural matters, V. S. Lebedev, who had helped to obtain his permission for the publication of *One Day in the Life of Ivan Denisovich*. Times had changed, however, since the height of the anti-Stalin campaign in 1961–2, and Khrushchev had been obliged to 'put up with' a great deal from other members of the Presidium for his authorisation of Solzhenitsyn's novella.[18] Lebedev regarded the 'lightened' *First Circle* as a libel on the Soviet system, objected to Solzhenitsyn's description of Stalin's everyday life, and asked: 'Do we really believe that officials in Soviet ministries worked at night? And – according to this author – spent their time playing draughts?'.[19] Realising that the novel was unlikely to be published in the USSR, Solzhenitsyn 'deepened' and 'sharpened' the manuscript which he had shown to Tvardovsky, and sent microfilms of this sixth version of the work abroad through someone whom the American journalist Olga Carlisle characterises as 'an exceptionally courageous man, an admirer of Solzhenitsyn's literary talent', whom we now know to be the son of the Italian Communist writer Vittorio Strada.[20] Although Solzhenitsyn allowed his novel to be read by a small circle of friends and acquaintances within the USSR,[21] it did not at that time circulate freely in *samizdat*. In September 1965 one manuscript of the novel was confiscated by the KGB from the flat of the author's friend V. Teush. It was not until 1967 that Solzhenitsyn authorised Olga Carlisle to publish it in the west, and it began to circulate in *samizdat* within the USSR.

In 1968, at the height of his struggle with the Soviet authorities, Solzhenitsyn rewrote the 96-chapter version of *The First Circle*, which was finished at about the same time that the 87-chapter version was being published in Europe. He 'saved' this version by keeping it in a provincial town where the KGB did not find it, and eventually sent it abroad. The 96-chapter *First Circle* was, therefore, entirely written in the USSR, when the author did not have full access to western sources on the biography of Stalin. We know that when Solzhenitsyn came to Zurich he rewrote *Lenin in Zurich*, making much fuller use of western material on

Lenin.[22] There is, however, no evidence that Solzhenitsyn rewrote *The First Circle* completely for the final version set in print for inclusion in his *Complete Works* in 1978 (although in 1976 he said that he had 'recently begun to re-read' his earlier works).[23] He admits only to some minor retouching: 'As I re-read it [*The First Circle*] I also perfected some things; after all, I was forty years old then, and now I am fifty'.[24] The 1978 edition of *The First Circle* can, therefore, be seen as a revised first version rather than a completely new version produced in the west.

It is significant that the reactions of Tvardovsky and his colleagues to the publicistic elements in the Stalin chapters coincide, to some extent, with criticisms levelled against them by some western commentators who considered that in these passages of *Circle-87* Solzhenitsyn's elementary irony degenerates into unsubtle sarcasm.[25] Solzhenitsyn's memoirs show that he himself was conscious of the fact that the Stalin chapters contained, in Tvardovsky's phrase, 'a little overweight . . . a little more than the minimum required by the structure of the novel', but that he agreed with Tvardovsky's view that such excess was legitimate in the furtherance of his psychological and political ends. Solzhenitsyn was also aware of certain weak points in his original portrait of Stalin, for example the description of the dictator's early life; it is, therefore, a reasonable assumption that he was prepared to change some factual details in the light of further evidence. However, Solzhenitsyn's approach to historical truth is somewhat inconsistent. Although he has indirectly admitted that he possessed insufficient evidence to be absolutely certain that Stalin was a Tsarist spy, Solzhenitsyn does not disguise the fact that he set out deliberately to present this controversial hypothesis in a convincing manner: 'I tried by psychological and factual arguments to prove the hypothesis that Stalin had collaborated with the Tsarist secret police'. When Tvardovsky reproached him with the historical inauthenticity of his depiction of Stalin as an Okhrana agent, his reaction clearly demonstrated that his attitude to Stalin was that of an artist rather than of an objective historian: 'My view was that Stalin should reap the harvest of his secretiveness. He had lived mysteriously – so now anyone was entitled to write about him as he thought fit. The author's right, the author's duty, is to give his own picture and stimulate the reader's imagination'.[26] However, this admission does not mean, as Alexander Flegon, an extremely hostile critic, implies, that Solzhenitsyn's portrait of Stalin is motivated only by revenge, and that he is entirely unconcerned about historical accuracy.[27] On the contrary, as Solzhenitsyn himself claims, he is 'not simply a belletristic writer', but places himself in all his books 'in the service of historical truth'.[28] Yet it is important to note that Solzhenitsyn's view of history differs considerably from the objective approach of modern western historians. Solzhenitsyn resembles a medieval chronicler rather than a modern historian; in the definition of the German critic Walter Benjamin, the historian writes history, but the chronicler narrates it.[29] Solzhenitsyn's attitude to Stalin is coloured by his personal experience, and the portrait of Stalin in *Circle-96* is more satirical and denunciatory than those of other dissident writers who have depicted Stalin in their literary works, such as Voinovich and Maksimov. However, the author does attempt to reveal Stalin's character from within through the use of direct and indirect interior monologue, managing to demonstrate that 'No man considers himself a villain'.[30]

As Solzhenitsyn is concerned with serious historical issues, his portrait of Stalin cannot be treated entirely as literature, but must also be examined critically and objectively by the historian. As a general rule, of course, the writer of fiction possesses full licence to make of historical characters what he will. In past centuries most authors of literary works based on historical personages or events were content merely to employ the sources of the day and use the past to illuminate certain general ideas. There is no need, for example, for us to examine Shakespeare's *Antony and Cleopatra* and *Richard III* or Schiller's *Maria Stuart* with a pedantic concern for historical accuracy. Usually the main historical interest of such works consists in an analysis of the way in which the writer has diverged from the available sources, or used myths for his own creative purposes. In the twentieth century, however, with the increasing concern for accuracy which has come to permeate historical scholarship, certain works of historical fiction have aroused controversy because of what Joseph W. Turner aptly calls 'the tension inherent in the genre'.[31] Is a historical novel history, or is it fiction? Writers of historical novels have held different views on this subject. Mary Renault, for example, is a staunch champion of the need for historical authenticity: 'One can at least desire the truth; and it is inconceivable to me how anyone can decide deliberately to betray it; to alter some fact which was central to the life of a real human being, however long it is since he ceased to live, in order to make a smoother story, or to exploit him as propaganda for some cause'.[32] Other writers, including Robert Penn Warren, have contended that factual accuracy is irrelevant; what matters is to convey the spirit of a historical period.[33] One of the most acrimonious disputes of recent years surrounding the genre of historical fiction arose over William Styron's novel *The Confessions of Nat Turner* (1968) which aroused the ire of black American writers for its suggestion that the leader of the only sustained, effective revolt in the history of American negro slavery, which occurred in south-eastern Virginia in 1831, was motivated in part by his desire for a white woman.

Such debates are of interest, because they demonstrate that historical accuracy is a conventional expectation of most readers of documented historical novels, even though it need not necessarily be a fundamental requirement of the genre or play any significant role in the critical assessment of a work of literature. The works of Solzhenitsyn raise a particular problem, both because he is a fiction writer who also has pretensions to being a serious historian of twentieth-century Russia, and because he is in practice a far more accurate historian than most Russian writers of historical fiction. The literary works of Pushkin or Tolstoy, for example, although based on historical research, cannot be treated as works of authentic historical scholarship. Pushkin used Karamzin's biased *History of the Russian Empire* as his sole source for *Boris Godunov*; while the satirical portrait of Napoleon and eulogistic portrait of Kutuzov in *War and Peace* have been demonstrated by Shklovsky and others to be mere caricatures designed to corroborate Tolstoy's theory of history.[34] Pushkin is the only Russian writer to have written both a history and a novel on the same subject – the Pugachev Revolt – and he deliberately kept his *History of the Pugachev Uprising* separate from his novel *The Captain's Daughter*.[35] By contrast, Solzhenitsyn frequently mentions Stalin in his political works, but has never written an actual biography of Stalin; he therefore attempts to be both historian and artist in one work, *The First Circle*. Rather than blaming Solzhenitsyn for his inconsistency and contradictions, it is perhaps more helpful to see him as the creator of unique new genres on the blurred border between history and literature. This is particularly evident in the case of *The Gulag Archipelago, The Oak and the Calf* and *The Red Wheel,* but it is also true of *The First Circle,* which deals directly with historical events and introduces real historical characters into the artist's fictional plot. *The First Circle* can be seen as a unique combination of fictional licence, historical accuracy and publicistic passion.

Solzhenitsyn's portrait of Stalin in the new version of the novel differs considerably from any other depictions of Stalin in dissident literature, whether published in the west or recently published in the USSR. In comparison with Voinovich and Iskander, whose works present Stalin in purely fictional terms as a comic, grotesque caricature, Solzhenitsyn attempts to provide a more extensive historical evaluation of Stalin. Moreover, in contrast with Bek and Maksimov, who present largely realistic, objective psychological portraits of Stalin at one particular moment in his career, Solzhenitsyn's aim is to analyse Stalin's entire biography up to 1949. Whereas the detailed portrait of Stalin in Maksimov's *The Ark for the Unbidden* appears similar in conception to Solzhenitsyn's depiction of Stalin in the 1968 version of *The First Circle,* the 1978 edition proved that Solzhenitsyn's intention was far more ambitious than that of Maksimov, or indeed, of most other liberal or dissident writers who have attempted to portray Stalin in their literary works. In breadth of scope the Stalin chapters in *Circle-96* brook comparison only with the portrait of Stalin in Rybakov's *Children of the Arbat,* which depicts Stalin at an earlier stage of his career. Solzhenitsyn's portrait can, therefore, legitimately be judged for its historical accuracy as well as for its literary impact.

The major problem in approaching the Stalin chapters in the new *First Circle* is the ambiguity of the author's role. Whereas as a writer of fiction Solzhenitsyn can treat Stalin in any way he wishes, as a conscientious biographer or historian he has a duty to analyse even such a monster as Stalin objectively. Solzhenitsyn, however, wishes to enjoy the benefits of both fiction and scholarship simultaneously. His partisan approach to his subject and desire to take revenge on Stalin for the secrecy of his life have already been noted. He also, apparently, wishes to use the medium of fiction as a defence against the criticisms levelled at him by many historians who have taken issue with certain interpretations in his overtly political or historical writings. In an interview with Nikita Struve, for example, Solzhenitsyn expressed regret at critics' tendency to place an excessive emphasis on the political, rather than the literary aspects of his work.[36] Similarly, when criticised by Boris Souvarine for certain alleged inaccuracies in *Lenin in Zurich*, Solzhenitsyn defended himself by arguing that Souvarine ignores the fact that it is a work of literature, and concentrates on minor historical details rather than on the depiction of 'Lenin as a psychological type, his character, his inner life and day-to-day behaviour', which, the author claims, is the main purpose of the work.[37] This response would suggest that in *The First Circle* too, Solzhenitsyn was more interested in the general 'psychological type' of Stalin than with fidelity to historical detail. However, he has also claimed to be deeply concerned with historical accuracy: he found it necessary to inform Souvarine that *Lenin in Zurich* 'is a literary work, yet I tried my utmost to make my presentation of the historical facts irreproachably accurate, even down to the last day and the last hour'. Evidently, Solzhenitsyn wishes at the same time to be regarded as a novelist, who possesses a freedom the conscientious biographer does not have, and as a historian objectively analysing the history of Russia. Indeed, throughout his career he has been attempting to evolve new forms flexible enough to convey the interrelationship between history and fiction which underlies all his creative work.

Such scholars as Lev Loseff[38] and Maria Shneerson[39] have argued that Solzhenitsyn's works are fictional, and therefore criticism based on historical criteria is misplaced. This point of view possesses some validity; it is certainly futile to approach Solzhenitsyn's literary works purely as historical treatises. I would, however, contend that in view of Solzhenitsyn's ambitious claims, and the possible influence which his views may exert among his fellow countrymen within and outside the USSR, it is legitimate, indeed vital, to discuss the historical facts and interpretations presented in his literary works. Unlike most authors of historical novels, who are content merely to use primary sources and the synopses of historians, Solzhenitsyn believes that he has been entrusted with a divine mission to reinterpret the history of Russia and communicate his viewpoint to his contemporaries. He feels that it is only through a truthful re-examination of Russia's past that Russians will be able first to repent of their sins, then to build a future.[40] Solzhenitsyn's expanded portrait of Stalin, when first published in 1978, possessed topical political significance in view of the attempts to rehabilitate Stalin since 1964 and the persistent nostalgia of Soviet people for the Stalin era. Events since the accession of Gorbachev demonstrate that Solzhenitsyn's work can still be seen as an important contribution to a vigorous and continuing debate about Stalin and Stalinism in the USSR. In the new conditions of *glasnost*' views on Stalin similar to those of Solzhenitsyn are now being openly discussed in the Soviet press.

Critics have correctly observed that Solzhenitsyn prefers to write from memory and finds it more difficult to create a character whom he has not met personally. His technique in the Stalin chapters is to present an accumulation of historical facts – what Georges Nivat has called Solzhenitsyn's 'heavy' historical method[41] – and to combine them with psychological and political speculations. As there is insufficient available evidence to produce a full psychological portrait of Stalin, Solzhenitsyn has a certain leeway to invent. Yet, in general, the Stalin chapters attest to Solzhenitsyn's painstaking historical research and contain very few inaccuracies of historical fact. The author's selection and interpretation of these facts is, however, a different matter. Solzhenitsyn's technique of character-delineation is the same as in the version of *The First Circle* published in 1968: 'infiltration' of Stalin's interior monologue and 'intellectual mimicry' of Stalin's own style.[42] This method, while of great value and expressiveness in portraying Stalin's character from within, must of necessity hold certain dangers for the objective biographer: it inevitably leads to a selective, impressionistic presentation of historical material. In the new version of *The First Circle* Solzhenitsyn selects certain details of Stalin's life which are, for the most part, factually correct, but which have been deliberately chosen to support the author's own conception of Stalin's character. Whereas in *Circle-87* Solzhenitsyn was careful to keep within the bounds of historical accuracy, confining himself to events which occurred in December 1949, *Circle-96* is an attempt to provide a complete psychological and political biography of Stalin, and thus is much more likely to contain controversial points of fact and interpretation. This chapter will concentrate on these debatable points, focusing particularly on the new Chapter 20.

Whereas the 1968 version of *The First Circle* did not attempt to show how Koba became Stalin, the new version is deeply concerned with the influence of Stalin's early life on the formation of his character.[43] However, as biographers of Stalin frequently complain, very little is known about Stalin's early life.[44] Little of substance is contained either in official biographies, for example those by Beria, Yaroslavsky and Barbusse or the *Short Biography*,[45] or in hostile ones by Trotsky and the Georgian Mensheviks.[46] Stalin came to power so silently and unobtrusively that few diaries and memoirs of his contemporaries even mention him. The versions which Stalin himself dictated contradict each other; records have been destroyed, altered or suppressed; many people involved in the events have subsequently been purged.

As a writer Solzhenitsyn does, therefore, possess a certain freedom in his depiction of Stalin's early life. His portrait, however, can by no means be considered an objective attempt to analyse the formation of Stalin's political personality in his early life and the psychological motivations which led him to seek unlimited autocratic power. In the first place, Solzhenitsyn omits certain factors which other biographers have considered to have exerted an important formative influence on Stalin's character. Unlike such writers as Iskander, Maksimov and Rybakov, Solzhenitsyn makes no mention of Soso's alleged illegitimacy,[47] or of the violent beatings which, many biographers suggest, he was subjected to by his father, a drunken bully.[48] Such treatment, it is claimed, made the son as grim and heartless as the father, and, perhaps, led him to erect a psychological defence mechanism of mistrust, evasion and dissimulation against the world. The suspicion that Solzhenitsyn has deliberately omitted any mitigating circumstances from his portrait of Stalin is intensified by the fact that he describes Soso's mother as uneducated, and omits any reference to her dignity and deep religious faith, or of Stalin's devotion to her, which is posited by some biographers.[49] Similarly, there is no mention of Stalin's first wife, Ekaterina Svanidze, whose early death is frequently assumed to have led

Stalin to repress all human feelings.[50] Solzhenitsyn does, however, refer to Stalin's alleged cohabitation with a Siberian woman in exile and to his illegitimate son by her – an unconfirmed fact mentioned in only two memoirs.[51] Solzhenitsyn's technique of presenting Stalin's personal life in the darkest possible light is also demonstrated by the fact that he largely passes over Stalin's relationship with his second wife, the intelligent and sensitive Nadezhda Allilueva, who is described only as a 'beauty', and that he includes the suggestion that Stalin consoled himself with many other women after her death.[52] All this could, however, be ascribed to Solzhenitsyn's somewhat dismissive attitude to women, a general feature of his world-view intensified in the new version of *The First Circle*.[53] Yet Solzhenitsyn also implies that Stalin deliberately avoided fighting for Russia in the First World War, whereas, in fact, he was originally exempted from military service because of a slight infirmity: he could not bend his left arm at the elbow because of a blood infection which developed out of an ulcer on his hand.[54] In fairness to Solzhenitsyn, it should, nevertheless, be pointed out that many of these details about Stalin's life are controversial or based on insufficient evidence. Except in a few cases (for example, Stalin's exemption from military service), Solzhenitsyn cannot be said to be deliberately concealing the truth or inventing implausible details.

Another important aspect of Stalin's early life which Solzhenitsyn completely ignores is the relationship between the individual and the whole environment of Tsarist Russia. The new version of *The First Circle* resembles Solzhenitsyn's political writings which frequently compare Tsarist rule favourably with the conditions in the USSR after the Revolution. The author omits certain factors which should have been included if he were genuinely trying to provide an objective analysis of Stalin's decision to become a Marxist. For example, Solzhenitsyn fails to mention that Stalin grew up in the climate of serfdom (his grandfather was a serf), which undoubtedly aroused his awareness of social injustice in Tsarist Russia. Whereas Deutscher suggests that the young Stalin was concerned about the consequences of the abolition of serfdom in Georgia,[55] Solzhenitsyn merely claims that the desire to rise from the poverty and humiliation of his origins acted as a spur to his personal ambition. Stalin's interest in the nationality question and in

Georgian-Russian relations may have been inspired by the Tsarist policy of ruthless Russification in Georgia[56] – another factor which Solzhenitsyn chooses to ignore.

Solzhenitsyn also fails to explain adequately the interplay between Stalin's psychological motivation and his political goals and ideas. He regards the Orthodox seminary as a powerful influence on Stalin, but overlooks the grimness of the institution – a fact attested by many memoirs and confirmed by most biographers.[57] The monks spied on their pupils and forbade them to borrow books; and the seminary itself was an instrument for the Russification of the local Georgian population.[58] Not surprisingly, the young seminarist rebelled against this harsh regime, smuggled the works of Darwin, Mill and Chernyshevsky into the seminary,[59] and was influenced by Georgian patriotism.

Solzhenitsyn also fails to discuss two important questions which have preoccupied other biographers: what made Stalin a Marxist, and why he became a Bolshevik follower of Lenin when most Georgian Marxists were choosing Menshevism. Solzhenitsyn does not refer to Stalin's love of books, or mention any intellectual influences which could have inspired him to become a Marxist. He projects his own scorn of Marxist thought on to the character in his novel, and fails to take Stalin's intellectual development seriously; his main purpose is to demonstrate Stalin's total lack of ideas or principles. All Stalin's actions are ascribed to personal ambition and the idea-less lust for power.

Solzhenitsyn does, however, attempt to answer certain other important questions raised by Stalin's early life: why he left the theological seminary at the age of twenty to pursue a revolutionary career, and what his personal goals in the revolutionary movement were. The author's technique is to fit certain selected facts into his own interesting, but often controversial psychological and philosophical interpretation of Stalin's character. Solzhenitsyn lays considerable emphasis on Stalin's religious upbringing, depicting the young seminarian Soso as a sincere believer in God. However, Soso's view of God is distorted: he regards him as a kind of celestial Tsar whose main attributes are power and the ability to humiliate his servants. Soso, who worships power, is prepared to work long and hard for the omnipotent master whose service, he hopes, will prove advantageous to him: 'Oh, with what zeal the boy began to serve God! How he trusted Him!'.[60] Solzhenitsyn's postulation of Stalin's sincere, if perverted, religious belief contradicts other bio-graphies of Stalin which suggest that he was never a true believer.[61] Solzhenitsyn takes the opposing view in order to make Stalin's later rejection of God stand out more clearly. Stalin forsakes God for the revolutionary movement, because he realises that he will never manage to forge a successful career in the Church: 'Clever people had for a long time been laughing at God'.[62] Solzhenitsyn implies that Stalin was prepared to serve and deceive both masters: he follows the laudatory biographies which suggest that for four years before his expulsion from the seminary Stalin attended social-democratic circles,[63] but also claims that he continued to go through the motions of religious observance 'as an insurance'. A similar point was made by Trotsky, who also regarded it as an example of Stalin's talent for dissimulation that 'the young atheist in the course of five whole years continued to explore the mysteries of Orthodoxy'.[64] How-ever, both the atheist Trotsky and Solzhenitsyn, the committed believer, fail to take into account the fact that Orthodoxy has a strong, perhaps dominant ritual aspect; strict observance of Orthodox rites does not necessarily imply either extreme hypo-crisy or whole-hearted commitment. It is necessary for Solzheni-tsyn to stress Stalin's dissimulation in order to provide a psychological precedent for his subsequent alleged career as a Tsarist agent. Unfortunately, however, Solzhenitsyn does not succeed in making Stalin's rejection of God appear sufficiently convincing as a crucial psychological factor in the formation of his evil character, since his perception of God has itself been shown to be distorted with visions of power and ambition.

Solzhenitsyn's interpretation is valid only on a metaphysical plane; Solzhenitsyn is more concerned with symbolic expressive-ness than historical accuracy. Critics have noted that Solzheni-tsyn's portrait of Stalin in *Circle-87* bears a close resemblance to the portrait of Satan in Canto XXXIV of Dante's *Inferno*.[65] *Circle-96* clearly demonstrates that the author was fully con-scious of the symbolic identification of Stalin with Satan, and, by placing emphasis on certain themes and introducing certain new details (discussed below, in Chapter 8), sought to reinforce this parallel. The detailed changes to the text necessitated by this intensified comparison suggest that in this respect at least Solzhenitsyn has in fact revised the original manuscript of *The First Circle* himself, not merely restored passages cut by self-censorship and editorial revisions. The clearest parallel with Dante is Solzhenitsyn's new emphasis on the theme of treachery. Dante reserves the bottom circle of hell, Judecca, for the great traitors of the world – Brutus, Cassius and Judas – and the greatest traitor of them all is Satan himself, who was guilty of the ultimate sin of treachery against the authority and grace which form the divine order of the world. In *Circle-96* Solzhenitsyn lays much more stress on Stalin's treachery to God, the revolutionary movement and his benefactor Lenin. Just as Satan accused God of betraying him, so Stalin finds that 'God has deceived him', and decides to join the revolutionary movement. After this first apostasy, betrayal becomes the mainspring of Stalin's life. He soon discovers that 'The Revolution has also betrayed him', and lays the third stake of his life on the Tsarist secret police. But when he finds that 'The Okhrana has also deceived him' his life as a double agent and, subsequently, as a revolutionary, becomes a complex network of betrayal and counter-betrayal.[66]

Solzhenitsyn emphasises the psychological and metaphysical springs of Stalin's conduct rather than the political climate in which he matured as a revolutionary. He makes no mention of the growth of radical circles of intellectuals and workers, or of the ideological conflict between Bolsheviks and Mensheviks in Georgia. Solzhenitsyn's Stalin is interested only in furthering his own career: he possesses zeal, dedication and fanaticism, but no revolutionary principles or loyalty to any particular cause. He soon becomes scornful of the petty nonentities in the Georgian Social Democratic Party, and realises that the local revolutionary movement will provide no outlet for his ambition. The author ascribes to the young Stalin a hatred of all free revolutionary discussion and a belief in power, order and hierarchy which, according to other biographers, only became apparent later in his life: 'The former seminarist had come to hate these chatterers worse than the governors and policemen (what was the point of getting angry with them? They served for an honest salary and were naturally obliged to defend themselves)'.[67] Solzhenitsyn suggests that even at this early stage Stalin betrayed revolutionary ideals: he feels nothing but contempt for the working class and his fellow revolutionaries, whom he regards as 'professional loudmouths'.[68] His main motive forces are self-love and the thirst for power, which he first experiences when he leads a demonstration of about 200 people in Batumi: 'Koba . . . sensed the germination of the seeds and the force of power. People were following him! – Koba had tried it and would never again be able to forget the taste of it . . . '. This experience shows him that his greatest ambition is not to accumulate wealth, but to wield power over people: 'This was the one thing that suited him in life, this type of life he could understand: you speak and people act; you point something out and people move. There is nothing better, nothing higher than this. It is beyond wealth'.[69] Solzhenitsyn's objective is to portray the makings of the future tyrant in the young Stalin – a legitimate literary aim, but somewhat controversial historically.[70] It is not certain that Stalin always had his eyes fixed on his possible future dictatorship, or that he himself wanted to be a tyrant. Moreover, as Ulam argues, there is no reason why we should analyse Stalin's motivation as the mere cynical craving for power.[71] What Solzhenitsyn does not admit is that Russian revolutionaries in the nineteenth century could act from a perfectly rational premise that the system they were fighting was oppressive and anachronistic.

The most controversial element in Solzhenitsyn's portrait is his depiction of Stalin as a Tsarist police spy. This is not, as Flegon suggests, a 'new' theory, or one which has absolutely no historical foundation,[72] but it is certainly new in twentieth-century Russian fiction.[73] It is a theory for which there is insufficient historical evidence, and which most biographers reject – even such hostile biographers as Trotsky.[74] As we have seen, Solzhenitsyn himself has admitted that it is only a hypothesis which he is trying to prove; he would like it to be true, but treats it as a psychological possibility rather than as a proven historical fact. His interpretation of Stalin's past can be accepted on literary grounds, if not on grounds of historical authenticity.

It is probable that Solzhenitsyn based his theory that Stalin was an Okhrana agent on the oral testimony of many former prisoners who believed this story, for example the Old Bolshevik E. P. Frolov, who claimed to have seen Djugashvili's denunciation of fellow Social Democrats in the archives of the Kutaisi prison.[75] The different 'documents' referred to in the west in support of this theory by Alexander Orlov and Isaac Don Levine have either been destroyed or proved to be forgeries;[76] and E. E. Smith, in a more scholarly book based on the Maklakov papers at Stanford University, claims in the text that Stalin's guilt has been proved, but only presents flimsy hearsay evidence.[77] Scholars such as Medvedev, Tucker and Ulam have dismissed such evidence on the grounds that it is based on questionable second-hand or third-hand stories, the purveyors of some of which spent years in Stalin's labour camps.[78] Naturally, Solzhenitsyn, another victim of Stalin's purges, also had good reason to be swayed by anti-Stalin feelings.

Solzhenitsyn attempts to justify his theory of Stalin's collaboration with the Okhrana on both factual and psychological grounds. His psychological speculations, like those offered by Smith, Levine and Orlov, are more convincing than his attempt to prove somewhat dubious factual points. We cannot know if Solzhenitsyn had read the works by these western authors at the time that he wrote *The First Circle*, but he includes some of the same hypotheses, and his method is similar to theirs: he provides a series of speculative interpretations of Djugashvili's early actions and of events in his life, treating possibility as though it were certainty. Solzhenitsyn does not mention the story of Stalin's alleged denunciation of some of his fellow seminarists,[79] but he suggests that Stalin's contempt for his colleagues in the Georgian revolutionary movement could have led him to denounce them to the police – as local Bolsheviks believed, for example, in the case of the arrest of Stepan Shaumyan in 1909.[80] Solzhenitsyn also lays great emphasis on the fact that Stalin was not imprisoned for as long as some of his fellow revolutionaries, and that he escaped easily five times from exile.[81] Like Levine, Solzhenitsyn suggests that Stalin stopped being a police agent after his election to the Bolshevik Central Committee in Prague in 1912; and that only an overwhelming sense of guilt and a haunting fear of discovery could account for his conduct in the 1930s: the eradication of documents, falsification of records and execution of people who knew.[82] Solzhenitsyn does not, however, include all the rather far-fetched allegations published in the west, for example Orlov's claim that Marshal Tukhashevsky was told by General Yakir about Stalin's 'secret', and that they and Kossior, a member of the Politburo, were executed in 1937 because they headed a conspiracy against Stalin.[83] He does, however, allude indirectly to this hypothesis when he says that Stalin's secret 'was almost revealed in 1937'.[84]

Solzhenitsyn adds an individual touch to his portrayal of

Stalin's career as a Tsarist agent, interpreting it as an inevitable result of his psychology. Sentenced to a year in prison, and informed by his jailer that he will be kept in prison until he dies of tuberculosis, Stalin realises that he has no firm revolutionary convictions, and regrets staking his life on the revolution, which may not occur for another fifty years. Extrapolating from Stalin's later introduction of officers' ranks and uniforms into the Soviet army, Solzhenitsyn suggests that the young prisoner admired the uniforms of the Tsarist gendarmes. The author implies that Stalin's respect for order and stability led him inexorably to serve the powerful Russian empire: 'He knew himself, his unhurried character, his thorough character, his love of stability and order. It was on just such thoroughness, unhurriedness, stability and order that the Russian empire stood, and why should he shake it?'.[85]

It is noticeable that when Solzhenitsyn is not sure of his facts, he tends to accumulate an excess of factual details which nevertheless fail to prove his point beyond all reasonable doubt. It is instructive, in this connection, that Solzhenitsyn goes into detail about Stalin's arrests, escapes and exiles, which he attempts to use in support of his spy theory, while giving only a very impressionistic account of the 1905 revolution. Moreover, some of his interpretations demonstrate that he has ignored all facts which do not support his point of view. In some cases this leads him into contradictory statements. For example, Solzhenitsyn stresses that Stalin was only imprisoned for brief periods, omitting the fact that first offenders were frequently given short sentences, that more prominent Bolsheviks than Stalin – for example Krasin and Lenin – were treated even more leniently by the Okhrana,[86] and that many other revolutionaries escaped from exile under Tsarism. This last point is one that Solzhenitsyn himself has made very forcibly in *The Gulag Archipelago*, where he tries to prove that exile and imprisonment under Tsarism were much less severe than life for prisoners in Stalin's camps.[87] Similarly, in *The First Circle* the ironic author intervenes to subvert Stalin's monologue, declaring: 'the Tsarist regime knew how to stick on ruthless sentences – four years, it's terrifying to relate'.[88] This is an occasion on which Solzhenitsyn looks back on the past with hindsight and ascribes his own feelings to Stalin, implicitly contrasting the lenient sentences in Tsarist times with the far longer sentences imposed in the Stalin era, when the minimum was usually ten years. Solzhenitsyn's insinuation that no one feared arrest in Tsarist times is not only a highly debatable point,[89] but also inadvertently undermines his own argument that the short sentences meted out to Stalin prove his complicity with the secret police.

Solzhenitsyn makes certain other uncertain or unverifiable statements. It seems improbable, for example, that Stalin lived under police protection in Vologda, as Solzhenitsyn suggests; it is more likely that he was under police surveillance.[90] Moreover, it is not necessary to assume, as Solzhenitsyn does, that the money Stalin possessed in the years 1905–12 was chiefly provided by the Okhrana; he could have acquired all this from his notorious 'expropriations' – a suggestion which Solzhenitsyn himself makes in *The Gulag Archipelago* [91] – or from party funds. It is also highly improbable that Stalin could have carried out such 'exes' as the Tbilisi bank robbery of 1908 without the knowledge of his police masters. Solzhenitsyn is also unconvincing in his attempt to explain why Stalin appeared to devote so much of his time furthering the revolutionary cause after he became a police spy. The author suggests that the 1905 revolution, which came as a surprise to all the revolutionary parties, demonstrates to him that he has once again made the wrong choice. He wants his 'revolutionary soul' back again, but by this time his denunciations of fellow revolutionaries have irrevocably compromised him. Solzhenitsyn is obviously on thin ground here, as he is obliged to attribute the lack of evidence for this theory to the systematic destruction carried out by Stalin during his lifetime of all the Okhrana files incriminating him.[92] Solzhenitsyn alludes to the destruction of many Okhrana archives by guilty revolutionaries, including Stalin, after the February Revolution, but does not mention that some of the surviving documents referred to Koba as a prominent Social Democrat,[93] thus actually contradicting the theory that he was a police spy.

Solzhenitsyn does, nevertheless, have some facts on his side. He quite correctly suggests that Koba was not squeamish in his choice of means, and that the Okhrana made a practice of pressurising arrested revolutionaries into becoming informers.[94] The most convincing arguments adduced by Solzhenitsyn to support his view, however, are not new facts, but speculative interpretations of Stalin's character. He shows that Stalin had the psychology of an *agent provocateur* (as some of his colleagues in the Social Democratic Party noted), and that it is not implausible that he did in fact give some information to the police, particularly after his first arrest in 1902 when he may have been subjected to pressure. While it is not necessary to imply, as Solzhenitsyn does, that Stalin was on a par with the two notorious double agents Azef and Malinovsky, he could, nevertheless, have given some information in his own personal and factional interests without becoming a full-scale *agent provocateur.*

Another debatable point in Solzhenitsyn's portrait is his dismissal of any serious psychological or intellectual reasons for Stalin's decision to become a Bolshevik. He presents ambition as one of Stalin's prime motives, but does not expand on this point, failing to discuss the situation in the Georgian Social Democratic Party in 1904–5. One important psychological motivation for Stalin's decision was, most probably, the fact that in Georgia to be a Menshevik meant to follow such acknowledged leaders as Zhordania and Dzhibladze, whereas to become a Bolshevik gave a much better chance of rapid promotion. Secondly, many biographers suggest that Lenin's writings made a great impression on him,[95] and that he later fell under the spell of Lenin's personality.[96] Solzhenitsyn, however, implies that Stalin agreed to become a Bolshevik under pressure from the Tsarist police, who allegedly instructed him – as they did Azef and Malinovsky – to infiltrate the most extreme trend in the revolutionary movement. Solzhenitsyn thus suggests that, from the beginning, Stalin had no belief in Lenin's ideas. Once again, Solzhenitsyn is extrapolating from Stalin's conduct in power, and projecting his later views on to the young Stalin. It is indisputable that Stalin was ambitious for political power, and that in the 1920s he sought the role of acknowledged leader of the Communist Party. However, although he eventually wanted to be Lenin's successor, he was at first content merely to assume the role of one of Lenin's closest comrades-in-arms. It is also unlikely that he could have come so close to Lenin if he had not shared at least some of Lenin's ideological aspirations.

The depiction of the relationship between Stalin and Lenin is an important aspect of *Circle-96*. In the earlier version Solzhenitsyn had implied that Stalin departed from Lenin, destroying the pristine aims of the Revolution; Lenin and Leninism were presented as positive ideals. In the new version, however, Solzhenitsyn's attitude is quite different, although somewhat inconsistent: while emphasising Stalin's lack of belief in Lenin's ideas, he stresses the similarity of temperament between the two men. In contrast with *Circle-87*, in which, as Robin Blackburn stated, 'Solzhenitsyn is less drawn to the purely political rejection of Stalinism',[97] in *Circle-96*, Solzhenitsyn analyses the historical and political roots of Stalinism, and advances the proposition that there is a basic continuity between Leninism and Stalinism.[98]

It is now clear that Solzhenitsyn's view that Stalinism was rooted in Leninism had developed as early as 1955, when he began to write *The First Circle*. Indeed, it can be dated back even further to his time in the special prison (June 1947 to May 1949) when, as Lev Kopelev states, Solzhenitsyn 'hated Stalin and had come to doubt Lenin'.[99] It is thus a fair assumption that since the late 1940s he had held the view expressed in *From under the Rubble* that 'Stalin was a very consistent and faithful – if also a very untalented – heir to the very spirit of Leninism'.[100] Similarly, in *The Gulag Archipelago*, conceived in 1958 and composed over the following ten years, Stalin receives only a rare mention, for example: 'The personal, individual imprint he left on events consisted of dismal stupidity, petty tyranny, self-glorification',[101] whereas the whole thesis of the work implicates Lenin in the mass terror and the formation of the camps from the beginning. The more positive view of Lenin presented in the 1968 version of *The First Circle* can therefore be ascribed to expediency: Solzhenitsyn's decision to cut the original manuscript and submit to Tvardovsky's corrections in the hope that the novel might be published in the USSR.[102]

In the 1978 edition of *The First Circle* Lenin and Stalin are shown to be alike in their approval of violence and robbery to further the revolutionary cause. Solzhenitsyn supports this view by quoting Lenin out of context: he implies that Lenin characterised Stalin as a 'wonderful Georgian' when he heard about the criminal 'expropriations', although, in fact, Lenin first used this phrase in a letter to Gorky in February 1912 in connection with the national question.[103] Solzhenitsyn later repeats this phrase to convey Lenin's alleged admiration of Stalin during the Civil War as a strong figure typical of the new-style party members who are now 'very necessary'.[104] What Stalin most admires about Lenin is his mastery of devious political tactics. Solzhenitsyn makes his character express the author's own view of Lenin's cynical political manoeuvres: 'He could simply amaze you: in one day he did an about-turn – "Land to the Peasants" (and then we'll see), in one day he thought up the Brest peace (it was painful not only for a Russian, but even for a Georgian to give up half of Russia to the Germans, but it wasn't painful for him!) . . . Not to mention NEP, which was the most cunning trick of all; it would be no shame to learn from such manoeuvres'. Solzhenitsyn suggests that Stalin was also impressed by Lenin's intolerance towards opponents in matters of theory, his firm grasp of dictatorial power, his realisation of the need for purges within the party, and his belief in execution without trial.[105] In his attempt to prove the continuity between Leninism and Stalinism Solzhenitsyn uses the persuasiveness of the novelist, but ignores certain significant historical factors: the conditions of civil war in which the Bolshevik terror was introduced, the different meaning of the word 'purge' in the 1920s and the 1930s, and Lenin's criticism in 1923 of Stalin's handling of the Workers' and Peasants' Inspectorate (the body responsible for supervising the whole machinery of government). Solzhenitsyn sometimes allows his desire to attack Lenin to contradict his other aims: for example, Stalin condemns Lenin for being 'so exemplary' and failing to be bold enough to escape from exile, thus inadvertently casting doubt on the author's earlier contention that Stalin escaped from exile because of his connections with the Okhrana.

Curiously, in his emphasis on Stalin's scornful attitude to Lenin, Solzhenitsyn and Stalin often appear to be allies. Stalin complains that Lenin has no true understanding of Russia because of his many years spent abroad. This both reflects the real Stalin's contempt for the Russian revolutionary emigration[106] and closely corresponds to the approach adopted by Solzhenitsyn in *Lenin in Zurich*, which emphasises Lenin's scorn for 'accursed Russia' and demonstrates how out of touch he was with his country on the eve of revolution.[107] Solzhenitsyn's Stalin also stresses, like his creator, that Lenin was a 'bookish theoretician' of bourgeois origin who had never known poverty and hunger. Furthermore, Solzhenitsyn attempts to puncture the myth of Lenin's infallibility, attributing to Stalin the opinion that Lenin miscalculated and was forced to flee to Finland in July 1917 to save his own skin. Stalin also claims that Lenin was not sufficiently realistic and reliable to master the government and economy of the country after taking power.

By emphasising the differences between Lenin and Stalin, Solzhenitsyn attempts to debunk the myth current in Stalin's time that Stalin was Lenin's best disciple and natural successor. Solzhenitsyn's Stalin has not read half of Lenin's theoretical writings, and is contemptuous of the 'fantasies' which Lenin shares with Trotsky, such as his belief in world revolution. Solzhenitsyn also emphasises that Stalin frequently disagreed with Lenin on specific political tactics. In 1917 Stalin originally considered Lenin an 'adventurer' for his policy of refusing to support the Provisional Government and for his alleged encouragement of the anarchic July demonstrations; he subsequently failed at first to understand the necessity for signing the Treaty of Brest-Litovsk. During the Civil War Stalin resented Lenin's decision to send him all over the country instead of keeping him at his side. Stalin regards himself as 'steadier and firmer than Lenin' and more aware of the realities of political power. Stalin is more adept than Lenin at the dirty business of subterranean political intrigue: 'the dark manoeuvrings of real politics'.[108]

Solzhenitsyn's depiction of the relationship between Stalin and Lenin also reinforces the symbolic identification of Stalin with Satan and the other great traitors in the deepest circle of the *Inferno*. Like Satan, Judas, Cassius and Brutus, Stalin is guilty of diabolic treachery towards his leader and benefactor, the man who allegedly saved him from the Okhrana by having him elected to the Central Committee of the Bolshevik Party in 1912. In 1917 Stalin is prepared to surrender Lenin to the Provisional Government in order that he should be put on trial. Later he deliberately deceives Lenin by showing only one side of his character, and is rude to Lenin as a matter of policy in order to win his respect.[109] Stalin deceives Lenin into believing that he alone stands for party unity and wants nothing for himself. Stalin's final betrayal occurs when he hastens Lenin's death and suppresses his *Testament*. His cynical attitude towards his leader is exemplified during Lenin's last illness, when he is made 'responsible for Comrade Lenin's health'.[110] Although Solzhenitsyn does not give credence to Trotsky's unproven allegation that

Stalin poisoned Lenin,[111] he suggests that Stalin secretly wanted Lenin to die. Stalin's hostility towards Lenin would, however, have been more convincing if Solzhenitsyn had dwelt more on Lenin's conflict with Stalin in the years 1921–4 and his preparation of an onslaught against him. This omission demonstrates that Solzhenitsyn has no wish to emphasise Lenin's foresight and awareness of Stalin's danger to the party. He presents speculation as historical fact, suggesting that Lenin's secretary brought Stalin a copy of the *Testament* in which Lenin stated that Stalin should be removed as General Secretary of the Party.[112] He also, more plausibly, alleges that Stalin's conflict with Lenin and Krupskaya hastened Lenin's death, which occurred at a very convenient time for Stalin. The ironic narrator declares: 'So all the efforts to save his life were in vain'.[113]

In *Circle-87* the name and policies of Trotsky were not mentioned, although the character of Adamson, the one oppositionist Communist arrested in the 1920s (perhaps a left-wing supporter of Trotsky) was not particularly attractive. In the new version of the novel Solzhenitsyn makes it clear that he does not – as some western radicals originally hoped – favour the Trotskyite alternative to Stalinism. Although Trotsky is depicted through the prism of Stalin's hatred, the author's own distaste for Stalin's enemy is also plainly expressed. Trotsky is shown to be arrogant, to favour the fantastic idea of world revolution, to propagate meaningless agitator's slogans like 'No peace, no war', and to be an even more ruthless supporter of execution without trial than Stalin himself.

Like most biographers, Solzhenitsyn is on surer historical ground when he depicts Stalin's career after the Revolution. However, in concentrating on the personalities rather than on the political factors involved in the power struggles of the 1920s and 1930s Solzhenitsyn inevitably oversimplifies the historical process. He leaves out a detailed consideration of the economic and political context of Stalin's actions, but quite correctly points to the tactical manoeuvres which enabled Stalin to establish dominance over the Communist Party in the 1920s: his painstaking administrative work, his promotion of cadres loyal to him, his mastery of the art of alliances and his ability to pass himself off as a man of the centre, a supporter of party unity who, unlike Trotsky or Zinoviev, would present no danger of dictatorship.

The ironic narrator uses an apt historical parallel to convey Stalin's apparent innocuousness: 'Like Misha Romanov, he was chosen because nobody feared him'.[114] (The young Mikhail Romanov was chosen as Tsar by the Russian boyars in 1615 to unify the country after the 'Time of Troubles'). Solzhenitsyn simplifies history by focusing on the intra-party struggles of the 1920s to the exclusion of political and economic discussions, omitting everything which might conceivably be used in Stalin's justification: for example, the broad support in the party first for Stalin's decision to continue the New Economic Policy and later to abandon it; the appeal of his slogan 'Socialism in one country'; and the mistakes and weaknesses of his opponents. Solzhenitsyn quite rightly shows how Stalin cynically appropriated the slogans of the defeated Left Opposition, for example 'An attack on the kulak' and 'Forced industrialisation!'. However, the author's own distaste for Marxist-Leninist ideology leads him totally to discount serious ideological discussion as a factor of any importance in Soviet history. Solzhenitsyn's position in *Circle-96* appears to be the somewhat controversial view that there was no difference between Stalin and other historical tyrants, and that Marxism-Leninism meant nothing at all. This is a dubious interpretation, for although it may be true that Stalin later used ideological formulae as a smokescreen to disguise his desire for naked political power, in the 1920s ideological disputes were real enough.

Solzhenitsyn's talent for psychological revelation of the mind of the tyrant is greater than his powers of historical analysis. His psychological interpretations of Stalin's character, although speculative, are based on the observations of people who knew Stalin. Solzhenitsyn is particularly successful at explaining Stalin's technique as a purge investigator, which springs from his 'four strengths'. His first and greatest strength is the 'force of the unspoken decision': 'Inwardly you have already taken a decision, but he whose head it touches doesn't need to know before time. (When his head rolls it'll be time enough for him to find out)'. His second strength is mistrust and deceit: 'Never believe other people's words and attach no importance to your own. Don't say what you intend to do (perhaps even you yourself don't know yet, you'll decide later), but say what will reassure the person you are talking to at the present moment'.[115] Solzhenitsyn's analysis

closely corresponds to the picture of Stalin's morbid suspiciousness painted by Khrushchev.[116] However, it is interesting that
Solzhenitsyn omits from the new version of the novel the
generalisation 'Mistrust was his world-view', perhaps because he
has demonstrated Stalin's suspiciousness more vividly through
the depiction of his actions and thoughts.

Stalin's third strength is one he learnt through the harsh
experience of having to let Trotsky go – the decision never to forgive an enemy: 'If someone has betrayed you, don't forgive him;
if you've got your teeth into someone, don't let him go . . . '. This
recalls Stalin's statement to Khrushchev and Dzerzhinsky in
1923 that 'his highest delight in life was to keep a keen eye on
an enemy, prepare everything painstakingly, mercilessly revenge
himself, and then go to sleep'.[117] Stalin's fourth strength, according to Solzhenitsyn, is his lack of any genuine belief in Marxist
theory and his cynical ability to use theory to justify his
manipulation of the realities of political power: 'Don't direct
your actions on the basis of theory, that never helped anyone
(you can always propound some sort of theory afterwards), but
constantly take note of who's going your way at the moment, and
until what point'.[118]

Solzhenitsyn's Stalin passes rapidly in his mind over the many
waves of purges in the 1930s. The author does not mention any
political or historical factors which might conceivably be used
to explain Stalin's actions: the isolation of the USSR and its
encirclement by hostile capitalist powers, or Stalin's desire to
industrialise the country rapidly to make it secure against
invaders. Solzhenitsyn does not even offer the psychological
explanation which he gave in the 1968 version of *The First
Circle*: the suggestion that Stalin conducted permanent purges
because he never felt secure in his own position. In the new
version Solzhenitsyn merely places an ironic emphasis on the
heroic efforts which Stalin believes he is making to cleanse the
party and country of 'enemies' and purify Leninist doctrine, 'that
faultless teaching which Stalin had never betrayed'. The author
once again stresses that the concept of the purge originated with
Lenin: 'He was doing exactly what Lenin had outlined, only a
little more gently and without any fuss'.[119] Solzhenitsyn refers to
the USSR's serious agricultural and social problems in the 1930s,

which are not mentioned in official Soviet histories: 'At times the Ukraine let its grain rot, the Kuban fired from sawn-off shotguns, even Ivanovo went on strike'.[120] The implication is that Stalin believed his own propaganda about 'sabotage' and used terror as a means of diverting attention away from his domestic failures. He continued the purges on the eve of the German invasion in 1941 because of the USSR's humiliating defeat in the Russo-Finnish War. Solzhenitsyn suggests that Stalin took a malign pleasure in the terror, referring to the rumour, also mentioned in *The Gulag Archipelago*, that Stalin sat in a closed room secretly watching the purge trials of his defeated opponents. Even if not historically authentic, it is certainly psychologically plausible. Solzhenitsyn depicts Stalin gloating over the humiliation of his enemies: in contrast with such weaklings, he prides himself on his 'knowledge of human nature' and 'sobriety'.[121]

Solzhenitsyn introduces into *Circle-96* a theme which possessed particular interest for him: Stalin's treatment of Soviet writers. He quite accurately suggests that Stalin did not move against erring writers immediately, but chose his victims carefully and bided his time, in order that the punishment should be more 'instructive'. Solzhenitsyn implies that Stalin blamed the censors for allowing one of Pilnyak's stories to be published which incriminated him in the murder of General Frunze (see above, pp. 20–2). The lack of any explicit reference to Pilnyak's *Tale of the Unextinguished Moon*, however, implies both that Stalin was not particularly interested in literature, and, as Nivat remarks, that 'the senile despot is capable of grasping only the general outline; details do not interest him'.[122] Solzhenitsyn also indicates that, although Stalin was 'advised to have Bulgakov shot', his partiality for some aspects of the old world led him to allow Bulgakov's play about White officers, *Days of the Turbins*, to be shown in one Moscow theatre.[123] Stalin's dealings with writers are presented as merely a product of caprice; unlike some commentators, Solzhenitsyn does not postulate any sympathy or respect for great writers on Stalin's part[124] – a respect which, it has been claimed, led Stalin to allow Zamyatin to emigrate and to spare the lives of Bulgakov and Pasternak.

In *Circle-96* Solzhenitsyn lays considerable emphasis on Stalin's relationship with Hitler. In *Circle-87* he had merely stated that Hitler was the one man whom Stalin trusted in his entire life (a suggestion which has been ably contested by Roy Medvedev, who argues that Stalin's relationship with Hitler was not based on 'trust', but on expediency).[125] In *Circle-96* Solzhenitsyn goes much further, stressing Stalin's similarity to Hitler and his admiration for him as a man of action, a ruthless dictator and military leader who 'sauntered through France brandishing a big stick'. Solzhenitsyn rejects the official Soviet line that Stalin merely used the Nazi-Soviet Pact to gain time for his country, suggesting instead that Stalin actively supported the Pact as a cynical means of acquiring territory and did everything possible to appease Hitler: 'He sent trainloads of raw materials to Germany and failed to fortify the frontiers, as he was afraid of offending his colleague'. He was totally devastated when Hitler 'deceived' him and invaded Russia: 'He attacked, and, to his bewilderment, spoilt such a good alliance'.[126] In the 'Stalin chapters' Solzhenitsyn touches on a theme which receives amplified expression in the rest of the novel, and in his political writings: the similarity between the Stalinist and Nazi terror. (In *The Gulag Archipelago*, however, Solzhenitsyn has drawn a favourable comparison between the way in which Germany after Hitler faced up to its past and the Soviet experience after Stalin.[127])

In *Circle-87* Solzhenitsyn's depiction of Stalin's unpreparedness for war in 1941 closely followed the line taken in Khrushchev's 'Secret Speech'.[128] In *Circle-96*, however, Solzhenitsyn ventures even further, laying greater emphasis on the somewhat controversial, unproven rumour that Stalin gave in to panic for the first time in his life and escaped from Moscow to Kuibyshev for a week in October 1941 when there was a danger that Moscow would fall.[129] Solzhenitsyn's intention is to demonstrate that it is not thanks to Stalin that Russia was not abandoned to the Nazis; and that later Stalin had to purge many people who knew that their Commander-in-Chief had fled in their country's hour of need. The ironic narrator notes that 'the nationality question laughed at him during those difficult years', as many nationalities revolted against Stalin during the war and 'only the Russians and Jews' – those who had suffered most in the purges – 'remained loyal to him'.[130] Solzhenitsyn repeats Khrushchev's dubious speculation that Stalin would have deported the entire

Ukrainian nation to Siberia in 1944 if there had not been so many of them.[131]

Another element in Solzhenitsyn's portrait of Stalin which echoes the author's own view expressed in his later political writings is his character's contempt for the weakness of the west.[132] In 1931–2, when it seemed as though Russia would crumble if she were attacked, Stalin whipped up war fever in order to strengthen his own position, although he knew that the western 'chatterers' would not intervene. Solzhenitsyn's attack on the stupidity and spinelessness of the west is particularly evident in his depiction of Stalin's cynical attitude towards Churchill and Roosevelt, whom he is shown to have completely outwitted at the Yalta Conference: 'Stalin made amends for a lot of things by outplaying Churchill and the sanctimonious Roosevelt. Ever since the 1920s Stalin had not had such a success as he had with those two blockheads . . . statesmen they may be, but however clever they consider themselves to be, they are sillier than babies'.[133] The feeble conduct of the western leaders at Yalta, where they effectively surrendered to Stalin most of eastern Europe and many hapless Russian prisoners-of-war, is a theme which Solzhenitsyn has developed at greater length in *The Gulag Archipelago*.[134] Stalin's cynical exploitation of western Communists is also emphasised: the dictator refers scornfully to the French Communist leader as 'that old fool André Marty'.[135]

Solzhenitsyn's portrayal of Stalin's dissatisfaction with all classes of the population after the war and his decision to renew the onslaught against them touches on another theme discussed elsewhere in the novel and in Solzhenitsyn's political writings: the tragedy of the post-war period in Russia, when Stalin imposed further suffering on those who had defended their country and hoped for some internal liberalisation. Solzhenitsyn's evocation of Stalin's conflict with Tito is retained from *Circle-87*, except that he uses stronger language to convey Stalin's feelings. Instead of saying 'And who on earth could build socialism without Stalin?', the new version declares: 'Socialism without Stalin is outright fascism!'. Solzhenitsyn emphasises that Stalin cannot forgive Tito's impudence in resurrecting the old, long-forgotten Bolshevik formulae, the 'soap bubbles of the first three years of the Revolution' such as 'workers' control' and 'land to the peasants' which he regards as 'trinkets for fools'.[136] Thus

Solzhenitsyn makes it quite clear that Stalin betrayed the original ideals of the Revolution – as, in his opinion, Lenin did before him.

Solzhenitsyn demonstrates even more plainly in *Circle-96* that Stalin is not a theorist possessed by the idea of communism, but a dictator who prostituted the original Marxist ideal for the idealess lust for power. This is shown by Solzhenitsyn's emphasis on Stalin's similarity to other autocratic rulers of the past, exemplified by the extended comparisons with Napoleon and Hitler and the reference to Shakespeare's *Richard III*. This allusion possesses a particular resonance in the Soviet context, as a production of the play in 1965–6 had aroused the apprehensions of Furtseva, the Minister of Culture, and had been hastily withdrawn. Richard's name evokes not only the sexual fascination of evil, but also the isolation of the tyrant, and, perhaps, the guilt he feels when his purge victims return to plague his dreams. Solzhenitsyn, like Rybakov, suggests that Stalin regards himself as continuing the line of Russian autocrats with their Great Russian chauvinism and dreams of territorial expansion. He is constantly portrayed as a 'Tsar', an 'emperor', and the Russian people are described as his 'subjects'.[137] Although in 1905, as a revolutionary, he was glad at the fall of Port Arthur and the defeat of the Tsarist regime in the Russo-Japanese War, he now, as a Russian nationalist and Soviet imperialist, feels proud that this lost territory of his empire has been regained. With clever sophistry he easily reconciles his imperialist ambitions with the Marxist concept of 'world communism'.

As Edward J. Brown has shown, Solzhenitsyn satirically dissects the poverty of thought, tedious style and teleological phraseology of Stalin's famous article of 1950, 'On Marxism in Linguistics'.[138] Yet, whereas the 1968 version of the novel had mercilessly exposed the academic pretensions of the 'Patron of Science' who pontificates on linguistics, despite his rudimentary knowledge of languages,[139] in the new version the author goes even further, suggesting that Stalin is merely following in the footsteps of his eminent predecessors Engels and Lenin in his aspiration to make an 'immortal' contribution to scholarship. In particular, Solzhenitsyn censures the readiness of Engels in *Dialectics of Nature* and Lenin in *Materialism and Empiriocriticism* to make dogmatic pronouncements on physics, although they knew little about the subject. He emphasises the fact that Lenin, a lawyer, argued that matter could not turn into energy,[140] thereby displaying complete ignorance of Einstein's discovery of matter-energy a few years earlier, which had totally dispensed with Lenin's static notions of matter. In the Stalin chapters of *Circle-96* Solzhenitsyn adumbrates an attack on dialectical and historical materialism which is expanded in the rest of the novel, especially in the new Chapter 88 entitled 'Dialectical Materialism – the Progressive World-View'. In his depiction of Stalin's conception of communism Solzhenitsyn derides certain Marxist dogmas with which Stalin cloaks his lust for world domination: the idea that 'existence determines consciousness', the whole notion of a future earthly paradise, and the problem of whether, when communism is attained, the dialectical process will cease.

Solzhenitsyn's portrayal of Stalin's view of the future closely corresponds to the author's frequently expressed idea that the Soviet regime has aggressive intentions of taking over the world. Solzhenitsyn implies that Stalin is obsessed by a similar dream to that of such tyrants as Bonaparte and Hitler: the desire to conquer the whole of Europe. Since 1944 Stalin has believed in the inevitability of a third world war which will lead first to the conquest of Europe and then to the establishment of his form of totalitarian rule throughout the world. Solzhenitsyn's evocation of Stalin's fantasy of a third world war, the occasion on which his character seems most deranged, has been subjected to criticism by some readers for its excessive satire.[141] Certainly, at first sight Solzhenitsyn's interpretation appears highly questionable from a historical point of view, as Stalin had the defence of the USSR to consider in 1944, and between 1945 and 1949 the USA had a monopoly of nuclear weapons; moreover, Stalin managed to assert dominance over eastern Europe without resorting to war. Although such imperialistic ambitions would have been more historically plausible in 1949, when the USSR was on the verge of acquiring the atomic bomb, it seems improbable, after the failure of the Berlin blockade in 1948, that Stalin would have envisaged a march through Europe. Nevertheless, Solzhenitsyn's presentation of Stalin's dream does have a basis in reality: Djilas relates that Stalin once expressed the desire to 'have another go' at conquering the whole of Germany in another fifteen to twenty years.[142] Solzhenitsyn betrays his own hostility towards western Communists through his depiction of Stalin's ambitious scheme: 'Neither Napoleon nor Hitler could take Britain because they had an enemy on the continent. But he wouldn't have. From the Elbe he would march at once to the English Channel. France would fall apart like rotten wood dust. (The French Communists would help)'.[143] He dreams of a Hitlerian Blitzkrieg which he will be able to unleash once atomic bombs have been constructed and the rear has been purged. Although extremely controversial historically, this passage is, nevertheless, acceptable in literary and psychological terms as a megalomaniac fantasy in which Stalin indulges before falling asleep.

The further suggestion that Stalin intends a Blitzkrieg in Korea as a rehearsal for the coming world war – a view Solzhenitsyn first propounded in prison camp[144] – is somewhat simplistic, as in actual fact the Russians encouraged the North Koreans to attack, while remaining aloof themselves and forcing the Chinese to intervene, thereby becoming involved in a local war with the USA. The author's emphasis on Stalin's belief in 'revolution from above' rather than the anarchic 'revolutions from below' favoured by Marx and Lenin, is, nevertheless, totally convincing. Solzhenitsyn's Stalin finally betrays the Marxist-Leninist concepts of revolution and internationalism, substituting military conquest and totalitarian political control for the idea of world revolution: 'With our tanks, artillery and aviation we might manage without a world revolution. In general the path to world communism would be simplest of all through a third world war. First unite the whole world, then establish communism. No more revolutions are necessary!'.[145]

Conclusion

The principal difference between the old and new versions of the Stalin chapters in *The First Circle* is that whereas Solzhenitsyn originally presented a largely moral critique of Stalin, and depicted him only at the height of his power, he now seeks to provide a complete political and historical analysis of Stalin's career up to 1949. Contrary to Kathryn Feuer's earlier judgement that

Solzhenitsyn, unlike Tolstoy, is merely a 'questioner',[146] he now clearly emerges as an 'answerer' who attempts to propose a highly individual 'solution' to the enigma of Stalin. Similarly, it is not now true to say, as Edward J. Brown did about the original portrait of Stalin, that 'Solzhenitsyn . . . expounds no theory of history and is not trying to prove anything'.[147] The revisions have the effect of introducing much greater political explicitness into the Stalin chapters and the novel as a whole. Whereas in the original version Solzhenitsyn did not venture much further in his criticism of Stalin than Khrushchev had done in his 'Secret Speech' of 1956, the new version contains many of the strong views familiar from his more recent political writings. In Georges Nivat's words, 'there is an obvious *double-jeu* between the ruminations of the Tyrant and the way Solzhenitsyn, the author, uses this character to settle old scores'.[148] Through the dictator's interior monologue Solzhenitsyn clearly conveys his own opinions: the October Revolution was simply a lucky accident which might easily have failed, and Stalin merely intensified the trend already inherent in Leninism. The author mercilessly dissects Marxist-Leninist ideology and exposes both the cruelty of Lenin and Trotsky, and Stalin's falsehood, tyranny and megalomania. Solzhenitsyn now sharply dissociates himself from Khrushchev's de-Stalinisation campaign, portraying Khrushchev, Malenkov and their colleagues as Stalin's toadies and accomplices.

One important question which cannot be adequately answered unless Solzhenitsyn himself chooses to provide the answer is: to what extent did the author rewrite the 96-chapter version of *The First Circle* for publication in 1978? Is it the very same manuscript that he revised in 1968 after restoring the cuts made for the benefit of *Novy Mir*? Our analysis of the Stalin chapters would seem to suggest that there is insufficient evidence to prove conclusively whether Solzhenitsyn made extensive use of any other sources than those available to him in the USSR which he used for the original 87-chapter version of the novel: Stalin's own writings, official and unofficial biographies of Stalin, literary works of the 'cult' period, Khrushchev's 'Secret Speech', Djilas's *Conversations with Stalin*, and, most probably, the manuscript of Roy Medvedev's *Let History Judge*. Medvedev's work contains many psychological interpretations of Stalin's character which are echoed in *The First Circle* and may well have exerted the most significant influence on Solzhenitsyn.

The author has also made certain minor revisions to his original manuscript since his deportation from the USSR, possibly with the benefit of access to new materials, such as Khrushchev's memoirs, Allilueva's *Twenty Letters to a Friend* and the memoirs of Stalin's former secretary Bazhanov. For example, he has made certain details of Stalin's everyday life more exact, giving a more authentic description of Stalin's dacha at Kuntsevo,[149] and showing that even Stalin's closest associates called him 'Comrade Stalin' rather than 'Iosif Vissarionovich' – a detail which he could have obtained from the memoirs of either Khrushchev or Bazhanov.[150] Most of the new points Solzhenitsyn includes in the Stalin chapters, such as the reference to 'Nikita the dancer' – an allusion to the occasion on which Stalin forced Khrushchev to dance the Ukrainian gopak[151] – could, however, have been gleaned from oral sources while he was still in the USSR. Some of these details are still inexact, or, at least, unverifiable: for example, Solzhenitsyn describes a lock on Stalin's decanter, whereas Allilueva merely speaks of Stalin sipping wine from small glasses, and Khrushchev comments on Stalin's refusal to touch a dish or bottle before someone else had tested it;[152] Solzhenitsyn mentions the metro line specially extended to Stalin's dacha, but according to Medvedev this was not completed at the time of Stalin's death.[153] Although Solzhenitsyn has deliberately left out everything that might humanise Stalin, such as his relationship with his family or his love of his garden, he also fails to include the more extravagant, farcical rumours about Stalin which have proved attractive to such satirists as Voinovich, for example Stalin's idiosyncratic classification of his record collection.[154] It would seem that Solzhenitsyn preferred to omit the accidental and eccentric in Stalin's biography in order to concentrate on the typical. The attempt to depict Stalin as a Tsarist police spy was made while Solzhenitsyn was still in the USSR,[155] and possibly, again, his main sources were Roy Medvedev's manuscript and the Russian oral tradition. Since coming to the west he may have bolstered his preconceived opinion by reading such works as Isaac Don

Levine's *Stalin's Great Secret* or E. E. Smith's *The Young Stalin*, but there is no conclusive evidence that he used such sources. Moreover, works of western scholars such as Deutscher, Tucker and Ulam which contain a more objective, scholarly treatment of Stalin do not appear to be familiar to Solzhenitsyn. If he used such works to check his facts, he has not attempted to follow their approach.

Another open question is whether Solzhenitsyn, at the time he wrote the original manuscript of *The First Circle*, held the political views expressed in the revised version of the novel. Zhores Medvedev suggests that Solzhenitsyn has recently been busily engaged in rewriting all his earlier works in order to attack Lenin and Marxism, and that in the late 1950s and early 1960s 'he was an absolutely different person'.[156] Medvedev's view that 'The meaning of the novel is transformed in a way that makes it clear that Solzhenitsyn is no longer writing so much for a Russian audience as for his own messianic vision of future generations' is an interesting speculation which, contrary to Michael Nicholson's strongly argued view, does not amount to 'imputations of textual fraud'.[157] Medvedev ventures no suggestion as to how much material was added in the new version; and Solzhenitsyn himself claims that he did not wish to make major alterations to his literary works, because they belonged to an earlier phase of his development which he felt he should not change.[158] Nevertheless, as yet it is a matter of conjecture where the material in the 96-chapter version of *The First Circle* came from, and whether much of it was added in the west. The text of the new edition strongly suggests that Solzhenitsyn has, in fact, added certain polemical passages aimed against his present-day opponents, including Sakharov and the Medvedev brothers, and has changed the characters of Rubin and Sologdin as a result of his quarrel with their prototypes, Lev Kopelev and Dimitry Panin.[159] He has also included new passages dealing with some of his current concerns, such as the weakness of the west and the possibility of another world war. Solzhenitsyn's awareness of the dangers of re-Stalinisation in the USSR during the Brezhnev period is demonstrated by the statement: 'Stalin knew that with time people would forgive all the bad things, even forget them, and even remember them as good'.[160]

171

If Solzhenitsyn's portrait of Stalin is to be judged purely from the point of view of historical accuracy, it has certain defects. Solzhenitsyn, almost inevitably, falls into the danger of 'psycho-history'[161] – the limited view that history is merely the activity of individuals. Unlike Tolstoy, who discounts the role of individuals in history, Solzhenitsyn emphasises the great impact on Russian history of one individual of great evil, Stalin. However, by omitting every mitigating circumstance which might conceivably be used to analyse Stalin's character or to explain his policies, and by failing to take full account of the relationship between the individual and his milieu, Solzhenitsyn oversimplifies Stalin's record. Moreover, by omitting wider historical factors: the evils of the Tsarist system; the grievances and aspirations of the workers and peasants; the history of the Russian Social Democratic movement; the failure of the liberals and socialists in the Provisional government; the complexity of the forces and issues involved in the Civil War; the alternative views of the other socialist parties and of the oppositionist Communists in the 1920s, Solzhenitsyn, inevitably produces a narrow, one-sided view of the elements which created both Stalin and the Soviet Communist Party.

Boris Souvarine has characterised Solzhenitsyn's *Lenin in Zurich* as a 'diatribe against historical truth in the name of artistic licence'.[162] Such a harsh judgement is not appropriate in the case of Solzhenitsyn's new portrait of Stalin, which is a masterly psychological characterisation 'from the inside', even if, as we have seen, the author does deliberately ignore important socio-political and ideological factors in order to fit Stalin into his own preconceived mould. Solzhenitsyn's portrait does, however, differ totally in conception from a dispassionate biographical study by a historical scholar. He has made skilful use of certain specifically literary techniques – direct and indirect interior monologue and multiple levels of irony – in order to unveil the mind of the tyrant. All mitigating circumstances have now been removed from the portrait, thus weakening its literary effect, but making the author's bitter condemnation of his subject even more evident than it was in the original version. We are no longer invited to feel compassion for Stalin's illness and approaching death: Solzhenitsyn has largely cut the references to Stalin's fading memory, which formerly evoked a certain sympathy for his old age; we are now permitted merely to understand his 'fear'. Stalin's illness is now presented as a result of his overindulgence in food and drink; and Solzhenitsyn omits the phrase: 'Death had already woven his nest in him'. The main-spring of Solzhenitsyn's portrait in *Circle-96* is hatred rather than pity; the falsehood, megalomania, paranoid suspiciousness and satanic pride which animate the tyrant are now stripped bare. The greater bitterness of the satire and the much more explicit political comments in these new Stalin chapters render them closer in tone to Solzhenitsyn's early works written in captivity: *Feast of the Victors, The Captives* and *Prussian Nights*. Yet although the restraint and absence of didacticism which formed such notable features of Solzhenitsyn's first published works *One Day in the Life of Ivan Denisovich* and *Matryona's Home* are missing from the new *First Circle*, the portrait of Stalin still possesses much greater psychological depth and historical validity than the schematic cartoon figures of such liberals as Kerensky, Chkheidze and Milyukov in Solzhenitsyn's present work, *The Red Wheel*.

Chapter eight

Solzhenitsyn's portrait of Stalin: the philosophical dimension

As we have seen, if Solzhenitsyn's portrait of Stalin is judged entirely on the grounds of historical accuracy, many controversies arise. From the literary point of view, however, these controversial points can be treated as myths which add psychological and philosophical depth to Solzhenitsyn's character study. Daniel Rancour-Laferrière has provided an interesting psychoanalytical study of the character of Stalin created by Solzhenitsyn in *Circle-96*, concentrating on the pathological aspects of his personality, and, particularly, on seven clinical clusters of symptoms: paranoia; hyperdeveloped narcissism; megalomania; agoraphobia; obsessive power hunger; sadism (with associated masochism); and a defective conscience (an underdeveloped superego). He concludes that Solzhenitsyn has created a convincing psychological portrait of a fragmented, perverse and psychopathic personality, whether or not this depiction bore any relation to the historical Joseph Stalin.[1] Closely linked with Solzhenitsyn's psychological analysis is the most original aspect of his new portrait of Stalin: the metaphysical interpretation of Stalin's character. As Georges Nivat has convincingly argued in relation to *The Red Wheel*, Solzhenitsyn's historical research only makes sense in a wider context: his main concern is the religious and eschatalogical dimension.[2] Whereas in *Circle-87* religious themes were only implicit in the figure of Agnia and the use of religious imagery, they assume a much greater significance in *Circle-96*. The author now suggests that it was Stalin's original betrayal of God and attempt to usurp his throne that turned him into a living Satan, or Antichrist.

It is now clear that Solzhenitsyn was a religious believer at the time he wrote the original manuscript of *The First Circle*. During his time in the camps and the special prison he was influenced by various religious men, including George Gammerov and Dimitry Panin,[3] and a fellow prisoner introduced him to the writings of Vladimir Solovyov,[4] but he was still reluctant to commit himself. His ex-wife Reshetovskaya claims that he did not express any clear religious views in the letters he wrote to her from the camps.[5] Solzhenitsyn's return to religious faith occurred in 1952, during his treatment in hospital for cancer, when he met Boris Kornfeld, a Jew who had converted to Christianity;[6] after a period of sustained meditation on his life he wrote a prayer.[7] He asked to be baptised into the Russian Orthodox Church in 1957,[8] but largely concealed his faith in his works published in the USSR (the conversation between Ivan Denisovich and the Baptist Alyosha, for example, is ambiguous and equivocal). After the publication of the 1968 version of *The First Circle* Solzhenitsyn confirmed the religious interpretation of his work offered by the priest Alexander Schmemann. However, as Solzhenitsyn also admitted that Schmemann had 'explained himself to himself',[9] it is a matter of conjecture whether the author subsequently rewrote *The First Circle* to make the religious elements more explicit, or whether they were present in the original version which he later cut to allow the possibility of publication within the USSR.

It is certainly possible that Solzhenitsyn might have consciously and deliberately altered the manuscript of *The First Circle* in order to make it correspond more explicitly to Schmemann's congenial interpretation. Schmemann claims that Solzhenitsyn's work is based on 'the triune intuition of creation, fall and redemption'.[10] For Solzhenitsyn the world created by God was originally good but now 'lies in evil' because man has fallen from a state of grace and freely *chosen* evil; the rediscovery of personal conscience will, however, offer man the possibility of rebirth and salvation. Solzhenitsyn's revised portrait of Stalin is, like Dante's *Inferno*, clearly intended to illustrate 'the drama of the soul's choice'[11] – the process by which a human being freely chooses great evil. However, the suggestion that Solzhenitsyn substantially revised his interpretation after coming to the west appears somewhat less plausible in view of the fact that Solzhenitsyn in *The Gulag Archipelago*, written in the USSR in the years

1958–68, stated that the central experience inculcated by his time in prison was an understanding of 'how a human being becomes evil and how good'. Solzhenitsyn writes: 'Gradually it was disclosed to me that the line separating good and evil passes not through states, nor between classes, nor between political parties either – but right through every human heart – and through all human hearts . . . Since then I have come to understand the truth of all the religions of the world: they struggle with the evil inside a human being (inside every human being)'.[12] Solzhenitsyn borrows from physics the concept of the 'threshold magnitude' to express his belief that it is possible for a human being armed with an evil ideology to transcend the moral flux which all people experience, and to cross over a mystical threshold of evil: 'Evidently evildoing also has a threshold magnitude. Yes, a human being hesitates and bobs back and forth between good and evil all his life . . . But when, through the density of evil actions, the result either of their own extreme degree or of the absoluteness of his power, he suddenly crosses that threshold, he has left humanity behind, and without, perhaps, the possibility of return'.[13] Solzhenitsyn's portrait of Stalin is designed to depict a soul which has already irrevocably crossed the boundary between good and evil.

As has already been mentioned, the parallel between Stalin and Satan present in *Circle-87* is intensified in *Circle-96*. The revolt of the biblical Satan was caused by an outburst of pride, which led to his attempt to supplant God himself: 'Thou hast said in thy heart . . . I will exalt my throne above the stars of God . . . Yet thou shalt be brought down to hell, to the sides of the pit'.[14] Similarly, Solzhenitsyn makes Stalin's apostasy the original sin from which his satanic pride and tyrannical mangodhood stem. Stalin's distortion of true religion, both in his pact with the Orthodox Church and his misuse of biblical terminology, becomes a constant theme. Like Satan, Stalin has attempted to replace God; he feels himself to be a lonely being of great power soaring in a realm far above the earth, with only God, if he exists, as his rival. Like Satan too, Stalin's proud revolt has ended in punishment; he is incarcerated in the private hell of his windowless underground bunker, an immobile prisoner of night, time, space, mortality and the MVD troops who surround him.

The clearest expression of Solzhenitsyn's religious conception is in his description of Stalin's conduct during the war. The author suggests that Stalin betrayed Russia by leaving his country open to the German invasion; and he accentuates the parallel with Satan by emphasising that it is only after this supreme treachery to the divine order of the world that Stalin suffers for his betrayal of God. The passage in the first version of the novel outlining Stalin's anti-religious beliefs has been cut, and Solzhenitsyn depicts Stalin as being beset by childhood memories of the icons in church and his singing of the 'Nunc dimittis', and by the memory of his mother's dying words: 'What a pity you never became a priest'.[15] Stalin feels that Hitler has betrayed him, just as he betrayed God, and the German invasion is God's punishment on him. He prides himself that, unlike the atheists Lenin, Bukharin and Trotsky, he never spoke out against God; and when Hitler invades, he prays. The passage describing Stalin shutting himself in his room and really praying for the first time in his life is much more detailed than in the original version of the novel. Stalin vows that if the danger of the first crisis passes, 'he will restore the Church in Russia, and services, and will not allow persecution and imprisonment'.[16] The fact that Stalin, in one of his few positive acts, keeps his vow to God about the restoration of the Church, illustrates Solzhenitsyn's view expressed in *The Gulag Archipelago* that 'even within hearts overwhelmed by evil, one small bridgehead of good is retained'.[17] Solzhenitsyn does, however, make it clear that Stalin's view of religion is perverted – he has no conception of humility or human freedom, and feels that God must be 'much too good-natured, too lazy . . . How could he possess such power and endure everything?'. His complaint that 'Apart from that salvation in 1941 he never noticed that anyone else besides himself was in control of things. Not once had he nudged him, not once had he touched him',[18] demonstrates Stalin's lack of understanding of the spiritual nature of God and the true meaning of faith. Nevertheless, Stalin feels that if God does exist, he should make his peace with him before it is too late.

Solzhenitsyn's disapproval of the official Orthodox Church for its accommodation with the Soviet state, which first received clear expression in his *Lenten Letter* to Patriarch Pimen (1972), adds a new significance to the author's ironic treatment of Stalin's relationship with the Patriarch, who praises him as 'the

Leader Elect of God'[19]. Solzhenitsyn suggests that Stalin's ultimate treachery is to resurrect a crude parody of the nineteenth-century Russian values of Orthodoxy and Nationality, and to pretend that the Soviet Union he has created can be presented to the Russian people as the traditional Russian motherland: 'In this way it was as if his own power acquired greater stability. It was as though it were sacred'.[20] For Solzhenitsyn, to whom the traditional Russian values are sacred, Stalin's emphasis on a form of Orthodoxy and Russian nationalism congenial to himself is yet another form of apostasy. This view is explicitly stated later in the novel when the autobiographical Nerzhin describes Marxism-Leninism as a mistaken attempt to impose a materialist caricature of New Testament ideals through violence.[21]

In the Stalin chapters of *Circle-96* Solzhenitsyn intensifies the oblique symbolic parallels with ideas and imagery associated with Dante and Dostoevsky which existed in the earlier version of the novel. Solzhenitsyn's technique is to describe an actual feature of the life of the historical Stalin, and to build a metaphysical dimension on to it. One clear example of Solzhenitsyn's stylistic retouching is the more detailed physical description of Stalin which he provides, laying emphasis on the colour of his features: 'a yellow-eyed old man with reddish hair (which was portrayed as coal-black in paintings) ... with dark, uneven teeth'.[22] Such details are based on real descriptions of Stalin in the memoirs of Djilas and Trotsky,[23] but they also possess a symbolic significance: yellow, black and red are the colours of the three heads of Dante's Satan. Other characteristics of Dante's Satan paralleled in Solzhenitsyn's portrait are Stalin's immobility and imprisonment. In *Circle-87* Solzhenitsyn mentioned Stalin's fear of space, especially at the banquet for his seventieth birthday, and his liking for his narrow, claustrophobic study. In *Circle-96*, however, more emphasis is laid on his immobility: 'it did not cost a great effort to exclude himself from world space, not to move in it'.[24] Rancour-Laferrière interprets this merely as an example of Stalin's agoraphobia,[25] but it also has a deeper metaphysical significance: just as Dante's Satan is held immobile in the eternal ice of Cocytus, so Solzhenitsyn's Stalin is cut off from all the movements and communications of human life.

The image of Stalin as a prisoner is more clearly emphasised in the new version of *The First Circle*, recalling Dante's Satan who is imprisoned by his own sin. Just as Satan's attempts to free himself through flapping his huge wings merely make the ice freeze more firmly, thereby imprisoning him more securely, so Stalin is his own tormentor. Stalin feels that he has to live and suffer for another twenty years for the sake of the Russian people, 'like a prisoner with a twenty year sentence';[26] and the new stress on Stalin's windowless underground bunker is reminiscent of Satan's imprisonment in the deepest dungeon of the *Inferno*. Stalin's feeling of imprisonment has a basis in fact, for, as both Khrushchev and Roy Medvedev have shown, Stalin in his last years had a paranoid fear of the Georgian MGB troops under the command of Beria and Abakumov who formed his household bodyguard.[27] Solzhenitsyn uses a military image – the impossibility of knowing at the front which troops surround which – to demonstrate that Stalin is to some extent a prisoner of the MGB: 'Stalin had included himself (and the whole Central Committee) in the MGB system – everything he wore, ate, drank, anything he sat or lay on, everything had been obtained by MGB men, and only the MGB guarded him. So in some ironic, distorted sense Stalin himself was Abakumov's subordinate'.[28]

Rancour-Laferrière has interpreted the complaint of Solzhenitsyn's Stalin that he is imprisoned by the Russian people as 'a kind of identification with the abused object typical of sadism',[29] but the metaphysical resonances of this image were probably more important to the author. As Georges Nivat has shown, Stalin's morbid attachment to his voluntary incarceration in the Kremlin bunker and his solitary rambling monologue are designed to afford a striking contrast to the spiritual freedom gained by the true captives in the special prison through intellectual exploration and dialogue. Solzhenitsyn's own interpretation of Stalin's lack of freedom was clarified in an essay in the collection *From under the Rubble*: 'The most important part of our freedom, inner freedom, is always subject to our will. If we surrender it to corruption, we do not deserve to be called human'.[30] Solzhenitsyn's Stalin, like Dante's Satan, is a prisoner of his own evil, and, like Dostoevsky's Grand Inquisitor, feels himself to be a prisoner of time who is condemned to live until the age of 90. This is, of course, highly ironic, for both the author and his readers know that death will release the condemned man long before the end of his sentence.

In his description of Stalin's insomnia and strange hours of work, a subject long banned in the USSR, although graphically evoked in Khrushchev's memoirs,[31] Solzhenitsyn invests another real feature of Stalin's life with a deeper metaphysical meaning. He emphasises that Stalin, like Satan, shuns the sun, the light of life and the symbol of God: 'Most intolerable of all for Stalin was the morning and noontime: while the sun rose, played, climbed to its zenith, Stalin slept in the darkness, shuttered, enclosed, locked in'. Just as in Dante's Judecca time is the opposite of time in the 'bright world' above, so Stalin sleeps during the hours of sunshine, the morning and afternoon; he livens up at sunset, although he is still 'mistrustful, gloomy'; it is only after the long meals with his cronies, at about 2 a.m., before dawn, that Stalin thinks up 'his chief directives, which ruled the great state'.[32] Solzhenitsyn omits from *Circle-96* the earlier reference to Stalin's sunny, book-lined day study, thus intensifying his fear of space and hatred of the light. Stalin's love of the dark is designed to contrast with the beautiful morning light which comes to baptise the prisoners of Marfino, offering them a mystical second birth. The repeated word *svetalo* ('it was getting light') is used to introduce the description at the end of Chapter 25 of the newborn light of day bathing the Church of the Martyr Nicetas (which Yakonov, the future governor of the special prison, shuns), and the scene at the beginning of Chapter 26 in which Sologdin, a prisoner who can 'only breathe fresh air at definite times permitted by the prison authorities', glories in the 'miracle' of the morning with a sense of 'unshakeable peace' and 'the fullness of being'.[33]

Solzhenitsyn himself has admitted that he feels 'spiritually close' to Dostoevsky.[34] Svyatoslav Ruslanov and Vladislav Krasnov have convincingly analysed the echoes of Dostoevskian themes in *Circle-87* and, in particular, demonstrated that Solzhenitsyn's Stalin is not only an epigone of the Grand Inquisitor in *The Brothers Karamazov*, but also a historical product of his spiritual crossbreeding with other Dostoevskian 'mangods' and 'devils', notably Shigalyov, Stavrogin and Pyotr Verkhovensky in *The Devils* and Svidrigailov and Raskolnikov in *Crime and Punishment*.[35] Both commentators, however, leave the question open as to whether this resemblance to Dostoevsky's 'devils' was a product of the writer's deliberate effort or based on certain actual features of the historical Stalin. *Circle-96* demonstrates conclusively that Solzhenitsyn was aware of these parallels and sought to strengthen them, drawing on certain of Stalin's character traits which are often highly speculative, but always grounded in possibility.

In *Circle-96* Solzhenitsyn lays more stress on Stalin's scorn of 'the people', a prominent feature which he shares with the Grand Inquisitor. Just as, for the Grand Inquisitor, the masses are a mere 'herd' of obedient, helpless sheep, for Stalin they are an expendable rabble: 'The crowd is like the matter of history. (Note that down!) However much disappears from one place will reappear in another. So there is no point in conserving it'.[36] Like the Grand Inquisitor, who believes the people need to be ruled by 'miracle, mystery and authority', and Pyotr Verkhovensky, who wishes to present Stavrogin to the people as a god, Stalin, conditioned by his religious upbringing, feels that the Russian people need a god to believe in, and constant 'correct explanations' to set them on the right course: 'The Revolution had left the Russian people orphaned and godless, and that was dangerous. For twenty years, as far as he could, Stalin had corrected this situation'. Stalin has created the 'personality cult' of himself for the benefit of the people, but, like the Grand Inquisitor, is a 'sufferer for humanity'; he gains no personal pleasure from his position: 'It was necessary, but not for the Leader – it no longer gave him any joy, he had become accustomed to it long ago – it was necessary for his subjects . . . '.[37] He removes the burden of thought from the people's shoulders: 'Thinking was his duty. And thinking was also his fate and his punishment'.[38]

Solzhenitsyn constantly stresses the emptiness and joylessness of Stalin's old age; even food and women have ceased to give him pleasure any more. Like Stavrogin, Stalin is 'neither cold, nor hot', but indifferent to everything; although he sets himself up as a rival to God – a point emphasised by Solzhenitsyn's use of the godlike attribute 'Almighty' – he lives in a metaphysical void and, like all Dostoevsky's atheists, is suffused with a cosmic boredom. He is spiritually isolated; his house is filled with a 'deaf-mute silence'; and he has to fight time like an illness, constantly thinking up things to do: 'It was necessary to find somewhere to put that empty, long time'. When he is not working or drinking with his lieutenants, life is an ordeal to him: 'And through the remaining hours it was necessary to crawl, as though along sharp stones'.[39]

The parallel with Dostoevsky's 'devils' and the Grand Inquisitor, who proves to be in league with Satan, 'the spirit of destruction and non-being', becomes even closer when Solzhenitsyn emphasises the unreality of Stalin's existence. He looks at his secretary Poskryobyshev with 'a listless, half-alive gaze' and feels 'alienation from all living things'; like Stavrogin, he is already spiritually dead and almost physically dead. His impression that nothing exists outside himself evokes the extreme spiritual isolation of Dostoevsky's atheists who set up their own self-will to rival the will of God. The mist which fills the garden of Stalin's dacha recalls both the fog in the abyss of Dante's Judecca and the mist swirling around Svidrigailov in *Crime and Punishment* as he goes to shoot himself. Stalin lives in a world of abstractions, and Russia itself has become a non-existent abstraction to him: 'He could not even see the country . . . When after the war he had travelled to the south several times he had seen only empty, dead space . . . nothing of the live Russia'.[40] Once again Solzhenitsyn starts from certain real features of Stalin's life – his total lack of contact with the real Russia, and the regal isolation in which he travelled[41] – in order to emphasise his spiritual isolation: 'If he travelled by car, the road stretched out empty, and there were no people on the strip alongside it. If he travelled by train, the stations died'. The repetition of the word 'empty' and the use of the words 'dead' and 'died' intensify the evocation of Stalin's loneliness and non-being. In *Circle-87* Solzhenitsyn had alluded to Stalin's desire to phone Beria for advice, perhaps as a concession to 'the Beria version' – the original story propagated by the Party leaders after Beria's execution in 1953 that Beria had been largely responsible for Stalin's crimes.[42] In the revised version, however, the reference to Beria is omitted, and Stalin's alienation from his daughter Svetlana is also emphasised. Solzhenitsyn now stresses Stalin's utter loneliness: 'He was feeling more and more strongly that he was alone, not only in his dacha in Kuntsevo, but in general, in the whole of Russia, that the whole of Russia was invented . . . Stalin was so alone that he had no one to check himself by, no one to whom he could relate'.[43]

Dostoevskian themes are also implicit in Solzhenitsyn's

portrayal of Stalin's political ideas. He suggests that Stalin's conception of communism is quite different from Lenin's prediction of 'the withering away of the state', nor is it identical to the Grand Inquisitor's dream of a happy, well-fed, but enslaved humanity. Solzhenitsyn deviates from his usual technique of reproducing Stalin's own words, altering Stalin's infamous statement of 1937 that class struggles intensify with the approach of socialism in order to convey his own view that Stalin has not only built socialism, but has already attained the stage of communism, which is nothing other than Stalin's totalitarian state. Here Solzhenitsyn comes close to the view of Alexander Zinoviev, who in the 1970s defined communism as the society which already existed in the USSR.[44] Solzhenitsyn may also be hinting that the official Soviet definition of the current state of the country's development as 'developed socialism', a phrase coined in Brezhnev's time, deliberately avoids the epithet 'communism', as this would mean that there was nothing further to strive towards, and would undermine the whole teleological basis of Soviet ideology: the aim of creating a perfect society. Indeed, the whole of *The First Circle*, with its extended image of hell, is an ironic comment on the Soviet dream of the 'earthly paradise'. In Solzhenitsyn's opinion the reality of Stalin's communist empire is worse even than the Inquisitor's fantasy of a human 'anthill'; it is closer to the view of Shigalyov, the gloomy theorist in Dostoevsky's *The Devils*, that 'All shall be equal and all shall be slaves'. Solzhenitsyn emphasises this view by omitting from *Circle-96* the reference in *Circle-87* to Stalin's desire to force people to be happy; Stalin's aim is not now, like the Grand Inquisitor's, to make people happy, but 'in a word, to build communism'. Through his subversion of Stalin's interior monologue Solzhenitsyn both distorts the Grand Inquisitor's dream and undermines the entire Soviet fantasy of the communist utopia: 'Short-sighted naive people imagine communism as a kingdom of plenty and freedom from necessity. But that would be an impossible society, everyone would be at everyone else's throat, such communism would be worse than bourgeois anarchy. The first main feature of true communism must be discipline, strict obedience to leaders and fulfilment of all orders'.

The second feature of Stalin's communism is a deliberate

policy of failing to give his people enough to eat in order to starve them into submission: 'People must only have a very moderate amount to eat, insufficient even, because totally replete people fall into ideological disarray, as we see in the West'. Just as the Grand Inquisitor claims to be acting in the name of Christ, so Stalin justifies his totalitarian state with a distorted version of Marxist dogma: 'If man stops worrying about his food, he will be free from the material force of history, existence will stop determining consciousness, and everything will be topsy-turvy'.[45] Stalin's attitude recalls Alyosha Karamazov's interpretation of the Grand Inquisitor's lofty-sounding scheme: 'It's the most ordinary lust for power, for filthy earthly gains, enslavement – something like a future regime of serfdom with them as the landowners – that is all they are after'. Alyosha's verdict is confirmed in *Circle-96* by Stalin's meditation on the coercion and violence necessary to force the reluctant peasants into the collective farms. Solzhenitsyn implies that collectivisation is indeed a new form of serfdom with Stalin and his henchmen as the new masters. The tyrannical lust for power enshrined in Stalin's communist system is emphasised by the renaming of the chapter 'Old Age' to 'The Emperor of the Earth', and the use of the epithet 'Ruler' instead of the ironic 'Immortal One'. Like Satan, Stalin has become 'the prince of this world', and his desire to become Emperor of the Earth resembles the 'Caesarian' dream of the Grand Inquisitor. Solzhenitsyn suggests that by rejecting the divine order of the universe and setting himself up as a rival to God Stalin has become the personification of Satan on earth,[46] a Dostoevskian 'man-god' for whom the existence of God and the 'God-man' Christ is 'an unclear question'.[47]

Chapter nine

Solzhenitsyn's portrait of Stalin: the literary aspect

A detailed examination of Solzhenitsyn's style in *Circle-96* is beyond the scope of this study.[1] The purpose of the present chapter is to examine Solzhenitsyn's technique of character portrayal, particularly in the new Chapter 20, concentrating on three main issues: point of view, use of irony and choice of vocabulary.

Point of view

Solzhenitsyn's skilful manipulation of points of view has frequently been noted, especially in connection with *One Day in the Life of Ivan Denisovich*.[2] Gary Kern, in the only detailed study of Solzhenitsyn's literary technique in the Stalin chapters of *Circle-87*, has distinguished four separate voices: the omniscient author; the character's 'indirect interior monologue'; the ironic author; and the character's 'direct discourse'.[3] Kern's analysis is useful and illuminating, but not entirely appropriate for the new version of the chapters. His approach is at one and the same time over-complicated, distinguishing as it does between four separate voices instead of the two main viewpoints – that of the narrator and the character – and over-simplified, because his choice of clear, unambiguous examples of the different 'voices' does not do full justice to the ambiguity of Solzhenitsyn's technique, in which the two voices of the narrator and character often blend together to such an extent that they cannot be distinguished apart with certainty.

Since Solzhenitsyn employs all his techniques of characterisation, including quoted dialogue, in the first of the Stalin chapters in *Circle-96*, the new Chapter 19 (whereas in *Circle-87* the dimension of dialogue was only added in the last Stalin chapter), the long biographical Chapter 20 represents a continuation, rather than a culmination of Solzhenitsyn's strategy of character portrayal. In Chapter 20 Solzhenitsyn intersperses two main techniques: authorial narration (omniscient and ironic), and the interior monologue of the character (indirect and direct). The narrative voice in the Stalin chapters has several functions. In the first place, it focuses attention on the character's surroundings, as, for example, in the description of Stalin's room at the beginning of Chapter 19. Secondly, it is used to convey the author's analysis of his character, presenting Stalin's psychology 'from the outside', often imparting information which was not available to Stalin himself. Solzhenitsyn employs this method to particular effect in describing Stalin's illness and emphasising the contrast between Stalin's extraordinary fame and his personal insignificance. Thirdly, authorial narration is used to express the author's own point of view. The most obvious examples of this are the occasional direct, sarcastic authorial interpolations, for example:

'Thus the future great marshal began his military career.'
'So even the nationality question laughed at him in those difficult years.'
'Stalin himself had no pretensions to fame or leadership.'[4]

It is significant that Solzhenitsyn uses authorial narration to depict most of Stalin's early life up to the 1917 revolution. This demonstrates Solzhenitsyn's desire to present an objective, rounded view of the young Stalin, and, at the same time, perhaps, betrays his awareness that his account of Stalin's youth and career as a police agent is not based on sufficient solid evidence to be more than just a 'version' which he has chosen to relate.[5] The main characteristics of Solzhenitsyn's narrative style are the use of literary sentences; an absence of direct emotional statements in conversational syntax; and the inclusion of more complex grammatical forms, such as participles and gerunds.[6]

In his presentation of the character's point of view Solzhenitsyn makes extensive use of the technique of 'narrated monologue', which has been defined by Dorrit Cohn as 'the rendering of a character's thoughts in his own idiom, while maintaining the

third-person form of narration'.[7] (The term 'narrated monologue' will be used in preference to the confused term 'indirect
interior monologue', since the form of narration, although
ambiguous, is not strictly speaking indirect.) This method
enables Solzhenitsyn to represent Stalin's silent thoughts without
a break in the narrative thread. The use of the third person
(occasionally the second person) and the past or conditional
tenses, the customary tenses of epic narration, eliminates the
explicit distance between the author and character, allowing
Solzhenitsyn to depict the inner and outer scene with continuity
and simultaneity and to glide imperceptibly from the author to
the character. The syntactical structure is that of direct discourse,
with the rhythms of spoken language rendered through exclam-
ations, rhetorical questions, repetitions and the idiosyncrasies
of Stalin's style. The technique of 'narrated monologue' is a
most powerful tool by which Solzhenitsyn locates the viewpoint
directly within the psyche of his character, plunging the reader
into the immediate here and now of Stalin's experiencing
consciousness. Moreover, it can transform itself easily into
something resembling 'direct discourse' – the representation of
Stalin's interior monologue in the present tense (although it
cannot strictly be called 'direct discourse', as Solzhenitsyn always
avoids the first person).

One short example will serve to show how skilfully and easily
Solzhenitsyn manipulates this interplay of voices: 'Koba was
surprised, bewildered [omniscient author]. Had he been mistaken again? [narrated monologue]. But why doesn't he see
anything beforehand? [narrated monologue in the present tense].
The Okhrana had deceived him! [narrated monologue and ironic
author]. His will then was not merely not made of steel, but was
completely split into two' (ironic author).[8] The transition
between past and present tense is achieved much more smoothly
and easily in Russian than in English, sometimes through the use
of indirect statement, sometimes without: 'The October Revolution was also an adventure, but it succeeded, so well and good. It
succeeded. Fine [narrated monologue]. Lenin can be given full
marks for that. What will happen in the future is uncertain, but
it's all right now. Commissar of nationalities? Fine, so be it.
Compose a constitution. Fine, so be it [interior monologue in
present tense]. Stalin got used to it' (authorial narration).[9]

Solzhenitsyn employs the present tense to convey the immediacy of Stalin's thoughts, and, sometimes, to evoke the dichotomy between Stalin's feelings and memories in the present and the authorial narrative about his past. One example of this occurs when Stalin looks at the photograph of himself as a young man: 'He is all ready to strive for something, but he doesn't know what for. What a nice young man! An open, clever, energetic face without a trace of the bigoted novice'.[10]

At the end of Chapter 20 Solzhenitsyn adds a new dimension to his representation of Stalin's interior monologue by rendering Stalin's thoughts in a Georgian accent to emphasise the dictator's growing anger as he is carried away by suspicion and hatred of Tito. Stalin's paranoia grows as he ponders on the reasons why communism has not yet been achieved in the USSR. The long list of obstacles to his plan is at first punctured by commas; then by exclamation marks as his targets become more and more unlikely: 'If it were not for greedy housewives! Spoiled children!'; then, finally, Stalin stutters in fury and breaks into direct speech in a heavy Georgian accent:

> 'When it was already clear to everyone that communism
> was on the right road and wasn't far from completion – that
> cretin Tito thrusts himself forward with his Talmudist
> Kardelj and states that communism must be built
> differently!!!' At this point Stalin realised that he was
> speaking out loud.[11]

Here Solzhenitsyn takes the mimicry of Stalin's interior monologue to its furthest extreme; he loses his sense of aesthetic restraint and allows sarcasm to express too obviously his hatred of his subject.

Although narrated monologue in the present tense is occasionally used to emphasise the present, immediate quality of Stalin's thoughts, narrated monologue in the past tense is Solzhenitsyn's basic method of character delineation. It is the most common technique used to relate Stalin's biography after 1917, when the facts are not in dispute. It is also the chief method by which irony is conveyed. When discussing the new version of the Stalin chapters Kern's term 'the ironic author' is misleading, for the author's irony is conveyed mainly through the character's narrated monologue. As Cohn has demonstrated, this technique is essentially ambiguous: in third person narration the author's intelligence is always felt behind the character's, and the presence of the unobtrusive narrator ensures the duality or ambiguity of the vision. The mimetic, imitative qualities of the narrated monologue admit of two divergent possibilities: a lyric fusion of the author with his subject or a distance from the subject, a mock-identification which leads to satire.[12] In Solzhenitsyn's portrait of Stalin the distance between author and character is immediately evident, although the use of narrated monologue means that the author's view remains implicit and ironic. Yet however devastating the irony, the attempted empathy implied in narrated monologue is not entirely cancelled, and the reader retains the impression of having understood Stalin 'from the inside'.

Irony

The principal irony in Solzhenitsyn's portrait lies in the contrast between the viewpoint of the author and that of the character. Stalin sees himself as a hero, whereas the author (and reader) see him as a monster. Stalin's view of the improvement in the party in the 1920s is diametrically opposed to the author's opinion that Stalin turned a revolutionary party into a bureaucratic apparatus. Other particularly blatant examples of the distance between author and character are the self-satisfaction which Stalin feels at the 'justice' he attained through the purges organised by the Workers' and Peasants' Inspectorate in the 1920s and the later strenuous 'efforts' he undertook to purge the party in the 1930s; his belief that 'it is necessary' to sacrifice even his friends and helpers for the cause; his faith in Hitler and his resentment at the Russian people's initial failure to resist the Germans (although he himself had weakened the country on the eve of war). Sometimes Stalin's statements are so grotesque that the satire becomes excessively bitter: for example, his view that executions without trial win people's respect; and his exaggerated opinion of his military prowess in the Civil War: 'And to tell the truth, he demonstrated himself to be a great soldier, the architect of victory'.[13] Solzhenitsyn subverts Stalin's inner monologue by emphasising his narcissism and high opinion of himself:

'And his whole great life would be cut short on some
Belorussian farm . . .'
'Only he alone, Stalin . . .'
'His iron will, his inexorable will.'[14]

Another source of irony lies in the contrast between Stalin's
perceptions and the reader's greater knowledge of the historical
process. When explaining Stalin's alleged decision to become a
police spy, Solzhenitsyn uses narrated monologue to convey
Stalin's mistaken view that revolution in Russia is improbable:
'The most unbridled imagination could not envisage revolution
in Russia in less than fifty years, when Joseph would be 73 years
old . . . Why would he need a revolution then?'.[15] Stalin's contemptuous attitude towards Khrushchev is also ironic in view of
the fact that Khrushchev denounced Stalin at the Twentieth and
Twenty-Second Congresses. Similarly, Stalin's conviction that
no other form of socialism than his own is possible is ironic in the
light of Tito's successful rule in Yugoslavia.

There are also occasions when Stalin himself appears to be
ironising about his past relations with his enemies within the
party. Stalin looks back with malign satisfaction at the series of
alliances he made with his rivals in the 1920s: at first, during
Lenin's illness, Kamenev and Zinoviev become his 'best friends',
and subsequently, in order to prevent the reading of Lenin's
Testament, 'He becomes even closer friends with Zinoviev'.
Solzhenitsyn shows that the triumvirate temporarily provides
Stalin with a useful support against Trotsky, but that he manages
at the same time to dissociate himself subtly from his colleagues,
since 'He foresaw that Kamenev was not immortal either'. Here
the author's heavy sarcasm mingles with the ironic hindsight of
his character, who caused the death of his erstwhile 'great
friends' in the 1930s. When Zinoviev and Kamenev 'suddenly
turned out to be hypocrites, double-dealers who wanted power',
Stalin forms a new 'great warm friendship' with the young
theoretician known by the pet name of 'Bukharchik', who later,
by some 'fatal surprise' also 'turned out' to be opposed to the
unity of the party.[16] By his ironic use of the impersonal verb
'turned out' (*okazalos'*) and such words as 'suddenly' and
'surprise' the author subverts his character's interior monologue,
implying that, although Stalin caused these events to happen, his
selective memory tricks him into believing that they occurred of

their own accord, independently of him. A similar technique is used to evoke Stalin's memory of the waves of purges in the 1930s. In these passages about Stalin's treachery towards his former associates the voice of the ironic author is perhaps most insistent, although by his use of narrated monologue Solzhenitsyn also tries to show that Stalin justified his actions by the firm belief that he alone was the guardian of party unity and the only 'sane' man capable of 'formulating the correct slogans' and leading the party.[17]

Another ironic technique used by Solzhenitsyn is the puncturing of the myths which the Stalin cult wove around the figure of the dictator. Throughout the novel he ridicules the titles which Stalin has taken to himself, some ludicrous, some blasphemous: the Leader of All Progressive Humanity, the Best Friend of Counter-intelligence Operatives, the Most Brilliant Strategist of All Times and Peoples, Little Father, Greatest Genius of Geniuses, the Omnipotent, the Immortal One. In the 'Stalin chapters' such epithets are frequently used in a context which underlines their absurdity: for example Stalin is referred to as 'the Nearest and Dearest' when he asks Abakumov if he is not afraid of being shot; 'the Greatest of the Great' when he remembers the possibility of God's existence; and 'the Wisest of the Wise' before he writes his pedestrian article on linguistics.

Solzhenitsyn constantly polemicises with writers of the 'cult' period whose eulogies of Stalin he read in his youth. The portrait of Stalin is introduced by a bathetic contrast between the hyperbolic exaltation of Stalin and the reality of the small, ugly, ailing man. Moreover, as Maria Shneerson has noted, Solzhenitsyn uses phrases culled from laudatory works about Stalin, such as 'Stalin said sincerely', 'he spoke so simply and benevolently', 'Stalin looked with a wise, penetrating gaze', in a context which emphasises their incongruity, such as Stalin's decision to reintroduce the death penalty and his announcement to Abakumov of a new wave of repressions.[18] Sometimes the irony resides in Stalin's use of false analogies typical of those used by his flatterers in works of the 'cult' period: as in a folk *bylina* he sees himself as a hero and Tito as the dragon; and although he is imprisoned in an underground bunker, he imagines himself, in Antonov-Ovseenko's phrase, as a 'mountain eagle'.[19] Solzhenitsyn explicitly ridicules the images of Stalin in Vishnevsky's

Unforgettable 1919 and a film based on Virta's play *Great Days*. Stalin feels that 'A much truer appreciation of the part he had played in the Civil War, not to mention his role in the War for the Fatherland, was emerging. It was now becoming clear what a great man he had been even then. He well remembered the many occasions on which he had had to advise and restrain the impetuous, superficial Lenin'. Virta's play particularly appeals to him because of the scene with the imaginary Friend, even though Stalin has never had such a close, devoted friend in his life.[20]

Solzhenitsyn also implies criticism of the cautious depictions of Stalin in Soviet fiction of the post-Stalin era. Lev Loseff has suggested that the depiction in *Circle-87* of a professor of medicine in danger of arrest for handing a medicine to a foreigner was a deliberate parody of Simonov's play *The Alien Shadow*, in which a scientist is condemned for 'cosmopolitanism'.[21] Since Simonov is the prototype of the opportunist writer Galakhov in Solzhenitsyn's novel, it can be assumed that Solzhenitsyn was familiar with the portraits of Stalin in Simonov's war novels of the 1950s and early 1960s, which, even at the height of de-Stalinisation, contained only half-truths.[22]

Solzhenitsyn also creates an ironic effect by suggesting that Stalin's real thoughts about historical events at the time were different from the later version propagated in official biographies of him. There is an irony, for example, in the difference between Stalin's real thoughts about Lenin and 1917, when he did very little to advance the Bolshevik cause and felt 'In general 1917 was an unpleasant year',[23] and the subsequent myth about his revolutionary career. Similarly, Solzhenitsyn deflates the myths about Stalin's great military genius in the Civil War and his claim to be Lenin's closest disciple and obvious successor. Behind Stalin's use of such loaded expressions as 'dear Ilyich', whom he did not allow to dictate for more than five minutes a day during his illness 'in the interests of his precious life', we learn that Stalin's real attitude to Lenin is diametrically opposed to the solicitude and compassion he pretends to feel.[24]

Solzhenitsyn also uses the ironic technique of saying the opposite of what the reader expects in order to emphasise the tortuous, amoral nature of Stalin's thought. During the Civil War Stalin learns through his conflict with Trotsky that 'not all methods are good in battle, there are forbidden methods'.

However, instead of presenting execution without trial as one of the 'forbidden methods', as conventional morality might dictate, Solzhenitsyn's Stalin learns the opposite: 'Even in the most intense battle you shouldn't appeal to good nature ... if you don't shoot without trial you can't do anything in history'.[25] The last sentence is an example of Solzhenitsyn's use of what Kern calls 'the falsely positive statement':[26] the categorical statement of a falsehood which exposes Stalin's perverted morality. Another example is Stalin's megalomaniac belief that he alone can lead the party.

Another source of irony is Stalin's characterisation of other people in terms which could equally well apply to him. Stalin complains of Trotsky's arrogant conduct during the Civil War: 'And what of his arrogance? Like the Tsar himself, he rushed about in a saloon carriage. And why try to climb up to be commander-in-chief if you haven't got a bent for strategy?'.[27] This is highly ironic in view of Stalin's later habit of travelling in sealed railway carriages, and his pretensions to brilliant strategic genius in the Second World War. Similarly, Stalin's characteris- ation of Tito as a 'vain, touchy, cruel, cowardly, revolting, hypocritical, base tyrant' covered with medals despite his lack of martial skills, is an appropriate depiction of Stalin himself.[28]

Another level of irony resides in the fact that, as has already been noted in Chapter 7, Solzhenitsyn and Stalin sometimes appear to share the same views (although, naturally, for very different reasons). Stalin, for example, pours scorn on the short sentences handed out to political prisoners by the Tsarist government – a point frequently made by Solzhenitsyn in *The Gulag Archipelago* in order to contrast the leniency of the Tsarist regime with the harshness of Stalin's penal system. Solzhenitsyn and his character also appear to be allies in their contempt for all the other Bolshevik leaders, in their belief that the October Revolution was merely a lucky accident, and in their mockery of Marxist-Leninist ideology. Stalin's view of Lenin, in particular, appears to correspond to Solzhenitsyn's presentation of Lenin's character in *Lenin in Zurich*.[29] For the reader aware of Solzheni- tsyn's political views, this alliance between author and character appears rather bizarre, and detracts somewhat from the credi- bility of Solzhenitsyn's Stalin as an autonomous character independent of his creator.

Vocabulary

Solzhenitsyn's successful imitation of the rhythms of Stalin's own style testifies to his close study of Stalin's writings. As Edward J. Brown has shown, this is particularly evident in the chapter 'Language as a Tool of Production', which contains direct quotations from Stalin's 1950 article on linguistics, interspersed with the author's representation of the train of thought leading to these statements.[30] In the new version of this chapter Solzhenitsyn cites a further section of the article and conveys Stalin's meditation on the need to revise Marxist teaching about revolution, replacing it with an emphasis on evolution or 'revolution from above'. Moreover, in his evocation of Stalin's interior monologue Solzhenitsyn uses a famous phrase from the article, 'an Arakcheev regime',[31] to evoke Stalin's totally disingenuous criticism of the cults of infallible authorities which had been created in many branches of science and scholarship on the model of the cult of Stalin's own personality. In Chapter 20, in the passage of narrated monologue rendered in a Georgian accent, Solzhenitsyn takes this mimicry even further, reproducing Stalin's liking for litany-like repetition and invocation of the same theme or person (possibly inherited from his Orthodox upbringing) and his use of the phrases 'it is clear to everyone' and 'it is not accidental' to introduce highly dubious statements.[32]

Another aspect of Stalin's style which Solzhenitsyn particularly emphasises is his predilection for biblical phraseology:

'The mills of history grind slowly, but they grind exceeding small . . . '
'Inscrutable are Thy ways, o Lord!'[33]

In *Circle-96* Solzhenitsyn seeks to demonstrate Stalin's distorted use of religious terminology directly through Stalin's own interior monologue; he omits certain explicit authorial interventions which were included in the first version of the novel, such as 'The angel of medieval teleology looked over his shoulder'.[34]

In *Circle-96* Solzhenitsyn lays more stress on Stalin's distortion of Marxist terminology to express his own un-Marxist ideas: for example, Stalin misuses such terms as 'basis' and 'superstructure' to express his belief that he is a realist, as opposed to impractical intellectuals like Lenin and Trotsky. When Stalin writes his article on linguistics the author's voice merges with the character's to allude to the narrowness of Marxist dogma: 'and there was no third way, as always in Marxism'.[35] This new emphasis in the Stalin chapters corresponds to the greater significance attached in the rest of the novel to a critique of Marxist-Leninist ideology, particularly in the new Chapter 88, 'Dialectical Materialism – the Progressive World-View'.

Throughout Stalin's monologue Solzhenitsyn emphasises Stalin's crudeness and sarcastic attitude towards his opponents. He showers vituperative abuse on the Georgian Mensheviks, Lenin and Trotsky, and subsequently on the 'enemies of the people' whom he purges, such as Tukhashevsky, Zinoviev and Kamenev, and on the inept western leaders Churchill and Roosevelt whom he outwits. Solzhenitsyn lays a special emphasis on Stalin's Great Russian chauvinism and anti-Semitism, which characterise his attitude to Trotsky, Zinoviev, Kamenev and the revolutionaries as a whole, whom he sees as 'babblers' and 'wedge-beards' who are undermining the very foundations of the Russian empire.[36]

A psycho-linguistic analysis of the vocabulary of Lenin and Stalin has established that Stalin's vocabulary contains more aggressive oral and anal imagery than Lenin's, and far more death imagery.[37] In his evocation of Stalin's interior monologue Solzhenitsyn sometimes reproduces such imagery: for example, Stalin speaks of the need to 'clear away' Ezhov and to 'root out' rebellious youth; and he reflects:

'all his enemies will go away, die, be ground into dung'
'those Western Social Democrats had to be smoked out of their holes and finished off like rabbits'
'he made his enemies trample themselves down.'[38]

However, Solzhenitsyn's use of such imagery is limited, and in *Circle-96* he actually omits some strikingly aggressive imagery contained in *Circle-87*: for example,

'he had to lead people to happiness and shove their noses into it, like making a blind puppy drink milk'
'First lash the executioners into a fury of activity, then disown them at the critical moment.[39]

Since such vocabulary was typical of Stalin's style, it can only be assumed that Solzhenitsyn decided to omit these powerful passages for reasons of taste, perhaps in order to tone down the aggressive force of the satire in *Circle-87*, which had aroused considerable criticism.

Conclusion

In his analysis of Stalin's character in *Circle-96* Solzhenitsyn uses the same techniques of character portrayal as in *Circle-87*, with a greatly expanded use of narrated monologue in both past and present tenses. Apart from his occasional use of narrated monologue in a Georgian accent, Solzhenitsyn follows the traditions of character delineation typical of nineteenth-century Russian novelists, especially Tolstoy and Dostoevsky. He makes extended use of both 'internal analysis' by the narrator and 'narrated monologue' – the presentation of a character's thoughts at the upper level of consciousness, which can be translated into articulate speech – but at no time does he approach the 'stream of consciousness' technique characteristic of many modern novels since James Joyce's *Ulysses*.

One question worth considering is whether Solzhenitsyn's technique can be termed 'polyphonic'. Solzhenitsyn himself borrowed the term 'polyphonic' from Bakhtin's famous analysis of Dostoevsky in order to describe his own favourite form of novel: 'What genre seems to me most interesting? The polyphonic novel with precise indications of time and place. The novel without a principal hero'.[40] Since Solzhenitsyn himself used this term and claimed that he had written two novels – *The First Circle* and *Cancer Ward* – using the 'polyphonic method',[41] many western commentators use it uncritically in their assessment of Solzhenitsyn's work.[42] However, Bakhtin used the expression 'polyphony' to mean that in Dostoevsky's work the voices of the characters attain independence from the voice of the author. There is no evidence that Solzhenitsyn was specifically using the term 'polyphony' in the Bakhtinian sense to describe his own work; indeed, he defines the term quite differently: 'What do I understand by polyphony? Each character becomes the central character when he enters the field of action.

The author is thus obliged to answer for 35 heroes. He gives preference to none of them. He must understand and motivate all his characters.'[43] If the word is defined in this way, Solzhenitsyn's technique in the Stalin chapters can be regarded as polyphonic, since Stalin becomes the central character in the narrative; however, Solzhenitsyn's method cannot be considered completely polyphonic in the Bakhtinian sense, because Stalin's consciousness is not presented entirely from the character's point of view. In any case, Bakhtin's use of the term 'polyphony' to describe Dostoevsky's method is itself controversial, because, as Roy Pascal demonstrates, he underestimates the importance of the narrator in Dostoevsky and the possibility of irony in narrated monologue.[44] Solzhenitsyn's technique does, nevertheless, bear some comparison with that of Dostoevsky, because his use of irony and occasional direct authorial intervention renders his attitude to Stalin as hostile as that of Dostoevsky towards his 'devils' Shigalyov and Pyotr Verkhovensky.

Chapter ten

Conclusion

Few historical figures have been the subject of as many biographies and literary portrayals as Joseph Stalin, and none has given rise to more varied and conflicting interpretations. Biographers and writers of fiction have been deeply divided in their assessment of Stalin's character and historical role, presenting him either as a great leader who turned his country into a superpower, or as one of the greatest criminals in history.

The image of Stalin in Soviet and dissident literature

The depiction of Stalin has become an established tradition in modern Russian literature, but writers living in the USSR have been severely restricted in their treatment of his character at any given time. In literature published in the USSR during the 'period of the personality cult' (1934–53) Stalin was portrayed with a limited number of epithets and images. In prose works such as A. Tolstoy's *Bread* and V. Ivanov's *At the Capture of Berlin* he figured as the calm, inspiring disciple of Lenin or the brilliant Commander-in-Chief responsible for the victory over Nazi Germany; in countless poems and folk tales he was presented as a hero, a gardener, a mountain eagle or the sun. In Stalin's lifetime few Soviet writers dared to criticise him openly, but some, such as K. Chukovsky in *The Big Bad Cockroach*, B. Pilnyak in *The Tale of the Unextinguished Moon* and E. Shvarts in *The Dragon*, managed to allude to Stalin obliquely, through Aesopian devices. After Stalin's death in 1953 Khrushchev's policy of de-Stalinisation enabled writers such as K. Simonov, in *People are not Born Soldiers*, to contrast the reality of Stalin's appearance with the idealised figure in the portraits, and to refer to such previously taboo subjects as Stalin's ruthlessness in purging the party and the army and his unpreparedness for war in 1941. After Khrushchev's fall in 1964 Soviet writers once again became more restricted in their choice of themes, and such works as A. Chakovsky's *Blockade* and *Victory* emphasised that Stalin, although occasionally fallible, had played a basically positive role in the development of the USSR. It is only since Gorbachev's accession that previously censored works have appeared, for example A. Bek's *The New Appointment* and A. Rybakov's *Children of the Arbat*, which analyse Stalin's psychology more deeply and do not disguise the negative aspects of Stalin's rule.

Until recent years the theme of Stalin and Stalinism has been a dangerous subject for Soviet writers. Of those heroic individuals who registered their opposition to Stalinism in the dictator's lifetime, Mandelstam and Pilnyak died in the purges; Bulgakov was persecuted and many of his works remained unpublished; Shvarts survived the terror, but his play *The Dragon* was never performed in his lifetime. In the post-Stalin period many writers who treated this theme, such as Solzhenitsyn, Sinyavsky, Maksimov, Gladilin, Voinovich, Aksyonov and Aleshkovsky, were forced to emigrate. Many others, such as Akhmatova, Tvardovsky, Bek, Grossman and Dombrovsky, did not live to see the publication of their anti-Stalin works in the USSR.

Few portraits of Stalin in literature published in the USSR since Stalin's rise to power have been loyal to historical, rather than to political values, although they are of great interest to historians of Stalinism and de-Stalinisation. Most writers whose work has been published in the USSR adhere to the injunction current in Stalin's time: 'History is politics applied to the past; historical events must be evaluated in relation to current party policy'.[1] Soviet writers who treat the subject of Stalin adhere to an age-old tradition whereby the role of the arts is to provide the ruler with a justification of his right to rule and with propaganda against his enemies. The representation of Stalin in fiction has changed under Khrushchev, Brezhnev and Gorbachev, but such portraits all serve the same purpose: to enhance the political authority of the current political leaders.

Fiction published in the USSR closely conforms to the party

line on Stalin at any given time and, for the most part, does not analyse Stalin's psychology very deeply; Stalin is usually portrayed through 'external characterisation'.[2] Despite changing attitudes to Stalin, one constant feature of works published in the USSR has been the seriousness with which writers treat their subject. With only a few exceptions, such as the Aesopian depictions in Stalin's lifetime by Chukovsky, Shvarts and others, Bulgakov's tale about Stalin related in Paustovsky's memoirs, and Mikhail Shatrov's recently published play *The Peace of Brest-Litovsk*, humour has usually been lacking in portraits of Stalin published in the USSR, partly because of the awe in which Stalin has been held, and partly because ridicule of Stalin could be interpreted as ridicule of the party whose leader he was.

Although literary portraits of Stalin published in the USSR generally reflect the fluctuating policies of the party leaders at the time when they appeared, some writers, such as Pilnyak, Grossman, Leonov, Rozen and Okudzhava, managed to express views of Stalin which were unorthodox at the time of publication. There are approximately nine main ways of criticising Stalin indirectly in Soviet prose fiction:[3] omitting his name in a context where it was expected; creating a villain who embodied certain features of Stalin's character; introducing portraits of, or references to, historical characters who bear some resemblance to Stalin; denouncing foreign institutions identical with those of Stalin's Russia; attacking policies and decisions recognised as his, without attributing them to him; referring to the mistakes made by 'somebody'; showing an admirer of Stalin to be a fool or a rogue; putting criticisms of Stalin into the mouth of an apparent fool; quoting Stalin's words and subsequently, in the course of narration, revealing the discrepancy between his words and actual events. Poets and writers of children's fiction have possessed greater freedom to refer to Stalin obliquely, through devices of allegory, fantasy and Aesopian allusion.

Within the general conformity of Soviet fiction, different writers have, since Stalin's death, adopted a variety of approaches to Stalin and Stalinism. Fiction on this theme published in the USSR has provided a valuable insight into the conflict between reformers and conservatives in Soviet society, since Soviet writers express their views on the present through their depiction of the past. The Gorbachev era has seen the republication of many previously banned literary works on the subject of Stalin and Stalinism, notably Akhmatova's *Requiem*, Tvardovsky's *For the Right of Memory*, Rybakov's *Children of the Arbat* and the plays of Mikhail Shatrov, which issue a challenge to Soviet historians to reappraise the Stalin era with greater frankness than ever before. The re-examination of Stalinism is now a highly topical subject in the USSR, but historians may continue to be limited by the official attitude, summarised by Gorbachev in his speech of 2 November 1987: 'If, at times, we scrutinise our history with a critical eye, we do so only because we want to obtain a better and fuller idea of the ways that lead to the future'.[4]

In works by dissident, *émigré* and western writers Stalin has been portrayed with greater frankness and by a variety of techniques, notably realism, allegory and fantasy, or comedy and the grotesque. Nevertheless, dissident writers, for all their individuality, frequently seize on similar details in their portraits, such as Stalin's yellow, suspicious eyes, his long drunken dinners, or the occasion when he compelled Khrushchev to dance the gopak. Such similarities suggest that most Russian writers, including Solzhenitsyn, base their portraits more on the oral tradition within the USSR than on extensive historical research.

Solzhenitsyn's Stalin

The most ambitious portrait of Stalin by a Russian writer which has not yet achieved publication in the USSR, that by Solzhenitsyn in the revised version of *The First Circle*, raises many interesting questions: not only specific points pertaining to Solzhenitsyn's own work and to Russian literature, but also wider literary, historical and philosophical issues, such as the status of the historical and political novel and the relationship between history and fiction.

The principal differences between the old and new versions of the Stalin chapters in *The First Circle* are firstly, the wider scope of Solzhenitisyn's biographical investigation; and secondly, the more explicit expression of the author's own political views, which correspond to those outlined in his polemic about Stalin and Stalinism with American scholars in 1980.[5] In *Circle-96* Solzhenitsyn clearly expresses the opinion that Stalinism was a continuation of Leninism, and sharply dissociates himself from the 'reformist' Soviet line propagated by Khrushchev, and, more recently, by Gorbachev.

Like all hostile biographers of Stalin, Solzhenitsyn makes value judgements about Stalin's character, portraying him as a very evil man. But he does not share the rigid presuppositions about the nature of history or the respectful attitude towards Lenin evinced by Marxist biographers such as Souvarine, Trotsky, Deutscher and Medvedev. Unlike some western biographers, notably Hingley and Tucker, Solzhenitsyn does not regard Stalin as an extremely intelligent man, but satirises his poverty of thought and intellectual pretensions. In contrast with laudatory Soviet and early western accounts, the views of Khrushchev and Gorbachev and some recent biographies like that of Ian Grey, Solzhenitsyn sees no positive side to Stalin's achievement, such as the rapid industrialisation of the country and Stalin's contribution to the Soviet victory over Hitler. Moreover, he includes some of the more sensational aspects of western popular biographies, particularly Stalin's alleged activities as a police spy and his attitude to women. The Stalin chapters in the new *Circle-96* therefore present a completely new and highly original interpretation of Stalin's character.

Solzhenitsyn's main aim in the Stalin chapters was to paint a convincing psychological portrait of a historical monster. He has succeeded remarkably well; Solzhenitsyn is, perhaps, one of the writers who has been most successful in conveying the real essence of historical personages and the spirit of their age without bending historical truth too far. In this he is far more successful than Tolstoy, whose Napoleon is merely a caricature, an abstract incarnation of the author's ideas drawn to support his theory of history. However, the 'Stalin chapters' in *Circle-96* manifest the characteristic limitations of much 'psycho-history'. By focusing on the negative aspects of one individual's role in history, and by concentrating on internal political factors to the exclusion of wider economic, ideological, international and historical issues, Solzhenitsyn produces an oversimplified view of the factors which created both Stalin and the Soviet Communist Party.

Solzhenitsyn's new portrait of Stalin possesses limitations both as a psychological analysis and as a historical biography. Although Solzhenitsyn explores the roots of Stalin's evil, portraying his motive forces as supreme egoism, driving ambition, morbid suspiciousness and the lust for power, he does not adequately analyse the psychological and social origin of these traits. Solzhenitsyn's Stalin, even as a young man, appears to be a fully formed monster. Although Solzhenitsyn's portrait is probably quite close to the historical Stalin, except for the unproven assertion that he was a police spy, it can by no means be considered an objective, authentic historical biography. Solzhenitsyn's most significant addition to the study of Stalin is not his psychological or historical analysis, but his effective use of parallels with Dante and Dostoevsky to suggest a metaphysical interpretation of Stalin as a satanic figure who vied with God for power over people on earth.

Solzhenitsyn's portrait of Stalin in the original *Circle-87* caused a great deal of controversy among literary critics: it was either regarded as a 'masterly portrait',[6] the best thing in the book, or as a mordant caricature, an excessively didactic element disrupting the unity of the novel – in Rothberg's view, 'the least satisfactory of the characters', or, in Barker's more ambiguous statement, 'an excellent and facile cartoon'.[7] These value judgements are also relevant to the new version of the novel, and relate directly to certain controversial questions of literary theory.

One debatable point is whether ideas have any place in a novel. A fashionable critical movement in the twentieth century, the American 'New Criticism' which came to Europe as 'critical analysis', saw literature as totally autonomous, apart from society, uncontaminated by ideas; criticism was an analysis of form, and anything else was extrinsic to the novel. Such a view sprang from a love of generalisation about 'all novels', 'all literature', and led to certain absurdities, for example Caroline Gordon's total rejection of the works of Aldous Huxley and all 'novels of ideas'. When a young friend who made the *faux pas* of liking Huxley asked her: 'Can't there be more than one kind of novel and one kind of novelist? Can't I admire X (someone Miss Gordon approved of) and Huxley too?', she answered, 'No, I'm afraid you can't'.[8] Some American 'New Critics' claimed to be following the Russian Formalists, but their claim was based more on the polemics provoked by Formalism than the real position of the Formalists, who had merely stated that history and fiction belonged to two different domains (*ryady*) and hence could not be directly compared.[9] Serious Formalism, even before it was under pressure, had not denied the existence of the 'social connection of literature'; it had simply said that this was not the proper object of study for a student of literature. Of course, later, in 1928, under the pressure of events, Yuri Tynyanov and Roman Jakobson attempted to redefine their position, stating that 'literary history is closely bound up with other historic series';[10] and Victor Shklovsky's studies of *War and Peace* demonstrate his deep interest in the way history is treated in literature.[11] Although the New Critics' distaste for history, for any unwelcome ideology, any commitment, especially political, is understandable after the horrors of the Second World War, their prescriptive attitude to literature has been ably refuted by Lionel Trilling, who speaks of one of the major characteristics of the novel as 'an unabashed interest in ideas ... The great novels, far more than we remember, deal explicitly with developed ideas'.[12]

If it is not ideas as such that some fastidious western commentators object to in Solzhenitsyn, Koestler and others, the problem may well be that these novelists deal with *political* ideas. Undoubtedly, the intrusion of politics into a novel changes our whole conception of literature. As Stendhal remarked, 'Politics in a work of literature is like a pistol-shot in the middle of a concert, something loud and vulgar, and yet a thing to which it is not possible to refuse one's attention'.[13] It is probably the distaste for 'accursed' political, historical and philosophical problems which makes so many Anglo-Saxon critics dislike the works of Solzhenitsyn. Some writers, however, would argue that in the twentieth century, the most violent of all centuries, a writer has no right to retreat into his ivory tower and ignore politics. In the words of the Indian Panait Istrati discussing Victor Serge, 'Literature destroys the total indifference which the man who writes and the man who reads display before the savagery of our time'. He repudiates 'art for art's sake' when 'in the streets congealed blood rises knee-high'.[14]

In Russia literature has always been deeply concerned with socio-political issues. In the nineteenth century the conditions of the Tsarist censorship meant that literature was the only means of expressing ideas on other subjects, such as politics, religion or philosophy. As the Populist Nikolai Chernyshevsky said: 'Literature in Russia constitutes almost the sum total of our intellectual life'.[15] Irving Howe has pointed out that 'in dealing with the Russian novel, one is obliged to take religion as a branch of politics and politics as a branch of religion'.[16] We do not object when Dostoevsky says of *The Devils*: 'I mean to utter certain thoughts, whether all the artistic side of it goes to the dogs or not . . . Even if it turns into a mere pamphlet, I shall say all that I have in my heart'.[17] If this was Dostoevsky's view, faced with the relatively lenient Tsarist censorship, surely it is even more valid in the case of Solzhenitsyn, writing in a Stalinist prison camp and having to contend with the much more oppressive Soviet censorship? Some critics, however, can accept political ideas in Dostoevsky, yet cavil at them in Solzhenitsyn. The difference is, clearly, that Solzhenitsyn is closer to our own time and therefore may conflict with our own deeply-held beliefs and prejudices. Any judgement of the political novel raises what T. S. Eliot called 'the problem of belief':[18] the question of how one responds to literature which expresses a set of beliefs with which one cannot agree. Many critics judge a work of literature not according to its literary merits, but according to whether they approve of the author or share his point of view. Some of Solzhenitsyn's critics fall into this trap: for example, the Marxist David Craig prefers the sketchy, but more sympathetic depiction of Stalin in Serge's *The Case of Comrade Tulaev* to Solzhenitsyn's portrait;[19] while Paul Siegel dismisses Koestler's *Darkness at Noon* because he disapproves of Koestler's equivocal behaviour in Spain and elsewhere.[20] Thus, before we condemn Solzhenitsyn, we should be aware of our own prejudices.

Another question raised by Solzhenitsyn's work is the problem of didacticism in literature. It is fashionable to expect an author to 'disappear' from his work altogether and allow the characters to speak for themselves. To some extent Solzhenitsyn does this in the Stalin chapters, but his own view of Stalin is always present through his use of irony and satire. It is, however, legitimate to ask: should we always expect an author to conceal his own viewpoint, and does didacticism inevitably detract from the literary merit of a work of fiction? If this is so, we may have to dismiss much of Russian literature. Or could it be said that Tolstoy and Dostoevsky are successful in spite of their moral intentions, since their characters manage to escape from their preconceived mould and assert their human reality?

Political didacticism in a modern novel is, however, likely to arouse far more controversy than the moralising of nineteenth-century classics. As Irving Howe says, 'politics rakes our passions as nothing else does' and 'we react with an almost demonic rapidity to a detested political opinion'.[21] The discussion of political ideas in a novel sometimes leads critics into absurdities: for example, even such an experienced critic as V. S. Pritchett, who regards the portrait of Stalin as a weakness in *The First Circle*, an example of 'a daring' he finds 'merely journalistic', commits the cardinal sin of confusing the views of the author and his character: 'I simply do not believe the following words: "Stalin knew that with time people would forgive everything bad, even forget it, even remember it as something good"'.[22] Moreover, Pritchett totally rejects the comparison which Solzhenitsyn's Stalin draws between whole nations and Lady Anne in *Richard III* who willingly surrendered to the victor. Pritchett's indignation seems to cloud his literary judgement: he fails to recognise the irony of the passage, and the fact that it is attributed to Stalin, not the author. Yet, in any case, the resurgence of neo-Stalinism in the USSR during the Brezhnev era showed Pritchett to be mistaken in his judgement of the idea as well.

Perhaps, in fairness to western critics, it should be emphasised that one aspect of Solzhenitsyn's work to which they frequently object – and this is truer of the new version of *The First Circle* than the 1968 edition – is that Solzhenitsyn does not allow sufficient weight to the whole idea of opposition, opposition to an author's own predispositions, feelings and fantasies. In Dostoevsky's *The Devils*, for example, the author's own opinion is one of the most important, yet not entirely dominating views. In *Circle-87* the viewpoint of the autobiographical Gleb Nerzhin did not attain complete dominance, whereas in *Circle-96* the characters of Rubin and Sologdin are treated more satirically (probably reflecting the author's quarrels with their prototypes Kopelev and Panin). The new version of *The First Circle* is in some ways closer to a *roman à thèse*, to propaganda fiction, than to a complex political novel. Another characteristic of the successful political novel is that it should always be in a state of internal conflict, because it exposes the impersonal claims of ideology to the pressures of private emotion. In *Circle-96*, however, Solzhenitsyn does not give enough credit to the richness of Stalin's own experience: for example, he omits the former compassionate references to Stalin's old age and his relationship with his daughter Svetlana.[23] Solzhenitsyn does, nevertheless, succeed in passing the ultimate test for the political novelist. Irving Howe has argued that in the political novel the writer and reader enter into an uneasy compact, and that to find some common ground it is necessary to discover some supervening human bond above and beyond ideas: 'It is not surprising that the political novelist, even as he remains fascinated by politics, urges his claim for a moral order beyond ideology, nor that the receptive reader, even as he perseveres in his own commitment, assents to the novelist's ultimate order'.[24] This is what Solzhenitsyn, like Dostoevsky, has managed to achieve: the metaphysical interpretation of Stalin's character is more interesting than the author's political and historical analysis.

History and fiction

Another general problem raised by Solzhenitsyn's work and that of all the works on historical subjects which we have considered is: what is the nature of the relationship between history and fiction? The borderline between them can often be blurred, as the fascinating episode of the fraudulent *Hitler's Diaries* graphically demonstrates. In recent years numerous disputes have surrounded the genre of 'faction' which is becoming increasingly popular: Thomas Kinneally's *Schindler's Ark* was awarded the Booker Prize for literature, although some protested that it was a historical work; and Trevor Griffiths's television series *Scott of the Antarctic* was heavily criticised for its allegedly distorted presentation of historical characters, in particular for the rendering of Captain Oates's famous last words: 'I am going out, and I may be some time' as 'Call of nature, Birdy'.

Fictionalised documentaries about such subjects as Churchill, the Suez crisis and Lloyd George are not generally taken seriously by historians. Martin Gilbert, the biographer of Churchill, said in a radio interview that the television programmes about Churchill were 'good fun', but not genuine history. On a deeper level, most modern historians would see a great difference between their work and that of the novelist, since their aim is to study sources and try to reach the truth about the past on the basis of an objective analysis of accurate and complete evidence. Such philosophers of history as Brooke, Collingwood and Croce, however, admit that that there is some similarity between their discipline and art: the historian uses his imagination to recreate a historical period, and inevitably selects and emphasises certain facts.[25] E. H. Carr, who refutes Collingwood's theory that history is merely spun out of the human brain, nevertheless says: 'The facts of history never come to us "pure"; they do not and cannot exist in a pure form: they are always refracted through the mind of the recorder . . . By and large, the historian will get the kind of facts he wants. History means interpretation'.[26] It could be argued that all history is fiction to some extent (although most working historians would, no doubt, indignantly refute this view), and that the difference between a historical biography and a biography in a work of fiction, such as Solzhenitsyn's portrait of Stalin, is one of degree rather than of substance.

C. N. L. Brooke, in his pamphlet *Time, the Archsatirist*, an interesting discussion of the difference between history and fiction, disputes Ranke's view that the historian is limited by the record of what has happened in the past – 'wie es eigentlich gewesen'. Alternative choices might have been made; speculation is permissible and even desirable. Brooke recognises the need for the historian to use his imagination, but argues: 'Imagination in this sense is not fancy; it must always be controlled by evidence, and thus must always be fragmentary'.[27] This does not always set history apart from imaginative fiction; Thomas Hardy, for example, described his own art as a kind of history. In a cancelled passage in the manuscript of *Tess of the d'Urbervilles* Hardy said: 'In typical history with all its liberty there are, as in real history, features which can never be distorted with impunity, and issues which should not be falsified'.[28] In Brooke's view the historian's aim is authenticity, whereas Hardy's is sincerity; and the main difference between his work and Hardy's is that in Hardy's case 'the liberty is there to fill the gaps; beyond evidence, and reasonable inference from evidence, the historian can never go'.[29] If we accept this vital distinction, all the writers discussed in this study – even Solzhenitsyn. who claims historical accuracy – have produced fictional interpretations of historical characters, not objective historical biographies.

The main difference between Solzhenitsyn and western European writers who create imaginative reconstructions of historical characters – for example Hughes and Yourcenar – is that he fails to reveal his sources, or to include a modest disclaimer stating that he is not intending full historical accuracy and is leaving certain issues deliberately ambiguous. Solzhenitsyn has no room for ambiguities, and presents his Stalin not merely as a subjective portrait, but as the one true conception of Stalin's character. He approaches history with a deep Christian commitment, perceiving no conflict between the study of history and the mantle of the prophet. Solzhenitsyn's view of history stands in total contradiction to the empirical school of western historians who try to approach their source material objectively, divesting themselves of prejudices as far as possible; he is, however, a direct heir to the Russian and Soviet historical tradition. He resembles Soviet historians in his unashamed bias, his willingness to read into his sources what he wants to see, his desire not merely to establish the truth about the past, but to use it for social engineering in the present and future. He has rightly been described by Alain Besançon as an 'inverted Communist'[30] and by Anna Akhmatova, who objected to the crude, heavy, plebeian elements of his art, as a 'Soviet man'.[31] To use Isaiah Berlin's term, Solzhenitsyn is a 'hedgehog': someone who relates everything to a monological central vision, a single, unilateral guiding principle in terms of which alone all that people say and do has significance.[32]

As several critics have pointed out, Solzhenitsyn follows Tolstoy's tradition of regarding the artist as the teacher and conscience of the nation, 'another government', as the writer Galakhov says in *The First Circle*.[33] In March 1967 Solzhenitsyn spoke of the social duty of the novelist in an interview with the Czech journalist Pavel Ličko: 'A writer is able to discover far earlier than other people aspects of social life . . . It is incumbent upon a writer to inform society of all that he is able to perceive and especially all that is unhealthy'.[34] In 1969, at a meeting of writers, Solzhenitsyn directly quoted Tolstoy as saying: 'The disease we are suffering from is the murdering of people . . . If we could recreate the past and look it straight in the face, the violence we are now committing would be revealed', and he directly related this to the need to tell the truth about Stalin's crimes.[35] Thus, like Tolstoy, who through his condemnatory portrait of Nicholas I in *Hadji Murat* bore witness to the injustice of the Tsarist state, Solzhenitsyn, through his portrait of Stalin, exposes the essence of the totalitarian Stalinist state. Isaiah Berlin's characterisation of Tolstoy's attitude to history could equally well apply to Solzhenitsyn: 'History alone – the sum of empirically discoverable data – held the key to the mystery of why what happened happened as it did and not otherwise; and only history, consequently, could throw light on the fundamental ethical problems which obsessed him as they did every Russian thinker in the nineteenth century. What is to be done? How should one live? Why are we here? What must we do?'.[36]

Solzhenitsyn, like Tolstoy, believes in the necessity of confronting history in order to understand the present. In his *Nobel Lecture* he spoke of the need to create works of art that 'have scooped up the truth and presented it to us as a living force' and will 'take hold of us, compel us and nobody ever, not even in ages to come, will appear to refute them'. In *The Gulag Archipelago* Solzhenitsyn expresses his faith in the absolute value of telling the truth about his country's past so that history can be reborn:

> And I . . . thought: if the first tiny droplet of truth has
> exploded like a psychological bomb, what then will happen
> in our country when whole waterfalls of Truth burst forth?
> And they will burst forth. It has to happen.[37]

Solzhenitsyn's unique moral and religious approach to history has been eloquently characterised by Georges Nivat: 'The great message of Solzhenitsyn is that the chain of history has been broken, that a methodical concentration of perversity has broken the line of generations and rendered void the heritage of culture. But, let man strip himself bare, let him thereby enact a new gesture of valour and courage, let him follow the example of Nerzhin and Volodin, and slowly, History will be reborn'.[38] For the western critic, however, Solzhenitsyn's work raises the problem of whether it is possible to judge a man who considers himself to possess a divine mission to tell the truth about his country and revise its moral and spiritual values in the same way that he would judge a western historian or historical novelist whose ambitions are much more modest. Does great seriousness of purpose justify either historical inaccuracy or a certain heavyhandedness in literary style?

The Stalin chapters in *Circle-96* are one of the most interesting sections of the novel from both the historical and human points of view; they are not superfluous, intrusive or detrimental to the rest of the book. Solzhenitsyn originally considered printing the Stalin chapters separately under the title 'One Night of Stalin',[39] but to have left them out of the novel would have weakened the depiction of Stalinist society as a whole; his *Inferno* would have been incomplete without the bottom circle of hell. Judgement must, however, be suspended as to whether the satire is too obvious, the portrait of Stalin too much of a caricature. If it is always difficult to produce a totally dispassionate analysis of a historical monster, it is *a fortiori* even more difficult for any writer who has lived in the USSR in Stalin's time to be completely objective in his assessment of Stalin. It could, perhaps, be argued that such a subject as Stalin can only be treated with excessive satire, mordant caricature; yet the realistic portraits by Rybakov, Bek, Dombrovsky, Maksimov and Grossman, as well as the more good-humoured caricatures by Voinovich, Iskander and Aleshkovsky, would seem to belie this view. Only Zinoviev, in *The Yawning Heights*, approaches the ferocity of Solzhenitsyn.

In my opinion Solzhenitsyn's portrait of Stalin has greater impact than the more neutral, compassionate studies by Bek, Rybakov, Dombrovsky, Serge and Maksimov, although judgement of Solzhenitsyn is, of course, bound to depend on one's political views and literary taste. Solzhenitsyn himself has admitted to a certain 'excess' in the portrait, but, as Tvardovsky said, to leave it out would have meant 'cheating', 'cowardice' on the part of the author.[40] Susan Richards, writing at a time when Solzhenitsyn's portrait of Stalin was unique in *samizdat* and *tamizdat* fiction, takes issue with Solzhenitsyn's didacticism and dismisses the portrait of Stalin in the patronising words of Dr Johnson discussing women preachers: 'It is not done well, but it is surprising to find it done at all'.[41] The didactic element in Solzhenitsyn's work cannot, however, be dismissed so easily; as Maria Shneerson argues, it is invalid to draw a distinction between Solzhenitsyn the great writer and Solzhenitsyn the poor political thinker, because an author's world-view cannot be separated from his creative work.[42] Solzhenitsyn is committed, and has good reason to be; his portrait cannot be judged as an objective, historically authentic picture of Stalin, a 'whole character', in Arnold Bennett's phrase. Solzhenitsyn's method is that of the committed novelist rather than the disinterested scholar; he has demonstrated himself to be a passionate polemicist raising problems of current concern both to the west and the east, but a biased historian. Many western critics would argue that the didacticism obtrudes in *Circle-96*, because they find Solzhenitsyn's religious, anti-socialist ideas objectionable. As far as the Stalin chapters are concerned, however, any reader with an 'unabashed interest in ideas' will find the new portrait of Stalin more interesting and thought-provoking, in both the political and philosophical senses, than the original version. Ironically, however, unless and until the new *First Circle* is published in its entirety in the USSR, the works of Rybakov, Bek, Shatrov and Grossman, and indeed any works on the theme of Stalin and Stalinism which may achieve publication in the USSR, will exert more influence on the minds of Solzhenitsyn's fellow countrymen than *Circle-96*.

In 1968, while praising *The First Circle* as a great achievement, Donald Fanger posed an important question about the possibilities and limitations of realism in dealing with such a theme as Stalin and Stalinism after all that twentieth-century literature has accustomed the reader to:

> One may be troubled by a suspicion that the themes treated here require by now not so much to be realistically dramatised as somehow encompassed and mastered, and that the language of everyday life may no longer suffice for the purpose. At this point in history it may be that some metalanguage is needed to deal freshly with such numbing enormities.[43]

Although realism is the only strategy available to the writer who wishes, like Bek, Rybakov, Maksimov and Solzhenitsyn, to make a serious contribution to the biographical and historical analysis of Stalin, the works of Voinovich, Iskander, Aleshkovsky, Sinyavsky and Zinoviev, as well as Abuladze's film *Repentance*, suggest that comedy, fantasy and the grotesque may be more satisfactory methods of evoking the essence of Stalin and Stalinism in artistic form.

Notes

Preface

1   The original version of *V kruge pervom* was published in
    A. Solzhenitsyn, *Sob. soch.*, vols. 3 and 4 (Frankfurt, 1969–70).
    The new version is in A. Solzhenitsyn, *Sob. soch.*, vols. 1 and 2
    (Vermont and Paris, 1978).

Chapter one   An approach to the presentation of historical
                character in European prose fiction.

1   G. Lukács, *The Historical Novel*, transl. H. and S. Mitchell
    (London, 1962), p. 15.
2   H. Butterfield, *The Historical Novel* (Cambridge, 1924);
    G. Nélod, *Panorama du Roman Historique* (Paris, 1969);
    H.E. Shaw, *The Forms of Historical Fiction* (Ithaca, NY, 1983);
    A. Fleishman, *The English Historical Novel: Walter Scott to
    Virginia Woolf* (Baltimore, 1971); H.B. Henderson III, *Versions
    of the Past: the Historical Imagination in American Fiction* (New
    York, 1974).
3   A. Skabichevsky, *Nash istoricheskii roman v ego proshlom i
    nastoyashchem, Sochineniya*, 2 vols (St Petersburg, 1890);
    S. Petrov, *Russkii istoricheskii roman XIX veka* (Moscow, 1964);
    M. Serebriansky, *Sovetskii istoricheskii roman* (Moscow, 1936);
    M. Karpovich, 'The Soviet Historical Novel', *Russian Review*, V
    (1946), pp. 53–63; X. Gasiorowska, 'The Soviet Postwar
    Historical Novel', *AATSEEL Journal*, 12 (1954), pp. 76–9.
4   Nélod, (see note 2 above), p. 19.
5   X. Gasiorowska, *The Image of Peter the Great in Russian Fiction*
    (Madison, 1979), p. 7.
6   K. Tillotson, *Novels of the Eighteen-Forties* (London, 1954;
    reprint, 1961), p. 13.
7   I. Howe, *Politics and the Novel* (Cleveland, Ohio and New York,
    1957), p. 17.

8   Fleishman, (see note 2 above) p. 15.
9   J.W. Turner, 'The Kinds of Historical Fiction: An Essay in Definition and Methodology', *Genre*, XII (Fall 1979), p. 337.
10 Lukács, (see note 1 above) pp. 37–8.
11 Shaw, (see note 2 above) p. 135.
12 Gasiorowska, (see note 5 above) pp. 6, 10.
13 Shaw, p. 131.
14 Taine, cited in D. Forbes, *The Liberal Anglican Idea of History* (Cambridge, 1952), p. 190, n. 202.
15 K. Hamburger, *The Logic of Literature* (Bloomington, Indiana and London, 1973), p. 336.
16 M. Yourcenar, *Les Mémoires d'Hadrien* (Paris, 1951).
17 J. Fest, *Hitler* (New York, 1974); M. Gallo, *Robespierre the Incorruptible* (New York, 1971); R.C. Tucker, *Stalin as Revolutionary, 1879–1929* (New York, 1973).

Chapter two   Tyrants in twentieth-century literature

1   L. Trilling, *The Liberal Imagination* (London, 1951), p. 265.
2   B. Pasternak, *Avtobiograficheskii ocherk*, in *Sochineniya*, ed. G. Struve and B. Filippov, vol. 2 (Ann Arbor, 1961), p. 52.
3   A. Kuznetsov, *Babi Yar. A document in the form of a novel*, transl. D. Floyd (Harmondsworth, 1982), p. 98ff.; first published in censored form in *Yunost*, 1966.
4   W. Vesper, *Dem Führer!*, in E. Loewy, *Literatur unterm Hakenkreuz. Das Dritte Reich und seine Dichtung. Eine Dokumentation* (Frankfurt, 1969), p. 256.
5   L. Feuchtwanger, cited in J.M. Ritchie, *German Literature under National Socialism* (London, 1983), pp. 202–3.
6   C. Chaplin, *My Autobiography* (Harmondsworth, 1966), pp. 387–8. Chaplin admits, however, 'Had I known of the actual horrors of the German concentration camps, I could not have made *The Great Dictator*; I could not have made fun of the homicidal insanity of the Nazis'.
7   R. Hughes, *The Fox in the Attic*, (London, 1961), p. 353.
8   Ibid. , p. 195.
9   Richard Hughes, 'Historical Note' to *The Wooden Shepherdess* (Harmondsworth, 1975), p. 397.

Chapter three   Historical treatments of Stalin and Stalinism

1   For a more detailed discussion, see F. Randall, 'Books on Stalin', *Problems of Communism*, XII, no. 2 (March–April, 1963) pp. 94–9; 'Afterword: Stalin Known and Unknown' in T.H. Rigby (ed.), *Stalin* (Eaglewood Cliffs, NJ, 1966) pp. 177–82; R. Hingley, 'Introduction', in *Joseph Stalin: Man and Legend* (London, 1984), pp. xix–xx; see also below, Bibliography, Section 1;

J.A. Getty, 'Bibliographic Essay', in *Origins of the Great Purges: The Soviet Communist Party Reconsidered, 1933–1938* (Cambridge, 1985), pp. 211–20.

2 L.P. Beria, *On the History of the Bolshevik Organisations in Transcaucasia*, transl. from 4th Russian edition (Moscow, 1939), p. 164; H. Barbusse, *Stalin: A New World seen through one Man*, transl. V. Holland (London, 1935), p. viii; E. Yaroslavsky, *Landmarks in the Life of Stalin* (London, 1942), p. 191.

3 For the legend, see *Joseph Stalin: A Short Biography* (Moscow, 1941); 'Bibliographical Chronicle' appended to each volume of Stalin's *Collected Works* (1946–52); for a critique of Stalin's self-made myths about his early career, see B.D. Wolfe, 'How History is Made', in *Three who Made a Revolution* (Harmondsworth, 1966), pp. 491–502.

4 M. Kol'tsov, 'Zagadka Stalina', *Pravda*, 21 December 1929.

5 S. Graham, *Stalin: An Impartial Study of the Life and Work of Joseph Stalin* (London, 1931); I. D. Levine, *Stalin* (New York, 1931). Two particularly fanciful early biographies were S. Dmitrievsky, *Stalin* (Berlin, 1931); E. Bey, *Stalin, the Career of a Fanatic* (New York, 1932).

6 Yaroslavsky, (see note 2), p. 4.

7 J. Iremaschwili, *Stalin und die Tragoedie Georgiens* (Berlin, 1932).

8 B. Svanidze, *My Uncle Joe* (New York, 1952); A. Amba, *I Was Stalin's Bodyguard* (New York, 1952).

9 B. Souvarine, *Stalin: A Critical Survey of Bolshevism* (London, 1939).

10 L. Trotsky, *Stalin: An Appraisal of the Man and his Influence*, ed. and transl. C. Malamuth (New York, 1941), pp. 420, xv.

11 I. Deutscher, *Stalin: A Political Biography*, 1st edn (London, 1949).

12 N.S. Khrushchev, *The 'Secret' Speech*, with an introduction by Zh. Medvedev and R. Medvedev (Nottingham, 1976); N.S. Khrushchev, *Pravda*, 18 October 1961, pp. 2–11.

13. See R. Medvedev, 'The Stalin Question', in S. Cohen, A. Rabinowitch and R. Sharlet (eds), *The Soviet Union since Stalin* (Bloomington, 1980), pp. 32–49; S. Cohen, 'The Stalin Question since Stalin', in Cohen (ed.), *An End to Silence: Uncensored Opinion in the Soviet Union* (New York and London, 1982), pp. 42–50.

14 See, for example, M. Gorbachev, *Pravda*, 3 November 1987.

15 M. Djilas, *Conversations with Stalin*, transl. from the Serbo-Croat by M. Petrovich (Harmondsworth, 1969); S. Allilueva, *Twenty Letters to a Friend*, transl. P. Johnson (London, 1967).

16 R. Medvedev, *Let History Judge: The Origins and Consequences of Stalinism* (London, 1972).

17 I.D. Levine, *Stalin's Great Secret* (New York, 1956); A. Orlov, 'The Sensational Secret Behind Damnation of Stalin', *Life*,

International Edition, vol. 20, no. 10 (14 May 1956), pp. 12–19; E.E. Smith, *The Young Stalin: the Early Years of an Elusive Revolutionary* (London, 1968).

18 Wolfe, op.cit. (note 3); R. Hingley, *Joseph Stalin: Man and Legend* (London, 1974); R.C. Tucker, *Stalin as Revolutionary, 1929–1979: A Study in History and Personality* (London, 1974); A.B. Ulam, *Stalin: the Man and his Era* (New York, 1974). Two recent works are A. de Jonge, *Stalin and the Shaping of the Soviet Union* (London, 1986); and R.H. McNeal, *Stalin, Man and Ruler* (London, 1988).

19 See, for example, G. Alperovitz, *Atomic Diplomacy: Hiroshima and Potsdam* (London, 1966); *Cold War Essays* (New York, 1970), pp. 51–73.

20 I. Grey, *Stalin, Man of History* (London, 1979).

21 See, for example, T. Dunmore, *Soviet Politics 1945–1953* (London, 1984); G.T. Rittersporn, *Phénomènes et realités staliniens: tensions sociales et conflits politiques en URSS, 1933–1953* (Paris, 1985); J.A. Getty, *Origins of the Great Purges* (Cambridge, 1985).

22 E. Hoxha, *With Stalin: memoirs*, transl. from the Albanian (Tirana, 1979), p. 5.

23 The military desk calendar for 1979, cited in Cohen, 'The Stalin Question' (see note 13), p. 44.

24 A. Solzhenitsyn, *The Gulag Archipelago*, 3 vols (Fontana, London, 1974–8); R. Medvedev, *Let History Judge*; Z. Medvedev, *The Rise and Fall of T.D. Lysenko* (New York, 1969); E. Ginzburg, *Into the Whirlwind* and *Within the Whirlwind* (New York, 1967 and 1981); N. Mandelstam, *Hope against Hope* and *Hope Abandoned* (New York, 1974); L. Chukovskaya, *The Deserted House* (New York, 1967), *Going Under* (New York, 1972); V. Shalamov, *Kolyma Tales* (New York, 1980); L. Kopelev, *Khranit' vechno* (Ann Arbor, 1975); E. Gnedin, *Katastrofa i vtoroe rozhdenie* (Amsterdam, 1977); A. Nekrich, *The Punished Peoples* (New York, 1978); M. Baitalsky, *Eto nasha shkola: vospominaniya* (Moscow: samizdat, 1970); S. Gazaryan, *Eto ne dolzhno povtorit'sya* (Moscow: *samizdat*, 1961); A. Antonov-Ovseenko, *The Time of Stalin: Portrait of a Tyranny* (New York, 1981).

25 Antonov-Ovseenko, p. xviii.

Chapter four The image of Stalin in Soviet literature during Stalin's lifetime

1 M. Friedberg, 'Solzhenitsyn's and other literary Lenins', *Canadian Slavonic Papers*, 1977, no. 2, pp. 123–37.

2 N. Mandelstam, *Hope Against Hope*, transl. M. Hayward (Harmondsworth, 1975), p. 190.

Notes

3   K. Chukovsky, *Tarakanishche*, in *Sob. soch. v 6 tomakh*, vol. 1
    (Moscow, 1965), pp. 173–80.
4   L. Loseff, *On the Beneficence of Censorship. Aesopian language
    in Modern Russian Literature* (Munich, 1984), pp. 201–2.
5   E. Zamyatin, *Iks, Novaya Rossiya*, no. 2 (February 1926),
    pp. 49–62. The 'spoof on Stalin' has been noted in A. Shane, *The
    Life and Works of Evgenij Zamyatin* (Berkeley and Los Angeles,
    1968), p. 177.
6   E. Zamyatin, *The Dragon and Other Stories*, transl. M.
    Ginzburg (Harmondsworth, 1975), pp. 227, 234.
7   E. Zamyatin, *We*, transl. B. Guerney (Harmondsworth, 1983),
    p. 169. See also E. Zamyatin, 'O literature, revolyutsii i
    entropii', first published 1924, reprinted in *Litsa* (Munich,
    1967), pp. 249–56.
8   Zamyatin, *The Dragon and Other Stories*, p. 226.
9   B. Pil'nyak, *Povest' nepogashennoi luny, Novy Mir*, 1926, no. 5,
    pp. 5–33.
10 Most commentators have emphasised Number One's
    responsibility for the murder; for an alternative view, see
    G. Browning, *Boris Pil'niak: Scythian at a Typewriter* (Ann
    Arbor, 1985), pp. 153, 201 (n. 19), which stresses the ambiguity
    of details in the story.
11 V. Reck, 'Introduction', in B. Pilnyak, *Mother Earth and Other
    Stories*, transl. and ed. V. Reck and M. Green (London, 1968),
    p. xii.
12 S. Allilueva, *Dvadtsat' pisem k drugu* (New York and Evanston,
    1968), pp. 150, 19; A. Barmine, *One who Survived* (New York,
    1945), p. 198. These and other similarities to the real Stalin are
    discussed at length in V. Reck, *Boris Pil'niak. A Soviet Writer in
    Conflict with the State* (Montreal and London, 1975), pp. 29–38.
13 Pil'nyak, *Povest'*, *Novy Mir*, 1926, no. 5, p. 13.
14 Ibid., p. 10.
15 Reck, 'Introduction', p. xii.
16 Pil'nyak, 'Predislovie', *Novy Mir*, 1926, no. 5, p. 5.
17 Ibid., p. 18.
18 E. Semeka, 'The Structure of Boris Pil'njak's "Povest'
    nepogasennoj luny": From the Structure to a Determination of
    the Genre', in A. Kodjak, M. Connolly and K. Pomorska (eds),
    The Structural Analysis of Narrative Texts (Columbus, Ohio,
    1980), p. 161.
19 Pil'nyak, *Povest'*, *Novy Mir*, 1926, no. 5, pp. 31, 32.
20 Semeka, p. 168; cf. Browning (see note 10), pp. 152–8.
21 O. Mandel'stam, 'My zhivyom, pod soboyu ne chuya strany',
    no. 286 (November 1933), in Mandel'stam, *Sob.soch. v tryokh
    tomakh*, ed. G. Struve and B. Filippov, vol. 1 (Washington,
    1967), p. 202.
22 N. Mandelstam, *Hope against Hope*, pp. 191–2, 29.
23 Ibid., p. 189.
24 Ibid., p. 239.

25 O. Mandel'stam, *Sob.soch.*, vol. 1, p. 227.
26 N. Mandelstam, *Hope against Hope*, p. 177.
27 A. Ulam, *Stalin. The Man and his Era* (New York, 1974),
    p. 436.
28 See below, p. 86.
29 L. Chukovskaya, *Pamyati Anny Akhmatovoi. Stikhi, pis'ma,
    vospominaniya* (Paris, 1974), p. 160; D. Shostakovich,
    Testimony. The Memoirs of Dmitri Shostakovich, as related to
    and edited by Solomon Volkov, transl. A. Bouis (London,
    1979), p. 210. See also M. Zoshchenko, *Lenin and the Sentry*,
    transl. with an afterword by R. Sobel, *Irish Slavonic Studies*,
    no. 4, 1983, pp. 106–8.
30 N. Tumarkin, *Lenin Lives!* (Cambridge, Mass., 1983), pp. 1–23;
    R. Tucker, 'The Rise of Stalin's Personality Cult', *American
    Historical Review*, 84 (April 1979), pp. 347–8.
31 I.V. Stalin, *Sochineniya*, vol. 13, pp. 84–102; discussed in
    Tucker, pp. 353–63.
32 Tucker, p. 348.
33 Ibid., pp. 348–9. For Louis Fischer's article, see *The Nation*, 13
    August 1930, p. 176.
34 A. Werth, *Russia, Hopes and Fears* (New York, 1969), pp. 305–6.
35 *Pesni o Staline* (Moscow, 1950).
36 A.A. Lakhuti, 'Vozhdyu, tovarishchu Stalinu', *Pravda*,
    29 November 1932.
37 D. Dzhabaev, 'Moi Stalin, tebe etu pesnyu poyu', in *Pesni o
    Staline*, pp. 48–9; D. Dzhabaev, 'Imya bessmertnoe – Stalin', in
    Samoe dorogoe. Stalin v narodnom epose, ed. Yu. Sokolov
    (Moscow, 1939), pp. 10–13.
38 I. Deutscher, *Stalin: a Political Biography*, 2nd edn
    (Harmondsworth, 1970), p. 366.
39 Shostakovich, pp. 161–2, 171.
40 A. Surkov, 'Na prostorakh rodiny chudesnoi', in *Pesni*,
    pp. 16–17; A. Zinov'ev, *Nashei yunosti polyot* (Lausanne, 1983).
41 V. Lebedev-Kumach, 'Pesnya o rodine', in *Pesni*, pp. 9–11; on
    the author, see G. Smith, *Songs to Seven Strings: Russian
    Guitar Poetry and Soviet 'Mass Song'* (Bloomington, Indiana,
    1984), pp. 14–15.
42 *Pesni*, p. 3; discussed in Smith, p. 60; Shostakovich, pp. 201–5.
    V. Aleksandrov, 'Kak sozdavalsya gimn Sovetskogo Soyuza',
    Moskva, 1988, no. 3, pp. 190–3.
43 For references to Stalin as 'father', see, for example, S. Alymov,
    'Rossiya'; L. Olshanin, 'Rozhdyonnyi v gorakh', in *Pesni*,
    pp. 12–13, 30–1; for other godlike attributes, see A. Churkin,
    'Est' na svete strana'; M. Isakovsky, 'Shumyat plodorodnye
    stepi'; A. Kovalenkov, 'Pesnya o yunosti vozhdya', in *Pesni*,
    pp. 18–19, 22–3, 32–3.

44 A. Surkov, 'Na prostorakh rodiny chudesnoi'; Ya. Shvedov, 'Noch'yu zvezdnoi', in *Pesni*, pp. 16–17, 147–8.
45 From the Georgian folk song 'Slavnyi kormchii', in *Pesni*, p. 49.
46 M. Inyushin, 'Ot kraya do kraya'; L. Olshanin, 'Rozhdyonnyi v gorakh'; M. Lisyansky, 'Pesnya o Staline'; A. Kovalenkov, 'Pesnya o yunosti vozhdya', in *Pesni*, pp. 20–1, 30–1, 36–7, 32–3.
47 M. Isakovsky, 'Shumyat plodorodnye stepi'; M. Matusovsky, 'Spasibo Stalinu!', in *Pesni*, pp. 22–3, 165–6.
48 Tucker, *Stalin as Revolutionary*, p. 470; A. Antonov-Ovseenko, *Portret tirana* (New York, 1980), p. 281. On bird imagery in Stalinist culture, see M. Ziolkowski, 'The Reversal of Stalinist Literary Motifs: The Image of the Wounded Bird in Recent Russian Literature', *Modern Language Review*, vol. 83, part 1 (January 1988), pp. 106–20.
49 M. Inyushin, 'Ot kraya do kraya'; A. Kovalenkov, 'Pesnya o yunosti vozhdya', in *Pesni*, pp. 20–1, 32–3. On Stalin's relationship with the young pilots, see Katerina Clark, *The Soviet Novel: History as Ritual* (Chicago and London, 1981), pp. 124–9, 137–9.
50 V. Lebedev-Kumach, 'Pesnya o stolitse'; 'Moskva, Moskva!'; A. Zharov, 'Golos Kremlya', in *Pesni*, pp. 59–60, 154–6, 149–51.
51 Ya. Shvedov, 'Noch'yu zvezdnoi', p. 147.
52 V. Lebedev-Kumach, 'Sadovnik'; D. Suleimanov, 'Velikii sadovod'; A. Surkov, 'Na prostorakh rodiny chudesnoi'; M. Isakovsky, 'Shumyat plodorodnye stepi', in *Pesni*, pp. 59–60, 61–2, 16–17, 22–3.
53 N. Nezlobin, 'Kolechko', in *Pesni*, pp. 159–60.
54 V. Lebedev-Kumach, 'Spoyom, tovarishchi, spoyom', in *Pesni*, p. 28.
55 *Doklad A.M. Gor'kogo o sovetskoi literature, Pervyi s'ezd pisatelei: stenograficheskii otchot* (Moscow, 1934), p. 6.
56 Clark (see note 49), pp. 148–50.
57 M.S. Kryukova, *Skazanie o Lenine, Krasnaya nov'*, 1937, no. 11, pp. 97–118.
58 F.A. Konashkov, *Samoe dorogoe*, in *Samoe dorogoe. Stalin v narodnom epose*, ed. Yu.M. Sokolov (Moscow, 1939), p. 31.
59 *O schastye*, in ibid., p. 36 (first published *Pravda*, 4 July 1935).
60 V. Bespalikov, *Tri syna*, in ibid., pp. 48–52; V.E. Khramov, *Solntse*, ibid., pp. 53–6.
61 Ibid., p. 56.
62 I. Kovalyov, *Ledyanoi kholm*, ibid. , pp. 65–72; Ayau, *Kak bogatyri pokorili Il'mukhanum*, ibid., pp. 73–8.
63 *Stalin i pravda*, ibid., pp. 79–91.
64 Clark, p. 150.

65 See, e.g., N. Leontiev, 'Zatylok k budushchemu', *Novy Mir*, 1948, no. 9, pp. 248–66. For Zhdanov's speech, see *Oktyabr'*, 1946, no. 9, pp. 5–20.

66 'Tovarishch Stalin, vy bol'shoi uchonyi', in anon., *Narodnye sovetskie pesni, Student*, 2/3 (1964), pp. 81–4; see also M. Mihailov, *Leto moskovskoe 1964* (Frankfurt, 1967), pp. 58–9; the song is attributed to Vysotsky in *Pesni russkikh bardov* (Paris, 1977), vol. 3, p. 31. The first authorised publication is Yu. Aleshkovsky, *Pesni, Kontinent*. no. 21 (1979), pp. 146–7. The reference to linguistics is an ironic allusion to Stalin's famous article of 1950, 'On Marxism in Linguistics'.

67 As translated in G. Smith, *Songs to Seven Strings*, p. 76.

68 A. Solzhenitsyn, *The Gulag Archipelago*, vol. 2 (Fontana, London, 1976), pp. 308–38.

69 A.N. Tolstoy, *Pyotr pervyi*, in A. Tolstoy, *Pol'noe sobranie sochinenii*, 15 vols (Moscow, 1946–53), vol. IX.

70 R. Taylor, *Film Propaganda: Soviet Russia and Nazi Germany* (London, 1979). p. 119. See also M. Ferro, 'The fiction film and historical analysis', in P. Smith (ed.), *The Historian and Film* (Cambridge, 1976), pp. 80–94.

71 H. Marshall, *Masters of Soviet Cinema: Crippled Creative Biographies* (London, 1983), p. 174.

72 I. Ehrenburg, *People, Years, Life*, vol. 3 (New York, 1963), p. 226. See also Marshall, pp. 228–32.

73 V. Kostylev, *Ivan groznyi*, 3 vols (Moscow, 1955); discussed in V. Alexandrova, *Literatura i zhizn'. Ocherki sovetskogo obshchestvennogo razvitiya* (New York, 1969), pp. 430–1.

74 Cited in M. Seton, *Sergei M. Eisenstein* (New York, 1960), pp. 436–7.

75 M. Romm, *Besedi o kino* (Moscow, 1964), p. 91.

76 N. Zabolotsky, *Goriiskaya simfoniya*, in *Sob. soch.*, vol. 1 (Moscow, 1983), pp. 184–6.

77 A. Tvardovsky, *Strana Muraviya*, in *Stikhotvoreniya i poemy* (Moscow, 1954), pp. 283–6.

78 M. Friedberg, *Reading for the Masses: popular Soviet fiction, 1976–80* (Washington, DC, 1981), p. 29.

79 On Tvardovsky's *For the Right of Memory*; see above pp. 74–5.

80 P. Yashvili, *Na smert' Lenina, Tridtsat' dnei*, 1934, no. 1, p.13; V. Gaprindashvili, *Oktyabrskie stroki*, transl. B. Pasternak, in *Poety sovetskoi Gruzii* (Tbilisi, 1946), p. 49.

81 N. Mitsishvili, *Stalin, Novy Mir*, 1934, no. 3; P. Yashvili, *Stalin, Krasnaya nov'*, 1934, no. 6.

82 L. Fleishman, *Pasternak v tridtsatye gody* (Jerusalem, 1984), pp. 151–2.

83 See, for example, *Poety sovetskoi Gruzii*, pp. 50, 81, 116, 132, 152, 154.

84 N. Mandelstam, *Hope against Hope*, p. 173.

85 B. Pasternak, *Doctor Zhivago*, transl. M. Hayward and

M. Harari (Fontana, London, 1961), p. 19.

86   N. Cornwell, *Pasternak's Novel: Perspectives on 'Doctor Zhivago'* (Keele, 1986), p. 112.

87   I. Berlin, *Personal Impressions* (London, 1980), p. 204.

88   Cornwell, pp. 65–7, 137, n. 50.

89   N. Mandelstam, *Hope against Hope*, pp. 237–44.

90   A. Akhmatova, *Slava miru*, first published *Ogonyok*, 1950, nos. 14, 36, 42.

91   A. Haight, *Anna Akhmatova: A Poetic Pilgrimage* (Oxford, 1976), p. 159. Her wishes were ignored: see A. Akhmatova, *Sochineniya*, vol. 2 (Munich, 1968), pp. 147–54.

92   A. Akhmatova, *Sochineniya*, vol. 1 (Munich, 1967), p. 364.

93   Akhmatova, vol. 2, p. 147.

94   Ibid., p. 150.

95   Akhmatova, 'Podrazhanie armyanskomu', cited in *Sochineniya*, 2, p. 139.

96   Haight, p. 159.

97   N. Mandelstam, *Hope against Hope*, p. 244.

98   Clark, *The Soviet Novel*, p. 127.

99   P. Pavlenko, *Na vostoke* (Moscow, 1937), pp. 438–9.

100 I. Ehrenburg, *Lyudi, gody, zhizn'*, *Novy Mir*, 1962, no. 4, p. 61.

101 Clark, pp. 61–3, 79.

102 A. Tolstoy, *Khleb* (Moscow, 1937), pp. 35, 191, 192.

103 Ibid., pp. 194, 257.

104 Ibid., pp. 35, 192.

105 I. Ehrenburg, *Lyudi, gody, zhizn'*, *Novy Mir*, 1963, no. 1, pp. 70–1.

106 A. Korneichuk, *Front, Pravda*, 24–7 August 1942. On Stalin's role, see A. Werth, *Russia at War 1941–45* (London, 1964), pp. 423–6.

107 L. Leonov, *Nashestvie*, *Novy Mir*, 1942, no. 8, p. 84.

108 A. Karavaeva, *Ogni*, *Novy Mir*, 1943, no. 12, pp. 38–40.

109 K. Simonov, *Dni i nochi* (M., 1946), pp. 167–8.

110 V. Kataev, *Syn polka*, *Oktyabr'*, 1945, nos. 1–2, pp. 67–8. See also V. Kozhevnikov, *Blizost'*, *Oktyabr'*, 1945, no. 3, p. 62, which depicts Stalin's great interest in testing a gun, and stresses how important it is for soldiers to gain strength by thinking of Stalin's face.

111 V Ivanov, *Pri vzyatii Berlina*, *Novy Mir*, 1946, no. 3, p. 22.

112 Ibid., *Novy Mir*, no. 6, p. 32.

113 N. Virta, *Velikie dni*, in *P'esy*, (Moscow, 1950), pp. 113–15.

114 A. Solzhenitsyn, *V kruge pervom*, in *Sob.soch.*, vol. 1 (Vermont and Paris, 1978), p. 119.

115 V. Vishnevsky, *Nezabyvaemyi 1919-yi*, in *Dramaturgiya i izbrannoe* (Moscow, 1953), pp. 399–400; mentioned in Solzhenitsyn, *Sob.soch.*, vol. 1 (1978), p. 119.

116 Shostakovich, pp. 197–8. See also Tucker, p. 436, on Stalin's liking for other films such as *Lenin in October* and *Man with a*

Rifle, in which he himself figured as a character.

117 A. Kron, *Kandidat partii*, *Novy Mir*, 1950, no. 10, p. 19.

118 A. Gribachev, *Vesna v Pobede*, *Znamya*, 1948, no. 12, p. 48.

119 G. Berezko, *Mirnyi gorod*, Book I, *Znamya*, 1951, nos. 2–4; Books 1 and 2, Moscow, 1955; M. Bubyonnov, *Belaya beryoza*, *Oktyabr'*, 1952, nos. 3–5.

120 G. Berezko, *Mirnyi gorod*, *Znamya*, 1951, no. 3, p. 49; no. 5, pp. 77–8.

121 M. Bubyonnov, *Belaya beryoza*, *Oktyabr'*, 1952, no. 4, pp. 71–4.

122 E. Evtushenko, *A Precocious Autobiography*, transl. A. MacAndrew (London, 1963), pp. 77–8.

123 M. Bulgakov, *Batum*, in *Neizdannyi Bulgakov. Teksty i materialy*, ed. E. Proffer (Ann Arbor, 1977), pp. 137–210 (for a discussion of the circumstances surrounding its conception, see the Preface by E. Proffer, pp. 7–8); V. Vilenkin, *Nezabyvaemye vstrechi*, in ibid., p. 58.

124 Ibid., p. 8.

125 Ibid., p. 58.

126 See above, pp. 42–3.

127 V. Petelin, 'M.A. Bulgakov i "Dni Turbinykh" ', *Ogonyok*, 1969, no. 11, pp. 26–8. It is true that works about Stalin's youth were not encouraged. An exception to this general rule was a children's play by two Georgians, G. Nakhutsreshvili and B. Gamrekeli, *Lado Ketskhoveli* (Moscow, Leningrad, 1940), first performed in Tbilisi, subsequently translated into Russian and produced in Moscow in 1939, which presents the twenty-year-old Soso Djugashvili as a leading figure in the Trans-Caucasus who was responsible for setting up a clandestine printing press. See E.J. Simmons, *Through the Glass of Soviet Literature* (New York, 1953; 1972 reprint), pp. 184–5.

128 L. Loseff, *On the Beneficence of Censorship*, pp. 223–6.

129 *Neizdannyi Bulgakov*, p. 141.

130 Ibid., pp. 201–2, 204, 209.

131 Ibid., p. 182.

132 Ibid., p. 195.

133 Ibid., pp. 163, 156, 203–4.

134 M. Bulgakov, *Master i Margarita*, *Moskva*, 1966, no. 11; 1967, no. 1.

135 D. Piper, 'An Approach to Bulgakov's *The Master and Margarita*', *Forum for Modern Language Studies*, 7, no. 2 (1971), pp. 146–7.

136 For criticism of Piper's interpretation, see E. Proffer, *Bulgakov. Life and Work* (Ann Arbor, 1984), p. 647, n. 45; A.C. Wright, *Michael Bulgakov. Life and Interpretations* (Toronto, 1978), p. 266.

137 M. Bulgakov, *Master i Margarita* (Frankfurt, 1969), p. 359. See also the epigraph, taken from Goethe's *Faust*:

That power I serve
Which wills forever evil
Yet does forever good.

A. Barratt, *Between Two Worlds. A Critical Introduction to The Master and Margarita* (Oxford, 1987), pp. 171–2, makes quite a convincing case for interpreting Woland as a 'gnostic messenger'.

138 Barratt, p. 70.
139 Bulgakov, *Master i Margarita*, p. 351.
140 Ibid., p. 383. G. El'baum, *Analiz yudeiskikh glav 'Mastera i Margarity' M. Bulgakova* (Ann Arbor, 1981), p. 114, points out that this toast bears a close similarity to a passage in Suetonius referring to Tiberius.
141 Ibid., p. 41.
142 See, in particular, Piper; E. Mahlow, *Bulgakov's 'The Master and Margarita': The Text as Cypher* (New York, 1975).
143 A. Sinyavsky, 'Literaturnyi protsess v Rossii', *Kontinent*, no. 1 (1974), pp. 158–61.
144 D. Kharms, *Maiskaya pesnya, Chizh*, 1941, no. 5.
145 Loseff, pp. 205–7.
146 E. Shvarts, *Drakon*, ed. with an introduction by A.J. Metcalf (Canberra, 1984). The first version was completed by November 1943. For a discussion of the play, see Loseff, pp. 125–42; A. Metcalf, *Evgenii Shvarts and his Fairy-tales for Adults* (Birmingham, 1979), pp. 47–68.
147 Shvarts, *Drakon*, p. 9.
148 Ibid., p. 8.
149 M. Slonimsky *et al.*, *My znali Evgeniya Shvartsa* (Leningrad, 1966), p. 183.
150 A. Metcalf, 'Introduction' to *Drakon*, p. vii.
151 L. Kassil', *Povest' o tryokh masterakh*, in *Dorogie moi mal'chiki* (Moscow, 1949).
152 V. Grossman, *Za pravoe delo, Novy Mir*, 1952, no. 7, p. 102. For a translation of this passage and a discussion of the attacks it engendered, see E.R. Frankel, *Novy Mir. A case study in the politics of literature* 1952–1958 (Cambridge, 1981), pp. 9–14.
153 V. Grossman, *Zhizn' i sud'ba* (Lausanne, 1980). See above, pp. 116–18.

Chapter five The image of Stalin in Soviet literature of the post-Stalin period.

1 Y. Glazov, *The Russian Mind since Stalin's Death* (Dordrecht, 1985), p. 1.
2 Ulam, *Stalin*, p. 6; S. Vasil'ev (Borogonsky), 'Solntse-Stalin s nami naveki', in *Severnye poemy* (Moscow and Yakutsk, 1953),

pp. 31–2; K. Simonov, 'Glazami cheloveka moego pokoleniya', *Znamya*, 1988, no. 4, p. 108.

3   L. Leonov, *Russkii les*, *Znamya*, 1953, nos. 10–12.

4   K. Simonov, 'Surovaya godovshchina', in *Sochineniya*, vol. 1 (Moscow, 1952), pp. 57–8.

5   K. Simonov, *Soviet Weekly*, 18 July 1987, p. 5; Simonov's article, published in *LG*, 19 March 1953, is discussed in *Znamya*, 1988, no. 4, p. 119.

6   V. Grossman, *Za pravoe delo* (Moscow, 1955), pp. 137, 139–40.

7   S. Smirnov, *Krepost' nad Bugom*, *Znamya*, 1955, no. 9.

8   G. Nikolaeva, *Bitva v puti*, *Oktyabr*, 1957, nos. 3–7.

9   *Oktyabr'*, 1957, no. 3, p. 6.

10   Ibid., pp. 4–6.

11   A. Tertz, 'Chto takoe sotsialisticheskii realizm', in *Fantasticheskii mir Abrama Tertsa* (New York, 1967), pp. 399–446; A. Zinov'ev, 'O Staline i stalinizme', in *My i zapad* (Lausanne, 1981), pp. 8–9.

12   E. Evtushenko, *A Precocious Autobiography*, transl. A. MacAndrew (London, 1963), pp. 89–92.

13   A. Nekrich, *Otreshis' ot strakha* (London, 1978), pp. 109–10.

14   K. Fedin, *No Ordinary Summer*, transl. M. Wettlin (Moscow, 1950), vol. 1, p. 489; cf. Fedin, *Sob.soch.*, vol. 7 (Moscow, 1961), p. 296.

15   A. Tvardovsky, *Za dal'yu - dal'*, *Novy Mir*, 1960, no. 5, pp. 3–22.

16   K. Simonov, *Zhivye i myortvye*, *Znamya*, 1959, nos. 4, 10–12 (especially no. 12, pp. 38–9).

17   J. Newton, 'The Role of Stalin in the Second World War as portrayed in Soviet Russian Prose Fiction 1941–72', unpublished D.Phil. thesis (Oxford, 1977), p. 169.

18   V. Ketlinskaya, *Inache zhit' ne stoit*, *Znamya*, 1960, nos. 6–10.

19   N.S. Khrushchev, *Khrushchev Remembers*, transl. S. Talbott, ed. E. Crankshaw (New York and London, 1971), pp. 343, 351–2.

20   A. Bek, *Neskol'ko dnei*, *Novy Mir*, 1960, no. 3, p. 121.

21   Cited in S. Cohen (ed.), *An End to Silence*, p. 174.

22   G. Konovalov, *Istoki* (Moscow, 1959); the scene where Stalin receives the German delegation was changed in the 1969 edition. N. Rybak, *Pora nadezhd i svershenii* (Moscow, 1961).

23   E. Evtushenko, 'Nasledniki Stalina', *Pravda*, 21 October 1962; transl. G. Reavey in P. Johnson, *Khrushchev and the Arts: the Politics of Soviet Culture*, pp. 93–5.

24   A. Solzhenitsyn, *Odin den' Ivana Denisovicha*, first published in *Novy Mir*, 1962, no. 11; the reference to Stalin is retained in A. Solzhenitsyn, *Odin den' Ivana Denisovicha*, *Sob.soch.*, vol. 3 (Vermont and Paris, 1978), p. 105.

25   Solzhenitsyn, *The Oak and the Calf*, pp. 32, 40; cf. Solzhenitsyn, *The Gulag Archipelago*, vol. 3, p. 477.

26   K. Simonov, *Soldatami ne rozhdayutsya*, *Znamya*, 1963, nos. 8–11; 1964, nos. 1–5; for a detailed account of Simonov's

meetings with Stalin, see Simonov, 'Glazami . . .', *Znamya*, 1988, nos. 3, 4.

27 *Znamya*, 1964, no. 2, pp. 40–1.

28 *Znamya*, 1964, no. 5, pp. 92–101.

29 K. Paustovsky, *Kniga skitanii* (Moscow, 1964), pp. 62–6, 146–8.

30 Ibid., p. 65.

31 Ibid., p. 148.

32. A. Rozen, *Poslednie dve nedeli*, *Zvezda*, 1965, no. 1, p. 3–152. Another controversial work of the immediate post-Khrushchev period which demonstrates Stalin's unpreparedness for war is G. Baklanov, *Iul' 41 goda*, *Znamya*, 1965, nos. 1–2.

33 Rozen, *Zvezda*, 1965, no. 1, p. 74.

34 Ibid., p. 113.

35 Ibid., p. 77.

36 V. Sokolov, *Vtorzhenie* (Moscow, 1965), pp. 265–6.

37 L. Brezhnev, *Pravda*, 8 May 1965.

38 Yu. Trifonov, *Otblesk kostra*, *Znamya*, 1965, nos. 2, 3.

39 Yu. Trifonov, *Otblesk kostra* (Moscow, 1966), p. 163.

40 Ibid., pp. 52–5.

41 B. Okudzhava, 'Chornyi kot', *Sel'skaya molodezh*, 1966, no. 1, p. 33.

42 B. Okudzhava, 'Chornyi kot', in Okudzhava, *65 pesen. 65 Songs*, ed. V. Frumkin, transl. E. Shapiro (Ann Arbor, 1980), p. 89.

43 M. Dewhirst, R. Farrell (eds), *The Soviet Censorship* (Metuchen, NJ, 1973), p. 91.

44 A. Nekrich, *1941, 22 iyunya* (Moscow, 1965).

45 A. Rothberg, *The Heirs of Stalin: Dissidence and the Soviet Regime 1953–1970* (Ithaca and London, 1972), p. 269; K. Simonov, 'Stalin i voina', *Znamya*, 1988, no. 5.

46 See, for example, G. Zhukov, *Vospominaniya i razmyshleniya* (Moscow, 1969, 1971); S. Shtemenko, *General'nyi shtab v gody voiny* (Moscow, 1968, 1973); K. Rokossovsky, *Soldatskii dolg* (Moscow, 1968).

47 A. Chakovsky, *Blokada*, vol. 1 (Moscow, 1969), pp. 152–6.

48 A. Chakovsky, *Pobeda*, vol. 1 (Moscow, 1980), p. 179.

49 I. Stadnyuk, *Voina*, 2 vols. (Moscow, 1974); criticised in V. Barabanov, 'Otvetstvennost' pered temoi', *Komsomol'skaya pravda*, 17 September 1974, p. 2.

50 Cited in S. Cohen, 'The Stalin Question since Stalin', in Cohen (ed.), *An End to Silence*, p. 47.

51 Z. Medvedev, *Gorbachev* (Oxford, 1986), p. 210.

52 'Otvety M.S. Gorbachova na voprosy gazety "Yumanite" ', *Pravda*, 8 February 1986, p. 2.

53 'Mr Gorbachev Meets the Writers', transl. R. Sobel, *Détente*, no. 8 (Winter 1987), pp. 11–12.

54 A. Wilson, 'Cinemas packed to see Stalin's ghost laid low',

Observer, 16 Nov. 1986, p. 17; A. Wilson, 'The Commissars gently let go the reins', *Observer*, 30 November 1986.
55 *Pravda*, 28 January 1987, pp. 1–5.
56 M.S. Gorbachev, 'Ubezhdyonnost – opora perestroiki. Vstrecha v TsK KPSS', *Pravda*, 14 February 1987, p. 1.
57 'Otvety M.S. Gorbachova na voprosy redaktsii gazety "Unita"', *Pravda*, 20 May 1987, pp. 1, 3, 4.
58 A. Akhmatova, *Rekviem*, *Oktyabr*, 1987, no. 3, pp. 130–5.
59 A. Urban, 'I upalo kamennoe slovo', *LG*, 22 April 1987, p. 4.
60 A. Tvardovsky, *Po pravu pamyati*, *Znamya*, 1987, no. 2; *Novy Mir*, 1987, no. 3, pp. 190–201.
61 See above, pp. 34.
62 *Novy Mir*, 1987, no. 3, p. 197.
63 Ibid., p. 198.
64 Ibid., p. 201.
65 E. Sidorov, 'Osvobozhdenie – o poeme Aleksandra Tvardovskogo "Po pravu pamyati"', *LG*, 4 March 1987, p. 4.
66 *LG*, 29 April 1987, pp. 1–6.
67 *LG*, 6 May 1987, pp. 7, 10.
68 A. Bek, *Novoe naznachenie*, *Znamya*, 1986, nos. 10–11; for the original publication in the West, see A. Bek, *Novoe naznachenie* (Frankfurt, 1971). For a discussion of the novel, see below, pp. 113–15.
69 G. Baklanov, *Znamya*, 1986, no. 10, pp. 3–4.
70 V. Dudintsev, *Belye odezhdy*, *Neva*, 1987, nos. 1–4.
71 M. Mihajlov, *Moscow Summer*, transl. A. Field (London, 1966), p. 44.
72 *Neva*, 1987, no. 2, p. 132.
73 V. Shaposhnikov, 'S gnevom, s gordost'yu. Roman Vladimira Dudintseva "Belye odezhdy"', *LG*, 13 May 1987, p. 3.
74 M. Shatrov, *Brestskii mir*, *Novy Mir*, 1987, no. 4, pp. 3–51.
75 Ibid., p. 6.
76 Ibid., p. 7.
77 Ibid., p. 16.
78 Ibid., p. 27.
79 Ibid., p. 48.
80 M.S. Gorbachev, *Pravda*, 3 November 1987.
81 Yu. Afanasyev, 'Unleash the energy of history', *Soviet Weekly*, 21 February 1987, p. 10.
82 'Afanasyev answers his critics', *Soviet Weekly*, 6 June 1987, p. 5. For a further contribution to this debate, see A. Samsonov, 'But we must not distort it either', *Soviet Weekly*, 11 July 1987, pp. 8–9.
83 A. Rybakov, *Deti Arbata*, *Druzhba narodov*, 1987, nos. 4–6.
84 F. Barringer, 'Soviets to read of mass terror', *International Herald Tribune*, Paris, 16 March 1987, p. 2.
85 Letter from A. Brandt, *LG*, 19 August 1987, p. 4.
86 Barringer, p. 2.

87 See Rybakov's interview with I. Kishina, 'Zarubki na serdtse', *LG*, 19 August 1987, p. 4.
88 A. Pugach, 'Prodolzhenie sleduet. Nash korrespondent beseduet s Anatoliem Rybakovym', *Yunost'*, 1987, no. 12, pp. 23–5.
89 The similarity to Avtorkhanov's work is suggested in N. Kuznetsova, 'Pokayanie ili preklonenie? O romane Anatolya Rybakova "Deti Arbata" ', *Russkaya mysl'*, 30 October 1987, p. 12. Cf. Trotsky, *Stalin*, p. xiii and Rybakov, *Deti Arbata*, *Druzhba narodov*, 1987, no. 5, p. 111. Rybakov was also familiar with Roy Medvedev's *Let History Judge*, since he calls for it to be published in A. Rybakov, 'S proshlym nado rasstavat'sya dostoino', *Moskovskie novosti*, no. 29, 17 July 1988, p. 11.
90 *LG*, 19 August 1987, p. 4.
91 *International Herald Tribune*, 16 March 1987, p. 2.
92 J. Barber, 'Children of the Arbat', *Détente*, no. 11 (1988), p. 9.
93 *Druzhba narodov*, 1987, no. 4, p. 10. On Lenin's *Testament*, see Deutscher, *Stalin*, pp. 250–3.
94 *Druzhba narodov*, 1987, no. 4, pp. 13–14.
95 No. 4, p. 65.
96 No. 4, p. 69.
97 No. 5, p. 79.
98 No. 6, p. 88. On Stalin's use of the third person, see above, p. 43.
99 No. 5, p. 111.
100 No. 4, p. 108.
101 No. 5, p. 111.
102 No. 6, p. 53.
103 No. 5, p. 73.
104 No. 4, p. 98.
105 No. 4, p. 106.
106 No. 5, p. 79.
107 No. 4, p. 107.
108 No. 4, p. 112.
109 No. 6, p. 47.
110 No. 5, p. 77.
111 No. 4, p. 113.
112 No. 4, p. 115.
113 No. 6, p. 122.
114 Barber (see note 92), p. 11.
115 A. Latsis, 'S tochki zreniya sovremennika: zametki o romane "Deti Arbata" ', *Izvestiya*, 17 August 1987.
116 B. Okudzhava, in *Ogonyok*, no. 27, July 1987, p. 5.
117 See letters from K. Sidorova, L. Strizhalova, *LG*, 19 August 1987, p. 4.
118 N. Kuznetsova, *Russkaya mysl'*, 30 October 1987, pp. 12, 13, 14.
119 See A. Rybakov, *Tridtsat' pyatyi i drugie gody*, *Druzhba narodov*, 1988, nos 9, 10. Part 2 of this work is announced for publication in *Druzhba narodov* in 1989.

120 Stalin's complicity in Kirov's murder is still a controversial issue for western historians. Cf. Robert Conquest, *The Great Terror: Stalin's Purge of the Thirties* (Harmondsworth, 1971), pp. 72–96, with Getty, *Origins of the Great Purges*, pp. 207–10.

121 A. Turkov, '... Chtoby plyt' v revolyutsiyu dal'she', *LG*, 8 August 1987, p. 4. For further evidence that literature had surpassed history, see the discussion between Feliks Kuznetsov and Yuri Polyakov, *LG*, 30 September 1987, p. 3.

122 Rybakov, *LG*, 19 August 1987, p. 4.

123 D. Volkogonov, *Triumf i tragediya: Politicheskii portret I.V. Stalina, Oktyabr'*, 1988, nos 9–11. Book 2 will be published in *Oktyabr'* in 1989. See also D. Volkogonov, 'The Stalin phenomenon', in *Current Digest of the Soviet Press*, vol. xxxix, 1987, no. 50, pp. 1–6. R. Medvedev, *Oni okruzhali Stalina* has been announced for publication in *Yunost'*, 1989.

124 *Observer*, 8 November 1987, p. 11.

125 Gorbachev, *Pravda*, 3 November 1987.

126 M. Shatrov, *Dal'she...dal'she...dal'she, Znamya*, 1988, no. 1, pp. 3–53. For a discussion of the play, see D. Kazutin, 'Istorii podsudny vse', *Moskovskie novosti*, no. 2, 10 January 1988, p. 12.

127 Cited in D. Spring, 'Stalin exits stage left', *The Times Higher Education Supplement*, 12 February 1988, p. 14.

128 B. Pil'nyak, *Povest' nepogashennoi luny, Znamya*, 1987, no. 12; E. Zamyatin, *My, Znamya*, 1988, nos 4–5; B. Pasternak, *Doktor Zhivago, Novy Mir*, 1988, nos 1–4; V. Grossman, *Zhizn' i sud'ba, Oktyabr'*, 1988, nos 1–4; Yu. Dombrovsky, *Fakul'tet nenuzhnykh veshchei, Novy Mir*, 1988, nos. 8–11.

129 A. Adzhubei, 'Te desyat' let', *Znamya*, 1988, no. 8, p. 101.

Chapter six Portraits of Stalin in western and dissident literature

1 A. Koestler, *Darkness at Noon* (Harmondsworth, 1969), pp. 83, 18, recently published in the USSR under the title *Slepyashchaya t'ma, Neva*, 1988, nos 7–8.

2 Orwell specifically called *Animal Farm* an 'anti-Stalin' work, but also warned of the danger of a total identification of Napoleon with Stalin and Snowball with Trotsky. See B. Crick, *George Orwell. A Life* (London, 1980), p. 310; *Animal Farm* was published in *Rodnik* (Riga), 1988, nos. 3–6.

3 G. Orwell, *1984* (Harmondsworth, 1984), pp. 19, 256. *1984* has been announced for publication in *Novy Mir*, 1989.

4 V. Nabokov, *Bend Sinister* (Harmondsworth, 1974), p. 6. For an interesting discussion of Nabokov's political ideas, see D. Rampton, *Vladimir Nabokov. A Critical Study of the Novels* (Cambridge, 1984), pp. 31–63.

5 V. Nabokov, *Conclusive Evidence* (New York, 1951), p. 217.

6   V. Nabokov, *Strong Opinions* (London, 1974), p. 148.
7   V. Nabokov, *Tyrants Destroyed and Other Stories*, transl.
    D. Nabokov in collaboration with the author (London, 1975),
    p. 2 (first published in *Russkie zapiski*, Paris, August 1938).
8   Nabokov, *Strong Opinions*, p. 58.
9   Pierre Dommergues, 'Entretien avec Vladimir Nabokov', *Les
    Langues Modernes*, vol. 62, no. 1 (January–February, 1968), p.
    102.
10 *Tyrants*, p. 6.
11 Ibid., pp. 13, 14, 7, 18.
12 Ibid., p. 36.
13 See *The Nabokov-Wilson Letters*, ed. S. Karlinsky (London,
    1979), p. 117.
14 Nabokov, *Bend Sinister*, pp. 127–8.
15 V. Serge, *Midnight in the Century*, transl. R. Greeman (London,
    1982), pp. 152, 150.
16 V. Serge, *L'Affaire Toulaev*, in Serge, *Les Révolutionnaires.
    Romans* (Paris, 1967), p. 658.
17 Stanislav Tokarev, Alexander Gorbunov, 'How the Central
    Army Team was disbanded', *Moscow News*, no. 28, 1988, p. 15;
    Y. Krotkov, *The Red Monarch. Scenes from the Life of Stalin*,
    transl. T. Mairs, ed. C.H. Smith (New York, 1979), 'From the
    Author', p. 9.
18 For a detailed treatment, see G.S. Smith, *Songs to Seven
    Strings*, (Bloomington, 1984).
19 V. Vysotsky, *Ban'ka po-belomu*, in *Pesni russkikh bardov*, vol. 3
    (Paris, 1977), pp. 54–5.
20 Smith, p. 162.
21 Ibid.
22 V. Vysotsky, *Ban'ka po-belomu*, in V. Aksyonov, V. Erofeev,
    F. Iskander, A. Bitov, E. Popov (eds.), *Metropol'* (Ann Arbor,
    1979), pp. 209–10.
23 A. Galich, *Pokolenie obrechonnykh* (Frankfurt, 1973).
24 A. Galich, *Poema o Staline*, in ibid., pp. 275–87.
25 A. Galich, *Nochnoi dozor*, in ibid., pp. 31–2.
26 N.S. Khrushchev, *The 'Secret' Speech*, introd. by R. and
    Zh. Medvedev, p. 63.
27 A. Bek, *Novoe naznachenie* (Frankfurt, 1971). For its
    republication in the USSR in 1986, see above, p. 76–7.
28 R. Medvedev, *Problems in the Literary Biography of Mikhail
    Sholokhov*, transl. A.D.P. Briggs (Cambridge and London,
    1977), pp. 122–3; G. Svirsky, *Na lobnom meste. Literatura
    nravstvennogo soprotivleniya (1946–1976 gg.)* (London, 1979),
    p. 307.
29 Bek (1971), p. 38.
30 Ibid., p. 34.
31 Ibid., p. 44.
32 Ibid., p. 51.
33 Ibid., p. 56.

34   Ibid., p. 100.
35   Ibid., p. 55. Cf. Rybakov's *Children of the Arbat*, discussed on pp. 84–5 above.
36   G. Smith, *Songs to Seven Strings*, p. 47.
37   Yu. Dombrovsky, *Fakul'tet nenuzhnykh veshchei* (Paris, 1978), p. 94.
38   Ibid., p. 308.
39   Ibid., p. 407.
40   Ibid., p. 408.
41   Ibid., pp. 368, 411.
42   V. Grossman, *Zhizn' i sud'ba* (Lausanne, 1980).
43   Ibid., p. 532.
44   Ibid., p. 443.
45   Ibid., pp. 449–50.
46   Ibid., p. 456.
47   Ibid., p. 588.
48   V. Maksimov, *Kovcheg dlya nezvanykh* (Frankfurt, 1979).
49   G. Hosking, *Beyond Socialist Realism* (London, 1980), p. 123.
50   V. Turchin, *Inertsiya strakha* (New York, 1977).
51   V. Maksimov, *Karantin* (Frankfurt, 1973).
52   Chapter 49 of A. Solzhenitsyn, *V kruge pervom* (1968) is entitled 'The Ark' and makes extensive use of this metaphor.
53   A. Teskey, review of V. Maksimov, *Kovcheg dlya nezvanykh*, *Irish Slavonic Studies*, 1981, no. 2, p. 91.
54   V. Maksimov, *Kovcheg*, p. 284.
55   A. Tertz (A. Sinyavsky), 'Chto takoe sotsialisticheskii realizm', in *Fantasticheskii mir Abrama Tertsa* (New York, 1967), pp. 444, 446.
56   A. Tertz, *Sud idyot*, in ibid., p. 267.
57   G. Vladimov, *Vernyi Ruslan* (Frankfurt, 1975).
58   A. Gladilin, 'Stal'naya ptitsa', *Kontinent*, no. 14 (1977), pp. 356–9. For its publication in the west, see V. Aksyonov, *Stal'naya ptitsa*, *Glagol*, no. 1 (Ann Arbor, 1977), pp. 25–95.
59   Cited in J.J. Johnson, Jr, 'Preface' to V. Aksyonov, *The Steel Bird and Other Stories* (Ann Arbor, 1979), p. xix.
60   D. Rancour-Laferrière, 'The Boys of Ibansk', *Psychoanalytic Review*, vol. 72, no. 4, 1985, p. 645; J.J. Johnson, op. cit., p. xxii.
61   V. Aksyonov, 'Na ploshchadi i za rekoi', in *Zhal', chto vas ne bylo s nami. Povest' i rasskazy* (Moscow, 1969), pp. 342–53.
62   Aksyonov, *Stal'naya ptitsa*, p. 71.
63   Ibid., pp. 74–5.
64   Ibid., p. 65.
65   A. Tertz (A. Sinyavsky), *Spokoinoi nochi* (Paris, 1984). See above, p. 121.
66   Tertz, *Fantasticheskii mir*, p. 446.
67   *Spokoinoi nochi*, p. 276.
68   Ibid., pp. 277–8.

69   Ibid., p. 282.
70   Ibid., p. 285.
71. Ibid., pp. 273–5.
72   Ibid., p. 279.
73   Ibid., p. 401.
74   A. Gladilin, *Repetitsiya v pyatnitsu* (Paris, 1978).
75   Ibid., p. 75.
76   V. Voinovich, *Zhizn' i neobychainye priklyucheniya soldata Ivana Chonkina* (Paris, 1976); announced for publication in the USSR in *Yunost'*, 1989.
77   V. Iverni, 'Komediya nesovmestimosti', *Kontinent*, no. 5 (1975), pp. 427–54.
78   Yu. Mal'tsev, *Vol'naya russkaya literatura 1955–1975* (Frankfurt, 1976), p. 346.
79   Voinovich, *Chonkin*, p. 168.
80   'An interview with Vladimir Voinovich. The newly-exiled Russian novelist is interviewed in Paris by Richard Boston', *Quarto*, April 1981, p. 7.
81   V. Voinovich, *Pretendent na prestol. Novye priklyucheniya soldata Ivana Chonkina* (Paris, 1979).
82   Ibid., p. 320.
83   V. Voinovich, *V krugu druzei*, in *Putyom vzaimnoi perepiski* (Paris, 1979), pp. 165, 190.
84   G.M. Shtemenko, *General'nyi shtab v gody voiny*, vol. 2 (Moscow, 1974), pp. 39–40; repeated in Voinovich, *Putyom*, p. 166.
85   N.S. Khrushchev, *Khrushchev Remembers*, Commentary and Notes by E. Crankshaw, transl. S. Talbott (London, 1971), p. 267.
86   N. Cornwell, 'Voinovich on the March', *Irish Slavonic Studies*, no. 1 (1980), p. 122.
87   *Quarto*, April 1981, p. 7.
88   Voinovich, *Putyom*, p. 188.
89   F. Iskander, *Sandro iz Chegema* (Ann Arbor, 1979), p. 199. The chapters of *Sandro iz Chegema* which were originally censored in the USSR have now been published: F. Iskander, *Sandro iz Chegema: glavy iz romana, Znamya*, 1988, nos 9–10.
90   *Khrushchev Remembers*, pp. 265–9; Djilas, *Conversations with Stalin*, pp. 85–91, 115–25.
91   Iskander, *Sandro*, p. 221.
92   Ibid., p. 210.
93   Ibid., p. 222.
94   Ibid., p. 213. A similar pun is used in E. Shvarts, *Drakon* (see above, p. 1.
95   Iskander, *Sandro*, p. 218.
96   Ibid., p. 220.
97   Ibid., p. 302.
98   A. Zinov'ev, *Ziyayushchie vysoty* (Lausanne, 1976); as

translated in A. Zinoviev, *The Yawning Heights*, transl.
G. Clough (Harmondsworth, 1981), pp. 178, 436.

99   Ibid., p. 426.
100 Ibid., p. 665.
101 Yu. Aleshkovsky, *Kenguru* (Ann Arbor, 1981), p. 40.
102 Ibid., p. 114.
103 Yu. Aleshkovsky, *Ruka: povestvovanie palacha* (New York, 1980).
104 Ibid., p. 137 (on Dzhabaev, see above, pp. 27–8).
105 Ibid., p. 153.
106 Ibid., p. 158.
107 Ibid., p. 222.
108 Ibid., p. 213.
109 Ibid., p. 216.
110 Ibid., p. 226.

Chapter seven   Solzhenitsyn's 'new' portrait of Stalin: fact or fiction

1   A. Solzhenitsyn, *Respublika truda*, in Solzhenitsyn, *Sob.soch.*, vol. 8 (Vermont and Paris, 1981), p. 258.
2   Solzhenitsyn, *Plenniki*, in ibid., p. 218.
3   The original version (henceforth *Circle-87*) was published as A. Solzhenitsyn, *V. kruge pervom*, in Solzhenitsyn, *Sob.soch.*, vols. 3, 4 (Frankfurt, 1969–70). For critical responses to the 'Stalin chapters' in *Circle-87*, see E.J. Brown, 'Solzhenitsyn's Cast of Characters', in Brown (ed.), *Major Soviet Writers* (London and New York, 1973), pp. 360–5; G. Kern, 'Solzhenitsyn's Portrait of Stalin', *Slavic Review*, vol. 33 (1974), pp. 1–22; S. Layton, 'The Mind of the Tyrant: Tolstoj's Nicolas and Solzhenitsyn's Stalin', *Slavic and East European Journal*, vol. 23 (1979), pp. 479–90; C. Moody, *Solzhenitsyn* (Edinburgh, 1976), pp. 110–15; V. Krasnov, *Solzhenitsyn and Dostoevsky: a study in the polyphonic novel* (London, 1980), pp. 24–34; H. Muchnic, 'Solzhenitsyn's "The First Circle" ', *Russian Review*, vol. 29, no. 2 (April 1970), pp. 159–61; S. Ruslanov, 'Epigon velikogo Inkvizitora', *Grani*, no. 92–3 (1974), pp. 179–94.
4   A. Solzhenitsyn, *V kruge pervom*, in Solzhenitsyn, *Sob.soch.*, vols. 1, 2 (Vermont and Paris, 1978); henceforth *Circle-96*. On this new version, see R. Wells, 'The Definitive Solzhenitsyn?', *Irish Slavonic Studies*, no. 1 (1980), pp. 115–20; E. Lehrman, 'Solzhenitsyn's "New" View of Stalinist Russia', *St Louis Post Dispatch*, 18 Nov. 1979, p. 4; H. Ermolaev, 'Solzhenitsyn's Self-censorship: Two versions of *V kruge pervom*', *Russian Language Journal*, XXXVIII, nos 129–300 (1984), pp. 181–3; G. Nivat, *Soljénitsyne* (Paris, 1980), pp. 103–4; G. Nivat, 'Solzhenitsyn's Different *Circles*: an Interpretive Essay', in J. Dunlop, R. Haugh and M. Nicholson (eds.), *Solzhenitsyn in*

Exile: Critical Essays and Documentary Materials (Stanford, 1985), pp. 211–28; S. Richards, 'Alexander Solzhenitsyn: the literary and didactic conflict in his prose 1954–1971' (unpublished D. Phil. thesis, Oxford, 1979), pp. 251–2; R. Hallett, 'Beneath a Closed Visor: Dimitry Panin and the Two Faces of Sologdin in Solzhenitsyn's "The First Circle"', *Modern Language Review*, no. 78 (1973), pp. 365–74; M. Shneerson, *Aleksandr Solzhenitsyn: ocherki tvorchestva* (Frankfurt, 1984), *passim*.

5   D. Rancour-Laferrière, 'The Deranged Birthday Boy. Solzhenitsyn's Portrait of Stalin in *The First Circle*', *Mosaic*, vol. XVIII, no. 3 (1985), pp. 61–72.

6   See, for example, B. Souvarine, 'Soljénitsyne et Lénine', *Est et Ouest*, no. 570 (1–15 Apr. 1976); L. Loseff, 'Velikolepnoe budushchee Rossii. Zametki pri chtenii "Avgusta chetyrnadtsatogo" A. Solzhenitsyna', *Kontinent*, no. 42 (1984), pp. 289–320.

7   Nivat, 'Solzhenitsyn's Different *Circles*', p. 220.

8   Solzhenitsyn's main source of information about these dinners was probably the Russian oral tradition, which also influenced other writers, such as Iskander and Voinovich (see pp. 127–30). He may also have been familiar with the manuscript of M. Djilas, *Conversations with Stalin* and also, perhaps, at a later date, N.S. Khrushchev, *Khrushchev Remembers*.

9   In the 1968 version of the novel Solzhenitsyn depicted the special prison, or *sharashka*, where he himself was confined, under the fictional name of Mavrino, but in *Circle-96* Solzhenitsyn reveals its authentic name, Marfino, and its precise location in Ostankino, a suburb of Moscow. The design of a special telephone for Stalin fitted with a 'scrambler' was an actual task assigned to prisoners at Marfino: see D. Panin, *The Notebooks of Sologdin*, transl. J. Moore (London, 1976), p. 272; A. Solzhenitsyn, *Bodalsya telyonok s dubom* (Paris, 1975), p. 94.

10 For a more detailed discussion of this theme, see Layton, pp. 483–9; Brown, pp. 362–3.

11 On the genesis of *V kruge pervom*, see Solzhenitsyn, *Sob.soch*, vol. 1 (1978), p. 7; vol. 2, p. 403; 'Interv'yu s norvezhskim korrespondentom Nil'som Udgordom', in Solzhenitsyn, *Sob.soch.*, vol. 10 (Vermont and Paris, 1983), p. 480; Solzhenitsyn, *Bodalsya*, pp. 11n, 16–17, 39, 43, 80, 84–6, 89–97, 99, 102–3, 114, 116, 243, 349, 430–1.

12 For Khrushchev's speech at the exhibition, see P. Johnson, *Khrushchev and the Arts: The Politics of Soviet Culture, 1962–1964* (Cambridge, Mass., 1965), pp. 101–5; on the 'camp theme', see Khrushchev, *Pravda*, 10 March 1963, p. 4.

13 See, for example, I. Ehrenburg, *Ottepel'*, Znamya, 1954, no. 5, pp. 23, 74; V. Kaverin, *Poiski i nadezhdy*, Literaturnaya Moskva II (1956), pp. 183, 275; L. Kabo, *Na trudnom pokhode*,

Novy Mir, 1956, no. 12, p. 130; G. Nikolaeva, *Bitva v puti*, *Oktyabr'*, 1957, no. 4, p. 29.

14 A. Solzhenitsyn, *The Oak and the Calf: Sketches of Literary Life in the the Soviet Union*, transl. H. Willetts (London, 1980), p. 77.

15 Ibid., p. 78.

16 Ibid., pp. 80, 82.

17 Ibid., p. 83. O. Carlisle, *Solzhenitsyn and the Secret Circle* (London, 1978), p. 18 quotes Solzhenitsyn as saying that *V kruge pervom* was his 'most important book, the one that mattered, the one that would strike at the core of the Soviet leadership'.

18 Nina Petrovna Khrushcheva, cited in Solzhenitsyn, *The Oak*, p. 87.

19 Solzhenitsyn, *Bodalsya*, p. 99. Apparently Lebedev was so incensed by Solzhenitsyn's chapters about Stalin's private life that he intended to refute them immediately.

20 Carlisle, p. 21; M. Scammell, *Solzhenitsyn. A Biography* (London and Melbourne, 1984), pp. 302-4.

21 Carlisle, pp. 76-7. Apparently the sculptor Ernst Neizvestny thought that the Stalin chapters were 'magnificent',

22 N. Struve, 'Solzhenitsyn o Lenine', *Vestnik RKhD*, no. 116 (1975), p. 187.

23 A. Solzhenitsyn, 'Interv'yu na literaturnye temy s N.A. Struve mart 1976', *Vestnik RKhD*, no. 170 (1, 1977), p. 154.

24 Solzhenitsyn, *Sob.soch*, vol. 1 (1978), p. 7.

25 See, for example, Kern, p. 2; Moody, p. 115; A. Rothberg, *Solzhenitsyn: the Major Novels* (Ithaca, New York, 1971), pp. 69-70; F. Barker, *Solzhenitsyn: Politics and Form* (London and Basingstoke, 1977), p. 39; V. Erlich, 'The Writer as Witness: The Achievement of Aleksandr Solzhenitsyn', in J. Dunlop, R. Haugh and A. Klimoff (eds.), *Aleksandr Solzhenitsyn: Critical Essays and Documentary Materials*, 2nd edn (London, 1975), p. 24.

26 Solzhenitsyn, *The Oak*, p. 78.

27 A. Flegon, *Vokrug Solzhenitsyna* (London, 1981), pp. 902-3.

28 A. Solzhenitsyn, 'On the Fragments by Boris Souvarine', in Dunlop *et al.* (eds), *Solzhenitsyn in Exile*, p. 338.

29 Walter Benjamin, 'Der Erzähler', in *Schriften*, vol. 2, no. 2 (Frankfurt, 1977), p. 451; cited in E. Markstein, 'Observations on the Narrative Structure of *The Gulag Archipelago*', in *Solzhenitsyn in Exile*, p. 179.

30 D. Atkinson, 'Solzhenitsyn's Heroes as Russian Historical Types', *Russian Review*, vol. 30, no. 1 (1971), p. 9.

31 J. Turner, 'The Kinds of Historical Fiction', *Genre* (Oklahoma), vol. XII (Fall 1979), p. 342.

32 M. Renault, 'Notes on *The King Must Die*', in T. McCormack (ed.), *Afterwords: Novelists on their Novels* (New York, 1979), pp. 84-5.

33   R.P. Warren, 'Foreword', in *Brother to Dragons: A Tale in Voice and Verses* (New York, 1953), p. xi.

34   See, for example, V. Shklovsky, *Material i stil' v romane L'va Tolstogo 'Voina i mir'* (Moscow, 1928), Chapters 7–9; I. Berlin, 'The Hedgehog and the Fox', in *Russian Thinkers* (London, 1978), pp. 22–81; R. Christian, *Tolstoy: a Critical Introduction* (Cambridge, 1969) , pp. 162–3.

35   On Pushkin's historical research, see J. Bayley, *Pushkin: a Comparative Commentary* (Cambridge, 1971), pp. 345, 350.

36   *Solzhenitsyn in Exile*, p. 298.

37   Ibid., p. 330.

38   Loseff, *Kontinent*, no. 42, p. 313.

39   M. Shneerson, *Aleksandr Solzhenitsyn*, p. 227.

40   A. Solzhenitsyn, 'Repentance and Self-Limitation in the Life of Nations', in Solzhenitsyn, Agursky *et al.* (eds.), *From under the Rubble*, transl. A.M. Brock et al. (London, 1975), pp. 105–43.

41   Nivat, *Soljénitsyne*, p. 159.

42   Ibid., p. 103; Brown, p. 363.

43   S. Allilueva, *Only One Year*, transl. P. Chavchavadze (London, 1969), pp. 341–2, considers Stalin's early life, especially his years in the seminary, important in the formation of his character. See also R. Tucker, *Stalin as Revolutionary* (London, 1974), pp. xiv-xv.

44   See, for example, B. Wolfe, *Three who Made a Revolution* (Harmondsworth, 1966), p. 455; I. Deutscher, *Stalin: A Political Biography*, revised edn (Harmondsworth, 1970), p. 18; R. Hingley, *Joseph Stalin: Man and Legend* (London, 1974), pp. xvii–xxii.

45. L. Beria, *K. voprosy ob istorii bolshevistskikh organizatsii v zakavkaz'ye*, 9th edn (Moscow, 1952); H. Barbusse, *Stalin: a New World Seen through One Man* (London, 1935); E. Yaroslavsky, *Landmarks in the Life of Stalin* (London, 1942); *Joseph Stalin: a Short Biography* (Moscow, 1941).

46   L. Trotsky, *Stalin: an Appraisal of the Man and his Influence*, transl. C. Malamuth (New York, 1946); J. Iremaschwili, *Stalin und die Tragoedie Georgiens* (Berlin, 1932); G. Uratadze, *Vospominaniya gruzinskogo sotsial-demokrata* (Stanford, 1968); R. Arsenidze, 'Iz vospominanii o Staline', *Novyi Zhurnal* (New York), no. 72 (1963), pp. 218–36.

47   This allegation is implied in Iskander, *Sandro iz Chegema*, p. 219; refuted in Rybakov, *Deti Arbata, Druzhba narodov*, 1988, no. 5. Maksimov, *Kovcheg dlya nezvanykh*, p. 63 suggests that the rumour of Stalin's illegitimacy made a deep impression on him.

48   The original source for this is Iremaschwili, pp. 6, 11–12; cited in Tucker, p. 73; Hingley, p. 2; Deutscher, p. 23. Allilueva, *Only One Year*, p. 340 passes on the family tradition about the beatings, but A. Ulam, *Stalin: the Man and his Era* (New York, 1973), p. 20 states that Stalin later denied them.

49   Ulam, p. 18; S. Allilueva, *Twenty Letters to a Friend* (London, 1967), pp. 164–5.
50   Iremaschwili, pp. 30, 39–40.
51   Allilueva, *Only One Year*, p. 359 says that her aunts told her this story; Ahmed Amba, Stalin's professed former bodyguard, also insists on it: see A. Amba, *I was Stalin's Bodyguard* (London, 1952), pp. 125–6.
52   E.E. Smith, *The Young Stalin* (London, 1968), p. 343 states: 'Various bits and pieces of information have suggested that he was rarely without women friends or a mistress, though no one has precise data'; cf. the memoirs of Stalin's former secretary Boris Bazhanov, 'Pobeg iz nochi. Iz vospominanii byvshego sekretarya Stalina', *Kontinent*, 1976, no. 9, pp. 381–2 which suggests that Stalin was not interested in women.
53   See Wells, *Irish Slavonic Studies*, no. 1 (1980), p. 118.
54   A.S. Alliluev, *Vospominaniya* (Moscow, 1946), p. 167.
55   Deutscher, pp. 31–2, 43–5.
56   Ibid., pp. 29–30.
57   Ibid., pp. 32–43; Tucker, pp. 82–91; Hingley, pp. 9–18. Ulam, p. 23, however, notes that the horrors of the seminary may have been exaggerated by Stalin himself in a statement to Emil Ludwig in 1931: I.V. Stalin, *Sochineniya*, vol. 13 (Moscow, 1951), pp. 113–14. But an independent source, the memoir of an anonymous Russian member of staff, corroborates these details: see *Iz vospominanii russkogo uchitelya Pravoslavnoi gruzinskoi dukhovnoi seminarii* (Moscow, 1907).
58   Tucker, pp. 82–3; Hingley, p. 12.
59   Yaroslavsky, pp. 16–17.
60   Solzhenitsyn, *Sob.soch.*, vol. 1 (1978), p. 125.
61   *Joseph Stalin: A Short Biography* (Moscow, 1952), p. 7; Yaroslavsky, p. 11 suggests that Stalin became an atheist 'at a very early age, while still a pupil in the ecclesiastical school'; see also Iremaschwili, p. 8; Ulam, p. 20; *Rasskazy starykh rabochikh zakavkaz'ya o velikom Staline* (Moscow, 1937), pp. 18, 20. Allilueva, *Only One Year*, pp. 341–2, 355 claims that he 'never had any feeling for religion'. Stalin's marriage and his mother's funeral were, however, performed under the Orthodox rite. R. Medvedev, *On Stalin and Stalinism*, transl. E. de Kadt (Oxford, 1979), pp. 1–2 cites stories about Stalin's refusal to arrest his former teachers from the seminary during the purges of 1936–8; also mentioned in Solzhenitsyn, *Sob.soch.*, vol. 1 (1978), p. 167.
62   Ibid., p. 125. This recalls R. Medvedev, *Let History Judge* (London, 1972), p. 337, which suggests that Stalin joined the revolutionary movement because he saw the impossibility of 'making a career' in the Russian Empire.
63   Yaroslavsky, p. 11 suggests that Stalin joined the revolutionary movement at the age of fifteen; see also *Short Biography*, p. 7. The myths surrounding Stalin make it difficult to determine

when he actually became a Marxist. Deutscher, pp. 41–2; Wolfe, p. 365 suggest that it was 1–2 years before he left the seminary.

64 Solzhenitsyn, *Sob.soch.*, vol. 1 (1978), p. 126. A similar view is expressed in Trotsky, *Stalin*, p. 22.

65 V. Grebenshchikov, 'Les cercles infernaux chez Soljénitsyne et Dante', *Canadian Slavonic Papers*, 13 (1971), pp. 147–63; V. Liapunov, 'Limbo and the Sharashka', in Dunlop, Haugh and Klimoff (eds), *Aleksandr Solzhenitsyn*, pp. 231–40.

66 Solzhenitsyn, *Sob.soch.*, vol. 1 (1978), pp. 125, 126, 128.

67 Ibid., p. 126.

68 Ibid., p. 127.

69 Ibid., p. 126.

70 Tucker, p. xv.

71 Ulam, p. 33.

72 Flegon, p. 902.

73 Solzhenitsyn first mentioned this theory in *The Gulag Archipelago*, vol. 1, pp. 67, 195; vol. 3, p. 84. Maksimov's *Kovcheg dlya nezvanykh* is a later literary work which makes a passing reference to Stalin's 'service in the Okhrana' (p. 63).

74 See Medvedev, *Let History Judge*, pp. 315–24; Medvedev, *On Stalin and Stalinism*, pp. 15–18; Hingley, pp. 33–9; Ulam, pp. 97–8. Trotsky, p. 53, rejects allegations that Stalin denounced a former colleague, but considers that 'It is no mere accident that so vicious an invention is connected with Stalin's name. Nothing of the kind was ever rumoured about any of the old revolutionists'.

75 For Solzhenitsyn's reliance on the testimony of prisoners, see *The Gulag Archipelago*, vol. 1, p. 67; his ex-wife Natalya Reshetovskaya, in *Sanya: My Husband Aleksandr Solzhenitsyn*, transl. E. Ivanoff (London, 1975), p. 110 speaks of 'exact' versions of Stalin's biography which were circulating in the camps. On Frolov, see Medvedev, *Let History Judge*, pp. 319–20; for the views of other Old Bolsheviks, see Medvedev, *On Stalin and Stalinism*, pp. 15–18.

76 I.D. Levine, *Stalin's Great Secret* (New York, 1956), p. 2 cites the 'Eremin letter', allegedly from Colonel A.M. Eremin of the Petersburg Police Department, purporting to prove that 'Djugashvili-Stalin' was a police agent; for evidence of forgery, see Tucker, p. 112, n. 94. A. Orlov, 'The Sensational Secret Behind Damnation of Stalin', *Life*, International Edition, vol. 20, no. 10 (14 May 1956), pp. 12–19 states that his cousin, an NKVD agent, saw the file of the deputy director of the Tsarist secret police Vissarionov, which allegedly contained a record of Stalin's activities as a police spy.

77 E.E. Smith, *The Young Stalin* (New York, 1967).

78 Medvedev, *Let History Judge*, pp. 315–24; *On Stalin and Stalinism*, pp. 15–18; Tucker, pp. 108–14; Ulam, p. 62; Hingley, pp. 87, 97–8.

79 S. Vereshchak, 'Stalin v t'yurme (vospominaniya politicheskogo zaklyuchennogo)', *Dni*, 22 Jan. 1928.

80 Uratadze, *Vospominaniya*, p. 67; Arsenidze, 'Iz vospominanii', p. 224.

81 This view is also expresed in Solzhenitsyn, *The Gulag Archipelago*, vol. 3, pp. 84, 338, 347.

82 See Levine, pp. 51–6. Levine, p. 52 also refers to Stalin's possible complicity in the death of his fellow Bolshevik Kamo, and the destruction of his personal files — something hinted at by Solzhenitsyn in the sentence: 'And then Kamo was run over by a car (he chattered a lot about the "exes") see Solzhenitsyn, *Sob. soch.*, vol. 1 (1978), p. 139. Orlov, in *Life*, vol. 20, no. 10, p. 14 suggests that Stalin continued to be an active spy as late as the first part of 1913.

83 Ibid., pp. 15–16; this had, earlier, been hinted at in A. Orlov, *The Secret History of Stalin's Crimes* (London, 1954), p. 240.

84 Solzhenitsyn, *Sob. soch.*, vol. 1 (1978), p. 132.

85 Ibid., p. 127. This corresponds to the view of the Old Bolshevik G. Frolov on Stalin's 'Caesarist' ambitions cited in Medvedev, *On Stalin and Stalinism*, p. 16.

86 Ulam, pp. 62, 87.

87 Solzhenitsyn, *The Gulag Archipelago*, vol. 1, p. 192; vol. 3, pp. 81–4.

88 Solzhenitsyn, *Sob. soch.*, vol. 1 (1978), p. 130.

89 Ulam, pp. 48, 121–2; A. Wood, 'Solzhenitsyn on the Tsarist Exile System', *Journal of Russian Studies*, no. 42 (1981), pp. 39–43.

90 Tucker, pp. 106–7 states that Stalin's residence in Vologda under surveillance conformed with the edict of 1910 in which the viceroy of the Caucasus banned him from residing in Transcaucasia for five years.

91 On the large sums acquired by the 'expropriations', see Solzhenitsyn, *The Gulag Archipelago*, vol. 3, p. 278n.; Tucker, p. 113.

92 Solzhenitsyn, *The Gulag Archipelago*, vol. 1, p. 67 suggests that Solzhenitsyn's source for this idea was V.F. Dzhunkovsky, a former police director who died in Kolyma.

93 Medvedev, *Let History Judge*, pp. 320–3; *On Stalin and Stalinism*, pp. 17–18.

94 For a detailed account of one such experience in the Tiflis prison in 1900, see S. Alliluev, *Proidennyi put'* (Moscow, 1946), pp. 69–72.

95 We do not know exactly when Stalin made his first acquaintance with Lenin's views. It would seem that he met a friend of Lenin's, the revolutionary Victor Kurnatovsky, in 1900, and first corresponded with Lenin in 1903, when he was in exile in Irkutsk province. However, some laudatory Soviet biographies claim he first became familiar with Lenin's writings

in the seminary (under the pseudonym of 'Tulin'): see *Rasskazy starykh rabochikh*, p. 26; Yaroslavsky, p. 16.
96 Tucker, pp. 122–30; Hingley, pp. 20–1; Deutscher, pp. 51–4, 90–1.
97 R. Blackburn, 'The Politics of the First Circle', *New Left Review*, Sept.-Oct. 1970, p. 61.
98 For a refutation of this view, see Medvedev, *On Stalin and Stalinism*, pp. 183–98; see also E. Mandel, 'Solzhenitsyn, Stalinism and the October Revolution', *New Left Review*, no. 86 (July–Aug. 1974), pp. 51–62; R. Tucker, 'Communism and Russia', *Foreign Affairs*, vol. 58, no. 2 (Summer 1980), pp. 1178–83.
99 L. Kopelev, 'Solzhenitsyn na sharashke', *Vremya i my* (Jerusalem), no. 40 (1979), p. 187.
100 Solzhenitsyn et al., *From under the Rubble*, p. 12.
101 Solzhenitsyn, *The Gulag Archipelago*, vol. 1, p. 605.
102 The evidence now supersedes the earlier interpretation by Richards, 'Alexander Solzhenitsyn', p. 89.
103 Solzhenitsyn, *Sob. soch.*, vol. 1 (1978), p. 129; the phrase was originally used in a letter to Gorky about the national question in February 1912: V.I. Lenin, *Polnoe sobranie sochinenii*, 5th edn, 55 vols (Moscow, 1958–65), vol. 48, p. 162.
104 Solzhenitsyn, *Sob. soch.*, vol. 1 (1978), p. 137.
105 Ibid., p. 134. Solzhenitsyn expresses similar views on Lenin in an essay, 'Misconceptions about Russia are a threat to America', *Foreign Affairs* (New York), vol 58, no. 4 (Spring 1980), p. 803; 'Mr Solzhenitsyn and his Critics', *Foreign Affairs*, vol. 59, no. 1 (Fall 1980), pp. 200–1.
106 See a personal letter from Stalin dated 24 January 1911 from Solvychegodsk to Vladimir Bobrovsky, published in *Zarya vostoka*, 23 Dec. 1925; cited in Tucker, p. 149.
107 Solzhenitsyn, *Lenin in Zurich*, transl. H. Willetts (Harmondsworth, 1978), pp. 89, 147, 162–3.
108 Solzhenitsyn, *Sob. soch.*, vol. 1 (1978), p. 134.
109 Solzhenitsyn's interpretation here tallies with that of Bazhanov, who says that Stalin was 'rude only when it was not necessary to be polite': see *Kontinent*, 1976, no. 9, p. 386.
110 Solzhenitsyn, *Sob. soch.*, vol. 1 (1978), p. 139.
111 Trotsky, pp. 376–82.
112 Medvedev, *Let History Judge*, pp. 25, 27n. states that the first part of Lenin's *Letter to the Congress* was sent to Stalin on the same day that Lenin dictated it; probably the secretaries on duty did not consider the matter secret. He regards it as improbable, however, that after Lenin had told his secretaries that the documents were absolutely secret, the second part of the *Letter* and the supplement known as the *Testament*, written on 4 January 1923, were communicated to Stalin by Fotieva or Volodcheva, as Solzhenitsyn alleges.

113 Solzhenitsyn, *Sob. soch.*, vol. 1 (1978), p. 140.

114 Ibid., p. 138.

115 Ibid., pp. 137–8.

116 N.S. Khrushchev, *The Secret Speech*, with an Introduction by Z. and R. Medvedev, (Nottingham, 1976), p. 46; *Khrushchev Remembers*, transl. S. Talbott (Harmondsworth, 1977), p. 328 cites Stalin as saying: 'I trust no one, not even myself'.

117 Trotsky, p. 378.

118 Solzhenitsyn, *Sob. soch.*, vol. 1 (1978), p. 138. On Stalin's misuse of Marxist terminology, see also Medvedev, *Let History Judge*, p. 333.

119 Solzhenitsyn, *Sob. soch.*, vol. 1 (1978), p. 142.

120 Ibid., p. 143.

121 Ibid., p. 142; cf. Solzhenitsyn, *The Gulag Archipelago*, vol. 1, p. 411 on Stalin's conduct at the trial of Yagoda.

122 Ibid., pp. 142–3; cf. Nivat, 'Solzhenitsyn's Different *Circles*', p. 222.

123 Solzhenitsyn, *Sob. soch.*, vol. 1 (1978), p. 169.

124 See M. Hayward, 'Introduction', in A. Gladkov, *Meetings with Pasternak*, transl. M. Hayward (London, 1977), pp. 8, 13–18.

125 Medvedev, *On Stalin and Stalinism*, p. 121.

126 Solzhenitsyn, *Sob. soch.*, vol. 1 (1978), p. 143.

127 Solzhenitsyn, *The Gulag Archipelago*, vol. 2, p. 598; B. Meyer, 'Solzhenitsyn in the West German Press since 1974', in *Solzhenitsyn in Exile*, p. 72.

128 Khrushchev, *Secret Speech*, p. 58.

129 Discussed in Medvedev, *On Stalin and Stalinism*, pp. 129–32; denied in Djilas, *Conversations with Stalin* (Harmondsworth, 1969), p. 34. For evidence that Stalin did abandon his post on the second day of the war, see Medvedev, pp. 122–4.

130 Solzhenitsyn, *Sob. soch.*, vol. 1 (1978), p. 144.

131 Khrushchev, *Secret Speech*, p. 58.

132 See, for example, Solzhenitsyn, *Le Déclin du Courage. Discours de Harvard* (Paris, 1978); *Warning to the Western World* (The 'Panorama' Interview — BBC Talk) (London, 1976); *Alexander Solzhenitsyn speaks to the West* (London, 1978); *Detente: Prospects for Democracy and Dictatorship* (New Brunswick, NJ).

133 Solzhenitsyn, *Sob. soch.*, vol. 1(1978), p. 144.

134 Solzhenitsyn, *The Gulag Archipelago*, vol. 1, pp. 259–60. See also Medvedev, *Let History Judge*, p. 331.

135 Solzhenitsyn, *Sob. soch.*, vol. 1 (1978), p. 147.

136 Ibid., p. 145; cf. Solzhenitsyn, *Sob. soch.*, vol. 3 (Frankfurt, 1969), pp. 130–1.

137 Solzhenitsyn's view corresponds to that of Roy Medvedev, who in *Let History Judge*, p. 325 suggests that Stalin believed the Russian people need a Tsar.

138 I.V. Stalin, 'Otnositel'no marksizma v yazykoznanii', *Pravda*,

20 June 1950, pp. 3–4; 4 July, p. 3; 2 August, p. 2; discussed in Brown, pp. 361–3.
139 See Deutscher, p. 615; Allilueva, *Only One Year*, p. 357.
140 Solzhenitsyn, *Sob. soch.*, vol. 2 (1978), p. 302.
141 Rancour-Laferrière, p. 66.
142 Djilas, pp. 91, 119.
143 Solzhenitsyn, *Sob. soch.*, vol. 1 (1978), pp. 176–7.
144 For further discussion of the Korean War, see Solzhenitsyn, *The Gulag Archipelago*, vol. 3, p. 47.
145 Solzhenitsyn, *Sob. soch.*, vol. 1 (1978), p. 177.
146 K. Feuer, 'Solzhenitsyn and the Legacy of Tolstoy', in Dunlop, Haugh and Klimoff (eds), *Aleksandr Solzhenitsyn*, p. 140.
147 Brown, p. 361.
148 Nivat, p. 221.
149 It is difficult to tell if Solzhenitsyn has read Allilueva's book, as she mentions many other details about Stalin's dacha which he could also have included.
150 Bazhanov, *Kontinent*, 1976, no. 9, p. 386; *Khrushchev Remembers*, pp. 292–3. Other details which Solzhenitsyn could have taken from Khrushchev include Lenin's reference to Bukharin as 'our Bukharchik' (p. 56); the security devices in Stalin's dacha (p. 320); Abakumov's power over Stalin (p. 334).
151 See above, p. 128
152 Allilueva, *Twenty Letters*, p. 78; *Khrushchev Remembers*, p. 329. See also Djilas, p. 118.
153 Medvedev, *On Stalin and Stalinism*, p. 151.
154 See above, p. 128. Other stories which Solzhenitsyn omits include the claim that Stalin threw a chicken out of a window in the 1920s; his predilection for hunting stories; his habit of listening to telephone conversations; his belief that Michael Arlen's book *The Green Hat* had influenced his wife to commit suicide.
155 Carlisle, p. 15.
156 Z. Medvedev, 'Russia under Brezhnev', *New Left Review*, no. 117 (Sept.-Oct. 1979), p. 25.
157 M. Nicholson, 'Effigies and Oddities', in *Solzhenitsyn in Exile*, pp. 130–1.
158 Solzhenitsyn, *Vestnik RKhD*, no. 120 (1, 1977), p. 154.
159 See R. Wells, 'The Definitive Solzhenitsyn?', *Irish Slavonic Studies*, no. 1 (1980), p. 115. For Solzhenitsyn's view of the scientists who made nuclear weapons for Stalin, see Solzhenitsyn, *Sob. soch.*, vol. 2 (1978), Chapter 81.
160 Solzhenitsyn, *Sob. soch.*, vol. 1 (1978), pp. 164–5.
161 This term, taken from the psychologist Erik Erikson, is used by Tucker, p. xvi.
162 B. Souvarine, 'Otvet Solzhenitsynu', *Vesnik RKhD*, no. 132 (3–4, 1980), p. 265.

Chapter eight Solzhenitsyn's portrait of Stalin: the philosophical dimension

1   Rancour-Laferrière, pp. 61–72.
2   G. Nivat, 'Solzhenitsyn i my', *Obozrenie*, 19 November 1985, pp. 3–10.
3   M. Scammell, *Solzhenitsyn*, pp. 179, 245–6, 301–4.
4   Solzhenitsyn, *The Gulag Archipelago*, vol. 2, pp. 179–80.
5   N. Reshetovskaya, *Sanya* (London, 1976), pp. 115, 152.
6   Scammell, pp. 302–4.
7   D. Burg and G. Feifer, *Solzhenitsyn* (London, 1972), p. 190.
8   A. Besançon, 'Solzhenitsyn at Harvard', *Survey*, vol. 24, no. 1 (106), p. 136.
9   A. Schmemann, 'On Solzhenitsyn', in Dunlop, Haugh and Klimoff (eds.), *Aleksandr Solzhenitsyn*, pp. 28–44; for Solzhenitsyn's reply, see ibid., p. 44.
10 Ibid., p. 39.
11 D.L. Sayers, *The Comedy of Dante Alighieri the Florentine*, Canto I (*L'Inferno*), transl. D.L. Sayers (Harmondsworth, 1949), p. 11.
12 A. Solzhenitsyn, *The Gulag Archipelago*, vol. 2, p. 597.
13 Solzhenitsyn, *The Gulag Archipelago*, vol. 1, p. 175.
14 Isaiah, 14, vv. 13, 15.
15 Solzhenitsyn, *Sob. soch.*, vol. 1 (1978), p. 166; cited in Allilueva, *Twenty Letters*, p. 165.
16 Solzhenitsyn, *Sob. soch.*, vol. 1 (1978), p. 167.
17 Solzhenitsyn, *The Gulag Archipelago*, vol. 2, p. 597.
18 Solzhenitsyn, *Sob. soch.*, vol. 1 (1978), p. 167.
19 Idem; for Solzhenitsyn's 'Lenten Letter', see 'To Patriarch Pimen of Russia', transl. A. Klimoff, in Dunlop, Haugh and Klimoff, *Aleksandr Solzhenitsyn*, pp. 472–8.
20 Solzhenitsyn, *Sob. soch.*, vol. 1 (1978), p. 168.
21 Ibid., p. 375.
22 Ibid., p. 116.
23 On Stalin's yellow eyes, see Djilas, *Conversations with Stalin*, p. 52; Trotsky, *Stalin*, p. 244.
24 Solzhenitsyn, *Sob. soch.*, vol. 1 (1978), p. 116.
25 Rancour-Laferrière, pp. 64–5.
26 Solzhenitsyn, *Sob. soch.*, vol. 1 (1978), p. 121.
27 *Khrushchev Remembers*, pp. 333–4; Medvedev, *On Stalin and Stalinism*, p. 151.
28 Solzhenitsyn, *Sob. soch.*, vol. 1 (1978), p. 153.
29 Rancour-Laferrière, p. 65.
30 Nivat, pp. 220–1; Solzhenitsyn *et al.*, *From under the Rubble*, p. 25.
31 *Khrushchev Remembers*, pp. 320–2.
32 Solzhenitsyn, *Sob. soch.*, vol. 1 (1978), p. 121.
33 Ibid., pp. 193–4; discussed in Nivat, pp. 220–1.

34   Solzhenitsyn, *Vestnik RKhD*, no. 120 (I, 1977), p. 156.
35   Krasnov, p. 24–34; Ruslanov, pp. 279–94.
36   Krasnov, p. 165. This is reminiscent of Gorky's comment on
     Stalin, cited in Medvedev, *Let History Judge*, p. 355: 'People for
     him are material; more suitable the less exalted it is'.
37   Solzhenitsyn, *Sob. soch.*, vol. 1 (1978), p. 118.
38   Ibid., p. 121.
39   Ibid., pp. 116, 121.
40   Ibid., pp. 123, 170, 174.
41   See Medvedev, *On Stalin and Stalinism*, p. 150.
42   See above, p. 59.
43   Solzhenitsyn, *Sob. soch.*, vol. 1 (1978), p. 174. In the new version
     the earlier references to Svetlana telephoning her father and
     being admitted to him on rare holidays are omitted: see ibid.,
     pp. 149, 170.
44   A. Zinoviev, *The Reality of Communism*, transl. C. Janson
     (London: Paladin, 1975).
45   Solzhenitsyn, *Sob. soch.*, vol. 1 (1978), p. 165.
46   Solzhenitsyn's presentation of Stalin as a rival to God is not an
     entirely new interpretation. Iremaschwili, p. 23, suggests that
     Stalin rejected Christianity because he perceived himself as a
     godlike figure. Medvedev, *On Stalin and Stalinism*, p. 2 quotes
     Stalin as asking the Georgian Catholicos: 'And whom do you fear
     most — me or God?'. When the Catholicos remained silent
     Stalin said: 'I know you're more afraid of me, otherwise you
     wouldn't have come to see me wearing ordinary secular clothes'.
47   Solzhenitsyn, *Sob. soch.*, vol. 1 (1978), p. 166.

Chapter nine   Solzhenitsyn's portrait of Stalin: the literary
                   aspect

 1   On Solzhenitsyn's style, see, for example, G. Gibian, 'How
     Solzhenitsyn returned his ticket', in K. Feuer (ed.), *Solzhenitsyn:
     a collection of critical essays* (Eaglewood Cliffs, NJ, 1976),
     pp. 112–9; V. Carpovich, 'Lexical Peculiarities of Solzhenitsyn's
     Language', in Dunlop *et al.*, *Aleksandr Solzhenitsyn*, pp. 188–94.
 2   V. Rus, '*One Day in the Life of Ivan Denisovich*: A Point of
     View Analysis', *Canadian Slavonic Papers*, 13 (1971).
     pp. 165–78; R. Luplow, 'Narrative style and structure in *One
     Day in the Life of Ivan Denisovich*', *Russian Literature
     Triquarterly*, no. 1 (1971), pp. 400–12; L. Rzhevskii, 'Obraz
     rasskazchika v povesti Solzhenitsyna "Oden den' Ivana
     Denisovicha" ', in R. Magidoff *et al.* (eds). *Studies in Slavic
     Linguistics and Poetics in Honor of Boris O. Unbegaun* (NY,
     1968), pp. 165–78.
 3   G. Kern, 'Solzhenitsyn's Portrait of Stalin', *Slavic Review*, 33
     (1974), pp. 1–22.

4   Solzhenitsyn, *Sob. soch.*, vol. 1 (1978), pp. 131, 144, 141.
5   See above, pp. 152–6.
6   Solzhenitsyn, pp. 116, 119, 121.
7   D. Cohn, 'Narrated monologue. Definition of a Fictional Style', *Comparative Literature*, XVIII, no. 2 (1966), pp. 110–12. Terms which have been preferred by other scholars include 'free indirect speech' (R. Pascal, *The Dual Voice. Free indirect speech and its functioning in the nineteenth-century European novel* (Manchester, 1977)); 'quasi-direct discourse' (Luplow, p. 400); 'represented discourse' (Rus, p. 167).
8   Solzhenitsyn, *Sob. soch.*, vol. 1, p. 128.
9   Ibid., p. 133.
10 Ibid., p. 125.
11 Ibid., p. 146.
12 Cohn, p. 102, 110–11; Kern, pp. 5–7.
13 Solzhenitsyn, *Sob. soch.*, vol. 1, p. 135.
14 Ibid., p. 131.
15 Ibid., p. 127.
16 Ibid., pp. 139–42.
17 Ibid., p. 142.
18 M. Shneerson, *Aleksandr Solzhenitsyn* (Frankfurt, 1984), pp. 222–3.
19 Solzhenitsyn, *Sob. soch.*, vol. 1, pp. 145, 148. See above, p. 29.
20 Solzhenitsyn, *Sob. soch.*, p. 119. On Virta and Vishnevsky, see above, pp. 42–3. These references are not omitted in the new version of the novel, contrary to the claim of Georges Nivat, 'Solzhenitsyn's Different *Circles:* an Interpretive Essay', in Dunlop *et al.* (eds), *Solzhenitsyn in Exile*, p. 222.
21 Loseff, pp. 156–62.
22 On Simonov, see above, pp. 56–7, 58–9, 61–2. Galakhov appears in Chapter 62 of *Circle-96* (Solzhenitsyn, *Sob. soch.*, vol. 2, pp. 95–100).
23 Solzhenitsyn, *Sob. soch.*, vol. 1, p. 133.
24 Ibid., pp. 139–40.
25 Ibid., p. 136.
26 Cited in Kern, p. 63.
27 Solzhenitsyn, *Sob. soch.*, vol. 1, p. 136.
28 Ibid., p. 147.
29 See above, pp. 158–9.
30 E.J. Brown (ed.) *Major Soviet Writers*, pp. 361–3.
31 I.V. Stalin, 'Otnositel'no marksizma v yazykoznanii', *Pravda*, 20 June 1951, pp. 3–4. See p. 240, note 138
32 Solzhenitsyn, *Sob. soch.*, vol. 1, p. 146.
33 Ibid., pp. 143, 132.
34 Solzhenitsyn, *Sob. soch.*, vol. 3 (Frankfurt, 1969), p. 139.
35 Solzhenitsyn, *Sob. soch.*, vol. 1 (1978), p. 173.
36 Ibid., p. 133.

37 D. Luck, 'A Psycholinguistic Approach to Leader Personality', *Soviet Studies*, vol. XXX, no. 4 (October 1978), pp. 491–515.
38 Solzhenitsyn, *Sob.soch.*, vol. 1 (1978), pp. 143, 147.
39 Solzhenitsyn, *Sob.soch.*, vol. 3 (Frankfurt, 1969), pp. 159, 158.
40 Interview with S. Komoto, 1966, in Solzhenitsyn, *Bodalsya telyonok s dubom*, p. 484. This term is borrowed from M. Bakhtin, *Problemy poetiki Dostoevskogo*, 2nd revised edn (Moscow, 1963).
41 P. Ličko, 'Odin den'' u Aleksandra Isaevicha Solzhenitsyna', *Posev*, 23 June 1967, pp. 3–4.
42 For uncritical acceptance of Solzhenitsyn's 'polyphony', see D. Watt, 'The Harmony of the World: Polyphonic Structure in Solzhenitsyn's Larger Fiction', *Modern Fiction Studies*, vol. 23. no. 1 (Spring 1977), p. 16; A. Rothberg, *Aleksandr Solzhenitsyn* (Ithaca, NY, 1971), p. 133; H. Eagle, 'Existentialism and ideology in *The First Circle*', *Modern Fiction Studies*, vol. 23, no. 1 (Spring 1977), p. 48; A. Kodjak, *Alexander Solzhenitsyn* (Boston, 1978), p. 140; W. Krasnow, 'Polyphonic Arrangement of Characters in Solzhenitsyn's *V kruge pervom*', *Russian Language Journal*, vol. 29 (Fall 1975), pp. 83–94. A different view is expressed in S. Richards, 'Alexander Solzhenitsyn', pp. 79–82; J. Curtis, 'Solzhenitsyn and Dostoevsky', *Modern Fiction Studies*, vol. 23, no. 1 (1977), pp. 141–2; M. Nicholson, *Slavic Review*, vol. 41. no. 2 (Summer 1982), pp. 393–4.
43 G. Nivat and M. Aucouturier (eds), *Soljénitsyne* (Paris, 1971), p. 118.
44 R. Pascal, *The Dual Voice*, pp. 133–4; W. Booth, *The Rhetoric of Fiction* (Chicago, 1961), pp. 16–20, convincingly argues that the author can *never* be totally eliminated from a work of fiction.

Chapter ten Conclusion

1 Cited in M. Slonim, *Soviet Russian Literature. Writers and Problems 1917–1967* (London and Oxford, 1967), p. 288.
2 H. Shaw, *The Forms of Historical Fiction*, pp. 135, 143. See also p. 3 above.
3 Seven of these Aesopian devices are mentioned in Newton, 'The Role of Stalin', p. 283.
4 M.S. Gorbachev, *Pravda*, 3 November 1987.
5 A. Solzhenitsyn, 'Misconceptions about Russia are a threat to America', *Foreign Affairs* (New York); vol. 58, no. 4 (Spring 1980), pp. 797–834; R.C. Tucker, 'Communism and Russia', *Foreign Affairs*, vol. 58, no. 5 (Summer 1980), pp. 1178–83; 'Mr Solzhenitsyn and his critics', *Foreign Affairs*, vol. 59, no. 1 (Fall 1980), pp. 187–210.

6   A. Swingewood, *The Novel and Revolution* (London and
    Basingstoke, 1975), p. 248.
7   A. Rothberg, *Aleksandr Solzhenitsyn: The Major Novels* (Ithaca,
    NY, 1971), pp. 69–70; F. Barker, *Solzhenitsyn: Politics and Form*
    (London, 1977), p. 39. For other negative assessments, see
    C. Moody, S*olzhenitsyn* (Edinburgh, 1976), p. 115; D. Jacobson,
    'The Example of Solzhenitsyn', *Commentary*, vol. 47, no. 5
    (Jan–June 1969), p. 83.
8   C. Gordon, *How to Read a Novel* (New York, 1957), pp. 10,
    222–4.
9   B.Eikhenbaum, 'Vokrug voprosa o formalistakh', *Pechat' i
    revolyutsiya*, V (1924); discussed in V. Erlich, *Russian
    Formalism: History and Doctrine* (The Hague, Paris, 1969),
    pp. 107–9.
10 Yu. Tynyanov and R. Jakobson, 'Voprosy izucheniya yazyka i
    literatury', *Novyi Lef*, 1928, pp. 26–37; on Formalism and
    Marxism, see Erlich, pp. 99–139.
11 See, for example, V. Shklovsky, *Material i stil' v romane L'va
    Tolstogo 'Voina i mir'* (Moscow, 1928).
12 L. Trilling, 'Art and Fortune', in *The Liberal Imagination*
    (London, 1951), p. 259.
13 Cited in I. Howe, *Politics and the Novel* (London, 1961), p. 15.
14 P. Istrati, in V. Serge, *Les Révolutionnaires: Romans* (Paris,
    1967), p. 12.
15 Cited in Howe, p. 51.
16 Ibid., pp. 51–2.
17 F. Dostoevsky, 'Pis'mo N.N. Strakhovu', 24 March (5 April),
    1870, in Dostoevsky, *Polnoe sobranie sochinenii v tridtsati
    tomakh*, vol. 29 *Publitsistika i pis'ma 1869–1874* (Leningrad,
    1986), pp. 111–12.
18 Cited in P. Siegel, *Revolution and the Twentieth-century Novel*
    New York, 1979), p. 8.
19 D. Craig and M. Egan, *Extreme Situations: Literature and Crisis
    from the Great War to the Atom Bomb* (London, 1979),
    pp. 105–111.
20 Siegel, pp. 120–1.
21 Howe, p. 24.
22 V.S. Pritchett, 'Hell on Earth', *The New York Review of Books*,
    19 December 1968, pp. 3–5.
23 Solzhenitsyn, *Sob. soch.*, vol. 3 (Frankfurt, 1969), p. 164.
24 Howe, p. 24.
25 C.N.L. Brooke, *Time, the Archsatirist* (Inaugural Lecture at
    Westfield College, London, 1968); R.G. Collingwood, *The Idea
    of History* (Oxford, 1946); B. Croce, *Philosophy, Poetry, History:
    an anthology of essays*, transl. C. Spriggs (London, 1966). See
    also H. White, 'The Fictions of Factual Representation', in *The
    Literature of Fact*, ed. A. Fletcher (New York, 1976), pp. 21–44

for an interesting discussion of the similarity between the writing of history and the writing of imaginative fiction.

26 E.H. Carr, *What is History?* (Harmondsworth, 1964), pp. 22–3.
27 Brooke, p. 8.
28 T. Hardy, cited in Brooke, p. 9 from original MS (British Museum, Addit. MS 182f 523).
29 Brooke, p.9.
30 A. Besançon, 'Solzhenitsyn at Harvard', *Survey*, vol. 24, no. 1 (106) (Winter 1979), p. 134.
31 Quoted in ibid., pp. 134–5.
32 I. Berlin, 'The Hedgehog and the Fox', in *Russian Thinkers* (London, 1978) , p. 24.
33 Solzhenitsyn, *Sob. soch.*, vol. 4 (Frankfurt, 1970), p. 503. (This phrase is omitted from *Circle-96*). For critical assessments of Solzhenitsyn's artistic vision and Tolstoyan heritage, see Feuer, pp. 129–46; R. Haugh', 'The Philosophical Foundations of Solzhenitsyn's Vision of Art', in Dunlop *et al.*, *Aleksandr Solzhenitsyn*, pp. 168–84; S. Layton, 'The Mind of the Tyrant: Tolstoj's Nicholas and Solzenicyn's Stalin', *SEEJ*, vol. 23, no. 4 (1974), pp. 479–90; A. Obolensky, 'Solzhenitsyn in the mainstream of Russian literature, *Canadian Slavonic Papers*, 13 (1971), pp. 131–8.
34 L. Labedz (ed.), *Solzhenitsyn: A Documentary Record*, 2nd edn (Harmondsworth, 1975), p. 42.
35 Ibid., p. 219.
36 Berlin, p. 30.
37 Solzhenitsyn, 'Nobelevskaya lektsiya', in *Sob. soch.*, vol. 9 (Vermont and Paris, 1981), p. 9; *The Gulag Archipelago*, vol. 1, p. 298.
38 G. Nivat, 'Solzhenitsyn's Symbolism', in K. Feuer (ed.), *Solzhenitsyn*, p. 59.
39 Solzhenitsyn, *The Oak and the Calf*, p. 32.
40 Ibid., p. 78.
41 S. Richards, 'Alexander Solzhenitsyn', p. 90.
42 M. Shneerson, *Aleksandr Solzhenitsyn*, pp. 48–9.
43 D. Fanger, 'Solzhenitsyn: Ring of Truth', *The Nation*, 7 October 1968, p. 341.

Select Bibliography

There are few works of scholarship directly relevant to the subject of this book: portraits of Stalin in literature. The following short bibliography is divided into three sections: Section 1 contains an annotated selection of biographies and memoirs of Stalin and studies of Stalinism; Section 2 consists of English versions of fictional works and cultural memoirs connected with Stalin which are mentioned in the text; and Section 3 includes those works of literary criticism which have been found particularly helpful in the preparation of this study.

1. Biographies of Stalin and studies of Stalinism

A. In Stalin's lifetime

1. Laudatory Soviet works (Stalin cult period, 1929–53)

Batumskaya demonstratsiya 1902 goda (Materialy, dokumenty, vospominaniya o Batumskoi stachke–demonstratsii 9 marta 1902 g. podgotovlennoi i provedyonnoi tov. Stalinym) (Moscow, 1937).

Beria, L.P., *On the History of the Bolshevik Organisations in Transcaucasia:* speech delivered at a meeting of party functionaries, 21–22 July, 1935, translated from the 4th Russian edn (Lawrence and Wishart, London, 1939)

'Biographical Chronicle' appended to each volume of Stalin's *Collected Works*, English translation, 13 vols. (Foreign Languages Publishing House, Moscow, 1952–5).

Kaminsky, V., and Vereshchagin, I., 'Detstvo i yunost' vozhdya: dokumenty, zapisi, rasskazy', *Molodaya Gvardiya*, 1939, No. 12, pp. 22–100.

Rasskazy starykh rabochikh zakavkaz'ya o velikom Staline (Moscow, 1937).

Yaroslavsky, E., *Landmarks in the Life of Stalin* (Lawrence & Wishart, London, 1942).

2.   Hostile Marxist Biographies

Iremaschwili, Joseph, *Stalin und die Tragoedie Georgiens* (Berlin, 1932), (personal memoir by a Georgian Menshevik).

Souvarine, Boris, *Stalin: A Critical Survey of Bolshevism*, transl. C.L.R. James (Secker & Warburg, London, 1939).

Trotsky, Leon, *Stalin: An Appraisal of the Man and his Influence*, ed. and transl. Charles Malamuth, 2nd edn (Harper, New York, 1941) (unfinished at the time of Trotsky's murder).

Deutscher, Isaac, *Stalin: A Political Biography*, 1st edn, (CUP, London, 1949).

3.   Early Western Biographies and Memoirs

Amba, Achmed, *I was Stalin's Bodyguard*, transl. Richard and Clara ⸝ Winston, (F. Muller, London, 1952).

Barbusse, Henri, *Stalin: A New World Seen through One Man* transl. from the French by Vyvyan Holland, (Workers' Bookshop, London, 1935) (laudatory).

Basseches, Nikolaus, *Stalin*, transl. from the German by E.W. Dickes (Dutton, New York, 1952) (neutral).

Essad, *Bey, Stalin; the Career of a Fanatic*, transl. from the German by Huntley Paterson (Viking Press, New York, 1932) (popular, hostile).

Graham, Stephen, *Stalin: An Impartial Study of the Life and Work of Joseph Stalin* (E. Benn, London, 1931) (popular, neutral).

Levine, Isaac Don, *Stalin* (Blue Ribbon Books, New York, 1931) (popular, hostile).

Svanidze, Budu, *My Uncle Joe* (Heinemann, London, 1952).

B.   Since Stalin's death

1.   Revisionist Soviet

Khrushchev, N.S., The 'Secret' Speech to 20th Party Congress, 1956: *The Secret Speech*, with an introduction by Zhores A. Medvedev and Roy A. Medvedev (Spokesman Books, Nottingham, 1976).

Khrushchev, N.S., Speech to 22nd Party Congress, *Pravda*, 18 October 1961, pp. 2–11.

2.   Dissident Soviet

Antonov-Ovseenko, Anton, *The Time of Stalin: Portrait of a Tyranny,* transl. George Saunders, with an introduction by Stephen F. Cohen (Harper & Row, New York, 1981)

Medvedev, Roy, *Let History Judge: The Origins and Consequences of Stalinism*, transl. David Joravsky and Colleen Taylor (Macmillan, London, 1972) (a Marxist-Leninist viewpoint).

——, *On Stalin and Stalinism*, transl. Ellen de Kadt (OUP, Oxford, 1979).

Solzhenitsyn, Alexander, *The Gulag Archipelago 1918–1956*, 3 vols, transl. Thomas P. Whitney and H.T. Willetts (Collins Harvill, London, 1974–8; Fontana, London, 1974–8).

Zinov'ev, Alexander, 'O Staline i stalinizme', in *My i zapad* (L'Age d'homme, Lausanne, 1981), pp. 7–14.

3.   Personal Memoirs

Allilueva, Svetlana, *Twenty Letters to a Friend*, transl. Priscilla Johnson McMillan (Harper & Row, New York 1967).

——, *Only One Year*, transl. Paul Chavchavadze, (Harper & Row, New York, 1969).

The Alliluev Memoirs: Recollections of Svetlana Stalin's Maternal Aunt Anna and her Grandfather Sergei Alliluev, compiled by David Tutaev (Joseph, London, 1968) (Harper & Row, New York, 1969).

Arsenidze, R., 'Iz vospominanii o Staline', *Novy zhurnal* (New York), no. 72 (June 1963), pp. 218–36.

Bazhanov, Boris, 'Pobeg iz nochi (Iz vozpominanii byvshego sekretarya Stalina)', *Kontinent* (Paris), Nos 8, 9 (1976).

Djilas, Milovan, *Conversations with Stalin*, transl. from the Serbo-Croat by Michael J. Petrovich, (Penguin, Harmondsworth, 1963).

Khrushchev, N.S., *Khrushchev Remembers*, transl. and ed. by Strobe Talbott, with an introduction, commentary and notes by Edward Crankshaw (Deutsch, London, 1971).

Uratadze, Grigory, *Vospominaniya gruzinskogo sotsial-demokrata* (Hoover Institution Foreign Language publications, Stanford, 1968).

4.   Sensational Western Works claiming that Stalin was a Tsarist Agent

Levine, Isaac Don, *Stalin's Great Secret* (Coward-McCann, New York, 1956).

Orlov, Alexander, 'The Sensational Secret Behind Damnation of Stalin', *Life*, International Edition, vol. 20, no. 10, (14 May 1956), pp. 12–19.

Smith, Edward Ellis, *The Young Stalin: The Early Years of an Elusive Revolutionary* (Farrar, Strauss & Giroux, New York, 1967).

5.   Serious Western Biographies (objective, but basically hostile)

Hingley, Ronald, *Joseph Stalin: Man and Legend* (Hutchinson, London, 1974).

R.H. McNeal, *Stalin, Man and Ruler* (Macmillan, London, 1988).

Tucker, Robert C., *Stalin as Revolutionary 1879–1929: A Study in History and Personality* (Chatto & Windus, London, 1974).

Ulam, Adam B., *Stalin: The Man and his Era* (Allen Lane, New York, 1974).

Wolfe, Bertram D., *Three who Made a Revolution: A Biographical History* (Thames & Hudson, London, 1956; Penguin, Harmondsworth, 1966).

6. Laudatory Modern Biographies

Grey, Ian, *Stalin: Man of History* (Weidenfeld & Nicholson, London, 1979; Sphere, London 1982).

Hoxha, Enver, *With Stalin: Memoirs*, transl. from the Albanian, (8 Nëntori, Tirana, 1979).

7. Assessments of Stalinism

Carrère d'Encausse, Hélène, *Stalin: Order Through Terror*, transl. Valence Ionescu, (Longman, London, 1981).

Conquest, Robert, *The Great Terror: Stalin's Purge of the Thirties*, revised edn (Penguin, Harmondsworth, 1971).

Daniels, Robert V., *The Stalin Revolution: Fulfillment or Betrayal of Communism?* (Heath, Boston, 1965).

Nove, Alec, *Was Stalin Really Necessary? : Some Problems of Soviet Political Economy* (Allen & Unwin, London, 1964).

Rigby, T.H. (ed.), *Stalin* (Prentice-Hall, Eaglewood Cliffs, 1966).

Urban, G.R. (ed.), *Stalinism: its Impact on Russia and the World* (Wildwood House, Aldershot, 1985).

8. Attitudes to Stalin in the Soviet Union

Roy Medvedev, 'The Stalin Question', in Stephen F. Cohen, Alexander Rabinowitch and Robert Sharlet (eds.), *The Soviet Union since Stalin* (Indiana University Press, Bloomington, 1980), pp. 32–49.

Stephen F. Cohen, 'The Stalin Question since Stalin', in Cohen (ed.), *An End to Silence: Uncensored Opinion in the Soviet Union* (Norton, New York, 1982), pp. 42–50.

2. Literature on Stalin

Akhmatova, Anna, *Requiem, 1935–1940*, in *Selected Poems*, transl. with an Introduction by Richard McKane and an essay by Andrei Sinyavsky (OUP, London, 1969), pp. 90–105

Aksyonov, Vassily, *The Steel Bird and Other Stories*, transl. Rae Slonek and others (Ardis, Ann Arbor, 1979).

Aleshkovsky, Yuz, 'Comrade Stalin, you're a real big scholar', transl. in Gerald Stanton Smith, *Songs to Seven Strings: Russian Guitar Poetry and Soviet 'Mass Song'* (Indiana University Press, Bloomington. 1984), p. 76.

——, *Kangaroo*, transl. Tamara Glenny (Farrar, Strauss & Giroux, 1986).

Bubyonnov, Mikhail, *The White Birch*, transl. L.Stoklitsky (Foreign Languages Publishing House, Moscow, 1949).

Bulgakov, Mikhail, *The Master and Margarita*, transl. Michael Glenny (Collins & Harvill, 1974; Fontana, 1969).

Ehrenburg, Il'ya, *The War 1941–45*, transl. Tatiana Shebukina in collaboration with Yvonne Kapp, vol. 4 of *People and Life*, 6 vols., (Macgibbon & Kee, London, 1961–6).

Evtushenko, Evgeny, *A Precocious Autobiography*, transl. A Mac-Andrew (Collins & Harvill, London, 1963).
——, 'Stalin's Heirs', transl. George Reavey, in Priscilla Johnson, *Khrushchev and the Arts: the Politics of Soviet Culture, 1962–1964* (M.I.T. Press, Cambridge, Mass., 1965), pp. 93–5.
Fedin, Konstantin, *No Ordinary Summer*, 2 vols., transl. Margaret Wettlin (Foreign Languages Publishing House, Moscow, 1950).
Galich, Alexander, 'Stalin', 'The Night Watch', in *Selections: Songs and Poems*, ed. and transl. Gerald Stanton Smith (Ardis, Ann Arbor, 1983), pp. 90–8, 99–100.
Gribachev, A. 'Spring in Pobeda', extract in Vera Dunham, *In Stalin's Time: Middleclass Values in Soviet Fiction* (CUP, Cambridge, 1976), p. 261, n. 26.
Grossman, Vassily, *Life and Fate*, transl. Robert Chandler (Collins Harvill, London, 1985; Fontana, 1986).
Iskander, Fazil, *Sandro of Chegem*, transl. Susan Brownsberger (Jonathan Cape, London, 1983; Penguin, 1985).
Kharms, Daniil, 'May Song', in Lev Loseff, *On the Beneficence of Censorship*, transl. Jane Bobko (Sagner, Munich, 1984), pp. 205–7.
Koestler, Arthur, *Darkness at Noon*, transl. Daphne Hardy (Jonathan Cape, London, 1940; Penguin, 1947).
Korneichuk, Alexander, *The Front*, in *Four Soviet War Plays*, transl. Gerard Shelley and adapted by Tyrone Guthrie (Hutchinson, London, 1944).
Krotkov, Yuri, *The Red Monarch. Scenes from the Life of Stalin*, transl. Tanya E. Mairs, ed. Carol Houck Smith (Norton, New York, 1979; Penguin, Harmondsworth, 1983).
Leonov, Leonid, *The Invasion*, in *Four Soviet War Plays*, transl. Gerard Shelley and adapted by Tyrone Guthrie (Hutchinson, London, 1944).
——, *The Russian Forest*, transl. Bernard Isaacs, 2 vols (Progress, Moscow, 1966).
Mandelstam, Nadezhda, *Hope Against Hope*, transl. Max Hayward (Harvill, London, 1970; Penguin, Harmondsworth, 1975).
——, *Hope Abandoned*, transl. Max Hayward (Harvill, London, 1974; Penguin, Harmondsworth, 1977).
Mandelstam, Osip, 'We live without feeling the country beneath us' (the poem about Stalin), in *Selected Poems*, transl. David McDuff (Rivers Press, Cambridge, 1973), p. 131.
Nabokov, Vladimir, *Bend Sinister* (Weidenfeld & Nicholson, London, 1972; Penguin, Harmondsworth, 1976).
——, *Tyrants Destroyed and Other Stories*, transl. Dmitri Nabokov in collaboration with the author (Weidenfeld & Nicholson, London, 1975; Penguin, 1981).
Okudzhava, Bulat, 'The Black Tomcat', in Okudzhava, *65 pesen. 65 Songs*, ed. V. Frumkin, transl. E. Shapiro (Ardis, Ann Arbor, 1980), p. 89.
Orwell, George, *Nineteen Eighty-Four* (Secker & Warburg, London, 1949; Penguin, Harmondsworth, 1954).

Pasternak, Boris, *Doctor Zhivago*, transl. Max Hayward and Manya Harari (Collins & Harvill, London, 1958; Fontana, London, 1961).

Paustovsky, Konstantin, *The Restless Years* (*A Book of Wanderings*), transl. Kyril Fitzlyon (Harvill, London, 1974), vol. 6 of *Story of a Life* (Harvill, London, 1964–74).

Pavlenko, Pyotr, *Red Planes fly East* (*In the East*), transl. Stephen Garry (G. Routledge & Sons, London, 1938).

Pilnyak, Boris (Boris Vogau), *The Tale of the Unextinguished Moon*, in *Mother Earth and Other Stories*, transl. and ed. Vera Reck and Michael Green (Praeger, New York, 1968).

Rybakov, Anatoly, *Children of the Arbat* (Hutchinson, London, 1988).

Serge, Victor, *Midnight in the century*, transl. Richard Greeman (Writers & Readers, London, 1982).

——, *The Case of Comrade Tulayev*, transl. Willard R. Trask (Hamish Hamilton, London, 1951).

Shostakovich, Dmitri, *Testimony. The Memoirs of Dmitri Shostakovich*, as related to and edited by Solomon Volkov, transl. Antonina W. Bouis (Hamish Hamilton, London, 1979).

Shvarts, Evgeny, *The Dragon. A satirical fable in three acts*, transl. Elizabeth Reynolds Hapgood (Heinemann, London, 1969).

Simonov, Konstantin, *Days and Nights*, transl. J. Fineberg (Hutchinson, London, 1945).

——, *Victims and Heroes* (*The Living and the Dead*), transl. R. Ainsztein (Hutchinson, London, 1963).

Solzhenitsyn, Alexander, *One Day in the Life of Ivan Denisovich*, transl. Ralph Parker (Gollancz, London, 1963; Penguin, Harmondsworth, 1970).

——, *The First Circle*, transl. Michael Guybon (Collins & Harvill, London, 1968; Fontana, London, 1970).

——, *The Oak and the Calf. Sketches of Literary Life in the Soviet Union*, transl. Harry Willetts (Collins & Harvill, London, 1980).

Tertz, Abram (Andrei Sinyavsky), *The Trial Begins and On Socialist Realism*, transl. Max Hayward and George Denis (University of California Press, 1982; London, 1977).

Tolstoy, Aleksei, *Bread*, transl. Stephen Garry (Victor Gollancz, London, 1938).

——, *Peter the Great*, transl. Edith Bone and Emile Burns (Victor Gollancz, London, 1936).

Tvardovsky, Alexander, *Horizon beyond the Horizon*, excerpts, transl. Alex Miller and A. Leksis, in Tvardovsky, *Selected Poetry*, compiled by M. Tvardovskaya (Progress, Moscow, 1981), pp. 266–91.

——, *Land of Muravia*, excerpts, transl. Dorian Rottenberg, in Tvardovsky, *Selected Poetry*, complied by M. Tvardovskaya (Progress, Moscow, 1981), pp. 231–44.

Vladimov, Georgy, *Faithful Ruslan*, transl. Michael Glenny (Simon & Schuster, New York, 1979; Penguin, Harmondsworth, 1979).

Voinovich, Vladimir, *In Plain Russian: Stories*, transl. Richard Lourie (Cape, London, 1980).

——, *The Life and Extraordinary Adventures of Private Ivan Chonkin*, transl. Richard Lourie (Cape, London, 1977; Penguin, Harmondsworth, 1979).

——, *Pretender to the Throne*, transl. Richard Lourie (Cape, London, 1981).

Vysotsky, Vladimir, 'Stoke me the Bathhouse Smokeless', in *Metropol': A Literary Almanac*, ed. Vasily Aksyonov, Victor Erofeev, Fazil Iskander, Andrei Bitov and Evgeny Popov (Norton, New York, 1982), pp. 35–6.

Zinov'ev, Alexander, *The Yawning Heights*, transl. Gordon Clough (Bodley Head, London, 1979; Penguin, Harmondsworth, 1981).

Zoshchenko, Mikhail, *Lenin and the Sentry*, transl. with an afterword by Ruth Sobel, *Irish Slavonic Studies*, no. 4, 1983, pp. 106–8.

3. Literary Criticism

Clark, Katerina, *The Soviet Novel: History as Ritual* (University of Chicago Press, Chicago and London, 1981).

Dunham, Vera, *In Stalin's Time: Middleclass Values in Soviet Fiction* (CUP, Cambridge, 1976).

Johnson, Priscilla, *Khrushchev and the Arts: The Politics of Soviet Culture, 1962–1964* (MIT Press, Cambridge, Mass., 1965).

Kern, Gary, 'Solzhenitsyn's Portrait of Stalin', *Slavic Review*, vol. 33 (1974), pp. 1–22.

Layton, Susan, 'The Mind of the Tyrant: Tolstoj's Nicholas and Solzenicyn's Stalin', *SEEJ*, vol. 23 (1979), no. 4, pp. 479–90.

Loseff, Lev, *On the Beneficence of Censorship: Aesopian Language in Modern Russian Literature* (Sagner, Munich, 1984).

Marsh, Rosalind J., *Soviet Fiction since Stalin: Science, Politics and Literature* (Croom Helm, London, 1986).

Newton, Jeremy, 'The Role of Stalin in the Second World War as portrayed in Soviet Russian Prose Fiction 1941–72', unpublished D. Phil. thesis, Oxford, 1977.

Rancour-Laferrière, Daniel, 'The Deranged Birthday Boy: Solzhenitsyn's Portrait of Stalin in *The First Circle*', *Mosaic*, vol. XVIII (1985), no. 3, pp. 61–72.

Index

Chuvash literature, 30, 31
Civil War, 12, 66, 73, 83, 158, 172,
192; in literature, 40, 58, 89, 101,
117, 159, 192, 193
Clark, K., 39, 40
Cohn, D., 186, 188
Cold War, 14, 43, 73
collectivisation, 22, 25, 92, 98–9; in
literature, 23, 30, 34–5, 74, 87, 91,
93, 96, 101, 117, 118, 130, 137, 184
Collingwood, R., 208
comedy, 7, 63, 78, 105–6, 107–8,
124–34, 200, 201, 212
Communism, 139, 166, 167, 183–4,
188, 209
Communist Party of the Soviet Union,
12, 13, 56, 156, 160, 172, 202; party
members, 13, 32, 85, 95, 96, 107,
158; *see also* Central Committee;
Conference; Congress; Komsomol;
Leningrad party organisation;
Politburo; Presidium; Stalin and the
party;
Conference of CPSU: Extraordinary
(19th) Party Conference (1988),
99
conformist writers, 57, 71: *see also*
Union of Writers of USSR
Congress of CPSU: Tenth (1921), 100;
Seventeenth (1934), 26, 35, 81, 82,
84, 85–6, 89, 94; Nineteenth (1952),
61; Twentieth (1956), 13, 56, 57, 59,
66, 71, 81, 83, 112, 190; Twenty-
Second (1961); 13, 59, 60, 63, 71,
190; Twenty-Third (1966), 13;
Twenty-Fourth (1971), 13; Twenty-
Fifth (1976), 13; of Komsomol, 63;
of Russian Social Democratic and
Labour Party: Fifth (1907), 89; of
Union of Writers of USSR: First
(1934), 27, 30, 34
Conrad, J., *Nostromo,* 2
Convention (in French Revolution),
81
Cornwell, N., 36, 128
Craig, D., 205
Crimean Tartars, 75, 118, 131, 132
critical realism, 113
Croce, B., 208
Cromwell, O., 3

Dagestan literature, 31
Daniel, Yu., 68

Dante Alighieri, 56, 178, 181, 203;
Inferno, 150–1, 159, 175, 179, 181,
210
Danton, G., 3
Darwin, C., 149
de-Stalinisation, 17, 28, 199; under
Gorbachev, 71–102, 201, 202;
under Khrushchev, 7, 11, 13, 15, 54,
56–64, 83, 85, 95–6, 112, 140, 169,
192, 198, 202
Dekanozov, V., 65
Dementiev, A., 139
Denikin, General A., 99
Deutscher, I., 13, 27, 148, 171, 202
didacticism: in Solzhenitsyn, 128, 139,
141, 203, 211
dissident writers, 14, 15–16, 17, 71,
90, 108–34, 144, 201; republication
in USSR, 102
Djilas, M., 129, 167, 169, 178
Djugashvili, J., 19, 130, 133, 152, 153;
see also Stalin, J.V.
'Doctors' Plot' (1953), 112, 138
dogmatists, 59
Dolmatovsky, Yu., 122
Dombrovsky, Yu., 113, 124, 199, 211;
The Faculty of Unnecessary Things,
102, 115–16, 134
Donbass, 114
Dostoevsky, F., 178, 181, 196, 197,
203, 205, 207; *Crime and
Punishment,* 180, 182; 'Legend of
the Grand Inquisitor' (in *The
Brothers Karamazov*), 130, 179,
180–3, 184; *The Devils,* 134, 180–3,
196, 205, 206
Dovzhenko, O., *Shchors,* 33
Druzhba narodov, 81
Dudintsev, V., 78; *White Robes,* 77
Duma, 66
Dzerzhinsky, F., 162
Dzhabaev, D., 27–8, 133
Dzhibladze, S., 156

Ehrenburg, I., 33, 39, 40
Einstein, A., 167
Eisenstein, S, *Alexander Nevsky,* 33;
Ivan the Terrible, 33
Eismont, V., 96
Eliot, G., *Middlemarch,* 2
Eliot, T.S., 205
Elizabeth I., 3
El-Registan, G., 28